WORLD GUIDE

TO

MAMMALS

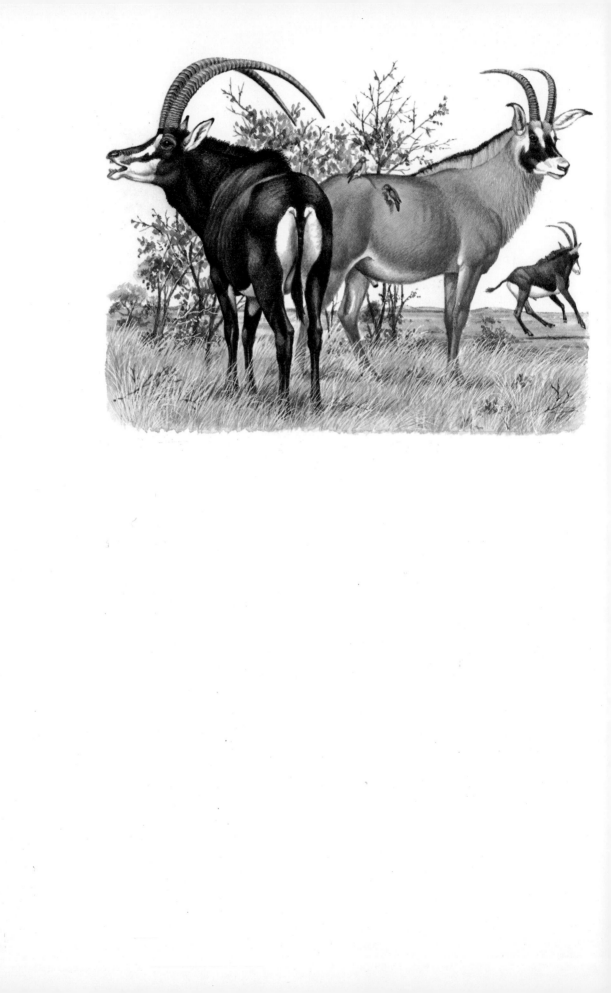

WORLD GUIDE TO
MAMMALS

by NICOLE DUPLAIX and NOEL SIMON

INTRODUCTION BY PRUE AND JOHN NAPIER

Illustrations by PETER BARRETT

CROWN PUBLISHERS, INC.
NEW YORK

ACKNOWLEDGMENTS

This guidebook has been an essentially cooperative venture. Many people helped us make a careful review of the available literature. Special appreciation must go to George Fichter for editing and refining the original manuscript, to Joseph A. Davis for his reading of the entire manuscript and review of the artwork and to Dr. George B. Schaller for correcting portions of the text. We gratefully acknowledge their assistance.

N.D.
N.S.

The illustration on p. 15 is adapted from Alfred S. Romer, Vertebrate Paleontology, © 1933, 1945, and 1966 by The University of Chicago. All rights reserved. Used with permission.

Published by
CROWN PUBLISHERS, INC.

An original work created and produced by
Vineyard Books, Inc.
159 East 64th Street
New York, N.Y. 10021

ISBN: 0-517-529203

Library of Congress Cataloging in Publication Data

Duplaix, Nicole.
　World guide to mammals.

　Includes index.
　1. Mammals. 2. Mammals—Identification.
I. Simon, Noel, joint author. II. Title.
QL703.D86　　599　　76-8391

Printed in Hong Kong by Mandarin Publishers Ltd.

USING THIS GUIDE

This is a book for everyone who enjoys watching and identifying mammals. The text covers the most common or most interesting species found in the world today. The illustrations accent physical features and behavioral traits that will help you recognize the mammals you see in the wild or in zoos.

First become familiar with the mammals in this guide. It is organized according to the principles of animal classification established by Linnaeus, which group animals according to their ancestral origin.

Mammals are more difficult to see in the wild than birds. Many are nocturnal, most are secretive, and you may catch only a glimpse of one as it darts across a road. Try to pick out the salient features, then thumb through the guide and choose the animal that comes closest to it.

Lengths given are usually the overall length from head to (and including) the tail; hoofed mammals are measured at the shoulder. The range maps, unless otherwise stated, show the present distribution of the mammals discussed on each page. The index lists both common and scientific names and will help you locate any mammal discussed in the book.

A Key to the Mammals of the World

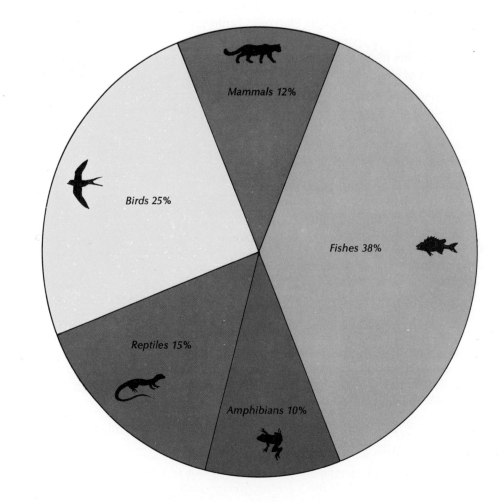

THE DISTRIBUTION
OF VERTEBRATE SPECIES

Introduction

Although mammals are the largest and most conspicuous animals on earth, they are by no means the most numerous. Among the vertebrates there are about 4,000 species of mammals, compared with roughly 3,000 amphibians, 8,500 birds and over 12,000 species of fishes. The animal kingdom is so vast that even the whole muster of vertebrates constitutes only 5 percent of all known animals. Invertebrates—animals without backbones—include insects, crustaceans, worms and minute creatures of all kinds, down to the single-celled amoeba. Spineless they may be, but invertebrate species represent 95 percent of the animal kingdom.

What mammals lack in numbers they make up for in ubiquity and diversity. On land and sea, from the little pika living high in the Himalayas to the blue whale of the ocean depths, mammals can be found in almost every ecological niche that will support life. The conquest of the air by bats is yet another example of mammalian versatility.

The secret of a mammal's success is the built-in thermostat that allows it to maintain its body temperature within certain limits. In the cold, the temperature is raised by the beating of the heart, by muscular activity and by increased metabolism. At the same time, heat loss is prevented by bunching the body and fluffing up the fur. An overheated mammal, on the other hand, assumes a spread-eagled attitude and loses heat by panting and by erecting its fur to expose the skin.

The most obvious characteristic of mammals—fur—is the most important factor in temperature control, but it also plays many other roles in their lives. One of the most important functions is to protect the skin from injury and to help arrest bleeding when the skin is broken. Hairs can also act as organs of touch; the sensitive whiskers around the muzzle of a nocturnal mammal help it to feel its way in the dark. Hairs are modified for both attack and defense—for

The quills of a porcupine (right) and a pangolin's protective scales (below) are composed of specially modified hair.

example, the rhinoceros's horn, the porcupine's quills and the pangolin's protective scales.

Several mammals have managed to dispense with fur altogether as part of their air-conditioning system. One of the smallest, the naked mole rat from East Africa, has only a few fine hairs scattered over its wrinkled four-inch body. It escapes changes of temperature by burrowing in sandy soil and rarely comes to the surface. A big mammal like the hippopotamus keeps cool by spending the day submerged in water, with only its eyes, nose and ears above the surface. The biggest mammals of all, the whales, have the fewest hairs—some vestigial whiskers around the mouth. To prevent heat loss in arctic seas, they have developed a blanket of blubber several inches thick beneath the skin. Man too utilizes a layer of subcutaneous fat to insulate his body from the cold but can lose heat quickly after bursts of activity by sweating, which has a dramatic cooling effect. Naturally sweating plays a much less important role in most mammals, as fur inhibits the process of evaporation.

Hibernating dormouse

Another means by which mammals combat the cold is by hibernation. They seek a nest or den and sleep away the winter, with their temperature control mechanism at least partially disengaged. The classic example, the dormouse, rolls itself into a ball, thus exposing the smallest possible surface area, and holds its muscles rigid, so that it can be rolled like a billiard ball without waking up. Its internal thermometer will alert it if the temperature falls below a certain point. Few vertebrates can survive being frozen, and this fail-safe mechanism rouses the dormouse so that it can seek a deeper frostproof retreat.

The advantages of a stable body temperature, and the accompanying insulating jacket that makes it feasible, are underlined by the fact that another vertebrate group has achieved exactly the same thing but using feathers instead of fur. Birds are an extremely successful group as far as numbers are concerned, but since their bodies need to conform to aerodynamic principles they have remained usually smaller in size and less versatile in behavior than mammals.

Mammals possess a relatively large brain and so respond to their environment in a more intelligent and varied way than other vertebrates whose behavior depends more on instinctive and programmed reactions. Mammals need a superefficient circulation to supply oxygen both to the brain and to the muscles of the body, as well as an intricate network of nerves linking the two, to ensure quick responses to stimuli and finely coordinated movements. The development of such a complex organism takes time, and to meet this need mammals have evolved a unique method of reproduction that lasts longer than that of any other animal. As the late Alfred Sherwood Romer, the paleontologist, once said, the accent is on "quality, not quantity." While reptiles may lay hundreds of eggs and abandon them to their fate, mammals produce relatively few young. The safety of these few offspring is thus of great importance, and the basic advantages of the mammalian reproductive system are that it is both slow and sure.

Mammal embryos develop inside the mother's body in a water-cushioned environment, well protected from harm and insulated from changes of temperature. They are nourished through an organ called the placenta that supplies nourishment from the mother's bloodstream through the umbilical cord. Unlike bird or reptile embryos, which are dependent on the limited amount of food contained in the yolk sac of the egg, embryos of placental mammals receive their nourishment directly from the mother over a lengthy gestation period and are born at an advanced stage of development. Even after birth the mother continues to feed her young with milk from her mammae and to care for them until they can fend for themselves.

Not all mammals develop a placenta. Marsupials, or pouched mammals, are born in a very undeveloped state. Though tiny and hairless, they manage to crawl to the security of the pouch and continue their development there. The monotremes, the duck-billed platypus and the echidna lay eggs, thus completely contradicting the basic concept of a mammal, but they suckle their young with milk as soon as they are hatched.

Marsupials, such as the great gray kangaroo (left), suckle their young from nipples inside the pouch. Egg-laying mammals such as the echidna (below) lack nipples; the young lick milk that flows from enlarged pores in the skin.

Mammals and Their Environment

In order to understand Darwin's theory of evolution through natural selection, it is essential to appreciate that more animals are born into the world than there is food to keep them alive. Thus the number of animals a given region can support is finite, and there is always competition for survival. Which creatures survive and which succumb depends on the "fitness" of the animal. This has nothing to do with health and beauty but is, rather, the sort of fitness by which a square peg fits a square hole. The hole is the particular aspect of the environment (or niche) concerned, and the peg is the animal. The tighter the peg fits, the more likely it is to remain in place.

For one animal to be more "fit" than another requires certain physical and behavioral characteristics that allow it, for instance, to run faster—either to avoid predators or, if it is a predator itself, to catch its prey. Similarly those animals that are better tree-climbers than others are more likely to be able to feed on the best fruit and tenderest leaves than their less well-equipped competitors. In evolutionary terms, characteristics such as these fostering fast running or better climbing are known as *adaptations*.

Adaptations are characteristics that have evolved in an animal species over time. For example, it has taken 40 million years for horses to grow from the size of a small dog to their present dimensions. A few mammals are in effect "living fossils," so termed because they have not changed in any important respect from their fossil ancestors. The classic example of a living fossil is the coelacanth, a fish that was thought to have been extinct for 60 million years—until it was found, quite unchanged, in South African waters in 1939. There are several examples among the mammals; the large American opossum, for instance, first crops up in the fossil record 100 million years ago.

The world has been in a constant state of flux since the time the first mammals appeared. The climate has changed, mountain ranges have appeared, sea levels have varied and the shape and connections of the continents have altered, and so has the vegetation. Throughout their history, mammals have been faced with environmental revolutions of one sort or another, and natural selection has been continually in action, weeding out the incompetent and clearing the way for those with new and more suitable adaptations. In the simplest terms, evolution is a process of change with time.

The ultimate test of survival in animal species is the ability to breed. Species that possess adaptations that make them stronger and better fed are more likely to produce many healthy and well-nourished offspring. The larger the number of offspring that grows to maturity, the greater the chance of advantageous adaptations becoming perpetuated in the species, whose chances of survival are thereby increased.

Unlike birds, reptiles and fishes, whose lives are governed by their instincts and reflexes, mammals are quite versatile creatures that are capable of initiating activities. In practice, such plasticity means that mammals have a certain amount of choice as to where they live and what they eat. There are a number of options open that gives them a greater chance of survival in times of stress. Monkeys and apes are particularly well equipped to survive under unusual or even adverse conditions. Their secret lies principally in the size and development of the brain, which, relatively speaking, is the largest of all mammals except man. There are very few places where man can live that monkeys cannot.

Although primates are particularly well equipped in this respect, all mammals have the potential to "do their own thing." However, some mammals have become specialists, and it is more difficult for them to adopt new patterns of behavior; their options are fewer. The survival of the koala bear, for instance, depends entirely on leaves of the eucalyptus tree; the giant panda mainly eats bamboo; anteaters must have ants or termites; baleen whales need plankton or krill. They are all specialists whose anatomy and physiology are geared for a particular type of food. In a world of plenty, specialists are at an advantage, but when conditions are adverse it is the Jack-of-all-trades that survives.

Monkeys, such as these red-faced Japanese macaques, can adapt to a variety of conditions. These macaques live throughout the year at a latitude equal to that of New York.

Most mammals are nonspecialists when it comes to moving about within their habitats. There are the obvious examples, such as squirrels, monkeys and leopards, which are as much at home in trees as on the ground. However, there are less obvious examples, such as goats, which are agile climbers, and the hippopotamus, which swims under water as gracefully as a ballet dancer.

There appears to be no limit to the number of ecological niches that the environment has to offer. Each mammal occupies a place in the ramifying network of interdependent life-styles that together form a community. A community is not a mutual-aid society; on the contrary, it is a matter of who eats whom. At the base of the food chain are the plants. The herbivores eat grass and leaves, the carnivores eat the herbivores, and the carnivores themselves, at their death, provide food for scavengers, such as vultures, jackals and rodents. What is left is returned to the soil, where it is broken down by bacteria into chemical units that are ultimately utilized by the plants. Thus the wheel has come full circle, and recycling is complete.

Classification

From the seventeenth century onward, in Europe and in the newly won American continent, the age of reason was dawning. All over the Western world scientists were beginning to try to make sense of the universe. Linnaeus, the famous Swedish naturalist, spent many years of his life arranging all the plant species then known into closely related groups. Later he turned his attention to the animal kingdom and in 1758 published a classification, *Systema Naturae*, that was both original and challenging. First, he coined a new name, "Mammalia," for animals that suckled their young, based on the Latin word *mamma*, meaning a breast. Second, he put man (*Homo sapiens*) fairly and squarely in the animal kingdom in the same group as the lemurs, monkeys and apes and placed them at the head of his list of mammals, calling them primates—"first mammals." Possibly his greatest contribution was in arranging animals in a unique hierarchical system of class, order, family, genus and species and, in naming them, using the international language of science at that time—Latin. For example, the zoological status of the timber wolf is as follows:

CLASS:	*Mammalia*	Mammals
ORDER:	*Carnivora*	Flesh-eating mammals
FAMILY:	*Canidae*	Fox, coyote, wolf
GENUS:	*Canis*	Coyote, wolf
SPECIES:	*Canis lupus*	Wolf
SUBSPECIES:	*Canis lupus griseus*	Timber wolf

The simplicity and flexibility of the system have made Linnaeus' *System of Nature* the foundation stone of modern zoology.

Linnaeus classified animals entirely on the basis of common characteristics and had no conception of evolutionary relationships. In the pre-Darwin era, each species of animal or plant was thought to have been created specially and to be incapable of change. With the publication of Darwin's revolutionary ideas in 1859, the old concept of species had to be discarded. A species is now considered as a group or population of animals that interbreed freely and naturally in the wild, even if they do not all look exactly the same. It is sometimes possible to confirm that two animals that look very much alike belong to separate species simply because they do *not* interbreed, even when living in the same place. In South America there are two small spotted cats, the margay and the slightly larger ocelot. The female ocelot and the male margay are virtually the same size, yet never interbreed. Clearly scent and other behavioral signals, not appreciated by a human observer, combine to prevent mating.

Darwin's principle of the evolution of species gave new impetus to the study of fossils. The fossil record goes back some 600 million years and shows a gradual increase in the complexity of living organisms from the Paleozoic era to the present day. As a record of change with time, spread over many millions of years, it has shed light on the interrelationships of the animal kingdom. The placental and marsupial stocks separated early in the Cretaceous epoch, so that any similarities between monkeys (placental) and opossums (marsupial) must be the result of a phenomenon known as convergence, where similar adaptations evolve in distantly related animals. Monkeys and opossums both have prehensile tails and opposable big toes, indicating that they have responded in a similar way to life in the tropical forests of South America.

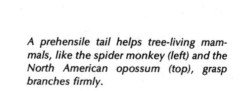

A prehensile tail helps tree-living mammals, like the spider monkey (left) and the North American opossum (top), grasp branches firmly.

Origin of Mammals

Mammals evolved from a group of primitive reptiles, called Pelycosaurs, some 200 million years ago. To begin with, they were as much reptiles as mammals, but as time passed certain characteristics foreshadowing those of true mammals appeared in the skull. For instance, the teeth, instead of being made up of a series of identical pegs, had become differentiated into sets each having a specific function: gripping teeth (incisors), puncturing and tearing teeth (canines) and crushing and slicing teeth (molars). The body of the mammallike reptiles slowly assumed a quadrupedal stance; the limbs supported the body off the ground in striking contrast to the sprawling posture of reptiles.

The first true mammals, free of reptilian characteristics, appeared during the Jurassic epoch 150 million years ago. They were small creatures varying from the size of a mouse to that of a cat. Most of the earliest mammalian lines disappeared from the fossil record, victims of competition from the much larger dinosaurs, but one line persisted and became the ancestor of modern mammals. They are the pantotheres, small ratlike creatures with furry coats. This statement is not so much of a guess as one might think; fur (or feathers) and warm-bloodedness almost inevitably go together.

Throughout the Cretaceous epoch, mammals are rare in fossil deposits compared with the ubiquitous dinosaurs, and there is little doubt which were the dominant animals for the 70 million years that the epoch lasted; but at the end of the Cretaceous everything changed. For reasons not fully understood, the dinosaurs suddenly vanished over a time span of less than five million years. Although five million years may seem a long time, it is sudden in geological terms. Many unlikely explanations have been put forward to explain the demise of the dinosaurs, from a star exploding near the earth to the wholesale destruction of dinosaur eggs by the up-and-coming mammals. Whatever the real explanation—the most generally accepted view is that the cold-blooded dinosaurs could not adapt to drastic climatic changes of the time—their disappearance radically altered the balance of power in the animal world. The beginning of the Paleocene 65 million years ago saw a dramatic increase in the number of mammal species. Old established orders such as the insectivores and the primates expanded in number and variety, and new orders such as hoofed animals (condylarths) and carnivores (creodonts) appear to have been followed rapidly by rodents, sea mammals, bats and the ancestors of all the rest of the incredible pageant of modern mammals.

The extinct mammallike reptile, Thrinaxodon (left), lived over 200 million years ago. The pantothere (below) was the earliest true mammal.

Tree of Mammals

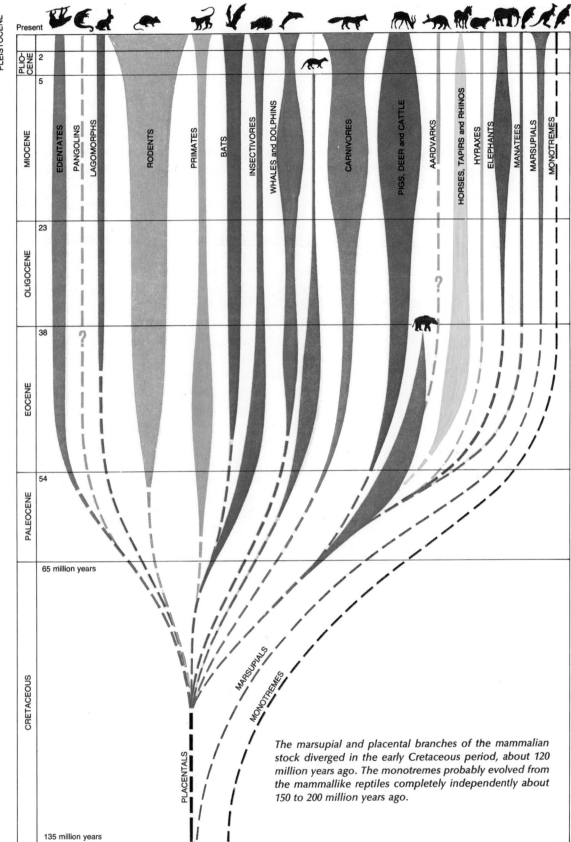

The marsupial and placental branches of the mammalian stock diverged in the early Cretaceous period, about 120 million years ago. The monotremes probably evolved from the mammallike reptiles completely independently about 150 to 200 million years ago.

Behavior of Mammals

Evolution is concerned with living animals, so it is inevitable that natural selection, the principle mechanism of evolution, should depend on behavior as a measure of fitness. A dead animal through its bones and other tissues tells us much about its adaptations but does not give us the whole story. A living, behaving animal can fill the gaps in the record by revealing facets of behavior that we could not have guessed at. For example, there is nothing in their structure to suggest that chimpanzees make and use tools, that Alaskan bears catch salmon in midstream or that wolverines cache their winter food in "deep-freeze lockers" above the snow line. The majority of behavior patterns, however, whether instinctive or learned, are correlated with structural adaptations.

Locomotion. Mammals are basically quadrupeds, as were their reptilian ancestors. The hindlimbs propel the animal, while the forelimbs support the rib cage. The forelimbs, being nearer the mouth end of the body, are more versatile than the hindlimbs and are used for a variety of activities, including handling food, reaching out to climb, digging, killing and capturing prey and in self-defense.

Quadrupedalism is a stable posture; the exact location of the center of gravity varies from animal to animal but is always within the area defined by the legs. A mammal has the equilibrium of a table, with a leg at each corner.

A few mammals have adopted a much more risky two-legged gait. Habitually bipedal mammals such as the kangaroo, the jerboa and the springhaas are ably assisted by their tails; in one sense they are tripedal. Occasional bipeds such as bears have a greater balancing problem.

Bipedalism is a special characteristic of all primates that probably developed out of their tree-climbing habit. All primates show bipedalism to some degree, particularly the apes, such as the gibbon and the chimpanzee, but the only real two-footed walker is man. As a result of the advantages bipedalism brings, particularly the liberation of the hands from a locomotor role, man has become, as it were, the President of the animal world.

Marine mammals have adapted to the environment in a somewhat different way. It is important to realize that whales and dolphins are not simply made-over fishes; they are land mammals that have reverted to the fish type. The seals have also reverted but to a somewhat later stage of evolution. They are more like ancestral amphibians, crawling out of the water to breed, moving awkwardly on their bellies and paddlelike limbs.

The gibbon is one of the most successful two-legged walkers, with the exception of man. The versatile forelimbs enable it to swing from branch to branch.

With its streamlined body and finlike limbs, a seal moves awkwardly on land but swims superbly in its natural element, the sea.

The bats are the only mammalian fliers, but there are a number of gliders that can cover considerable distances in a downward direction from tree to tree or from tree to ground. Gliding is achieved by spreading the loose skin between the arms and legs and the side of the body. There are several species of gliding mammals, including squirrels, but the best glider is the colugo, which may travel up to 100 yards by this method.

Locomotion is the basis of survival. A mammal needs to move to eat and to eat to live, but without the special senses movement would be useless. The mammal must be able to see where it is going, feel the nature of the ground as it moves, smell or hear its prey and taste it when it is captured.

In some animals one or more senses may be more highly developed than the others. The dominant sense of fishes is probably smell and of birds sight. Among mammals the twin senses of smell and hearing are basically the most important, but for primates, including man, the important combination is touch and sight.

Certain ways of life favor different combinations of senses. Nocturnal mammals, for instance, rely heavily on hearing, smell and touch, and, as a corollary, many of them have large ears like radio scanners, long inquisitive snouts and prominent facial whiskers. They sometimes have big eyes, too, but this is an adaptation for collecting as much available light as possible in their moonlit world, not evidence of an acute visual sense. Few nocturnal mammals possess the color vision or stereoscopic vision of many diurnal mammals. Predatory animals depend more on sight than prey animals, which are quite vulnerable unless thay have an acute sense of smell. Rooting animals such as pigs, aardvarks and anteaters rely most on their sensitive snouts.

The use of sonar (echolocation) by bats was not suspected until man had invented the identical principle, which he called radar. Later it was discovered that whales and dolphins also use this special hearing technique for navigation in dark or turbid waters. It is thought that some species of seals also use sonar. For all we know, many other mammals may be relying on this "sixth" sense to aid them in their nocturnal movements.

Social Behavior

Mammals suckle their young. The first hours, days and weeks of a mammal's life are spent in the society of its mother, so it is inevitable that social bonds develop between them. In later life males and females consort to mate. Thus there are at least two phases of social activity in every mammal's lifetime, even in the case of so-called "solitary" mammals.

Mammals adapt their life-styles to a wide variety of habitats in basically similar ways. Whales form the same kinds of social groups as do land mammals. The pygmy sperm whale is solitary; the blue whale forms a "family" group consisting of a male, a female and her calf; and pilot whales form large schools of fifty or so. At certain seasons the sperm whale adopts a "harem" formation, a single male keeping in close contact with a herd of females and their calves. Gray whales of the Pacific form large herds during their annual migration from the feeding grounds of the Bering Sea to the breeding grounds of Lower California. This behavior parallels that of the ungulate (hoofed mammal) migrations of Africa, when vast herds of wildebeest and zebra move westward during the dry season in search of better grazing.

Food is the key to the size of mammal societies. Grazers like the ungulates, or plankton feeders like baleen whales, can gather in large numbers, as their food supply is both abundant and widespread. For predators, on the other hand, finding food is unpredictable, so they cannot afford to congregate. Stealthy hunters like the leopard fare better in solitary pursuit of their prey, while cooperative hunters like wolves or killer whales form small cohesive packs.

While some animals migrate in search of food, others assure their food supply by establishing themselves in a fixed territory and defending it against invasion by others of their own species. Territorial behavior was first observed in songbirds, the song being an integral part of territorial defense, but it has also been effectively exploited by the noisy primates, the howler monkey, the gibbon and the siamang, whose "dawn chorus" advertises their presence and acts as a warning to intruders.

The mammalian system of reproduction entails a long period of infant dependence and so gives time for close social bonds to form between mother and young. There is time too for learning the skills that will mean survival. Through imitation, trial and error and play, young mammals learn how to find food, how to avoid danger and how to fit into the social system.

The learning process is aided by the ability of mammals to communicate with one another. Scent can give a lot of information. By leaving a few drops of urine on a branch, a potto indicates its presence, its sex and its reproductive condition to another potto, thus facilitating the meeting of these solitary animals.

Visual signals are equally important. Patches of color, stripes and spots are a means by which species recognize one another, and they may also serve as camouflage, either by blending with the background or by breaking up the animal's outline and making it difficult to see.

Vocal communication is as diverse as the mammals themselves, from the haunting song of the humpback whale to the faint squeaks of the smallest pygmy shrew. Calls have the advantage that they can convey a message in thick jungle

Chimpanzees communicate through an elaborate series of postures and facial expressions, such as this plea for a banana.

or over long distances, so it is not surprising that chimpanzees are among the noisiest mammals. Living either in dense forest or woodland, they keep in touch with one another through a wide variety of hoots, barks and screams. At close range, soft whimpers or grunts convey feelings of discomfort or pleasure. Chimpanzees cannot communicate with one another through speech or language as we know it. Their calls are an integral part of a sophisticated repertoire of postures, gestures and facial expressions that can convey factual information as well as very fine shades of feeling.

Language, and its expression through the mechanism of speech, is one of the few human talents not found in other mammals. Humans, on the other hand, fall short in many aspects of communication, in echolocation and scent perception, for instance, as well as in the more important fields of individual understanding and social awareness. True communication has little to do with words.

In this brief introduction it has been possible only to touch on the many interesting aspects of the life of mammals—their diversity, their evolution, their role in the animal kingdom and their physical and behavioral adaptations. Common to all these aspects is the influence of the environment, which dominates all animal affairs. It is easy to see how interference with the environment will immediately feed back on the welfare and, indeed, the very existence of wildlife; and this is exactly what man is doing. Day by day he is destroying wildlife habitats by a dozen different methods—not consciously but in his greed for timber, minerals, water power and agricultural products. The obliteration of the passenger pigeon and the wild horse and the near extinction of the blue whale pale to insignificance compared with the continual loss of wildlife from man's inexorable erosion of the natural environment. It is not only the animals on the official Endangered Species List that are in jeopardy—*all* wildlife is.

PRUE AND JOHN NAPIER

WORLD GUIDE
TO
MAMMALS

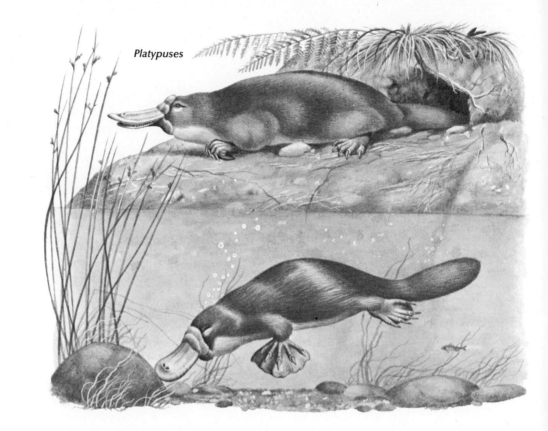

Platypuses

MONOTREMES: EGG-LAYING MAMMALS
(ORDER MONOTREMATA)

Monotremes are the most primitive mammals, sharing features with birds and reptiles. They are the only mammals that lay eggs, which are rubbery-shelled.

Monotremes, which occur only in Australia, Tasmania and New Guinea, have a lower body temperature than any other mammal, and it fluctuates with the temperature of their surroundings. Their single excretory opening, or cloaca, serves for reproduction and elimination. As in birds and reptiles, the male's testes are located internally. Males—and some females—bear horny spurs on their ankles. In male platypuses, the spurs are poisonous.

PLATYPUS (FAMILY ORNITHORHYNCHIDAE)

The platypus *(Ornithorhynchus anatinus)*, maximum length 20 in., weight 2–4 lbs., is the only member of its family. It occurs in Tasmania and eastern Australia — from sea level to 6,000 feet and from the tropics to near-freezing conditions. Once widely trapped for its fur, the platypus is now protected.

Wholly aquatic, living in lakes and streams, the platypus has a streamlined body and webbed feet. The short, dense fur extends onto the flat tail, and the pliable, ducklike bill is used to sift mud for the small aquatic animals it eats. While submerged, the platypus stores food in its cheek pouches. It lacks external ears but has ear holes that close when the animal is underwater. Most of its time is spent in its burrow or basking in the sun.

The female incubates her eggs (normally two) by wrapping herself around them for 7–10 days. She does not develop even a rudimentary pouch.

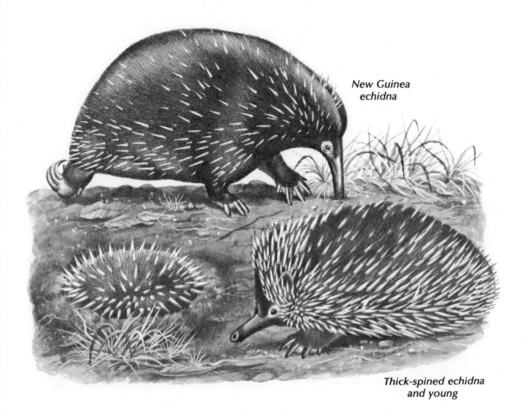

New Guinea
echidna

Thick-spined echidna
and young

ECHIDNAS (FAMILY TACHYGLOSSIDAE)

Echidnas (*Zaglossus*, 3 species, and *Tachyglossus*, 2 species) are widespread and common, occupying habitats ranging from deserts to rain forests and from sea level to more than 9,000 feet, wherever they can find termites and ants, their exclusive diet. In hot deserts they remain in cool underground burrows during the day, emerging at dusk to feed. They cannot tolerate heat and soon die at temperatures of 100°F. In cold weather they become dormant, entering a state of torpor similar to hibernation.

Echidnas are 1½ to 2 ft. long. They have short, powerful legs and large claws that equip them for breaking into hard termite mounds. The long, slim, rubbery snout has a small opening at the tip for the whiplike tongue, which is sticky with saliva. With this snout, the animals can reach deep into the galleries of ant and termite nests to get their meals.

During the breeding season, the female develops a rudimentary pouch— no more than a depression on her belly. Here she places a single egg, which is incubated for 10–11 days. The "hatchling" emerges into the pouch and there feeds on the thick, creamy milk that exudes from pores in the mother's skin rather than from teats as in other mammals. As soon as its spines begin to develop, the young echnida is forced from the pouch. The mother will continue to suckle it, however, until it is about 90 days old.

Echidnas are solitary in habit. They are remarkably agile and can run and climb well. If frightened, they will burrow quickly into the ground, leaving only their spines exposed. In the New Guinea echidna (*Z. bruijni*), the spines are almost hidden in the thick fur.

Left: Large American opossum and young   *Right: Large American opossum feigning death*

MARSUPIALS: POUCHED MAMMALS
(ORDER MARSUPIALIA)

Most marsupials have a fold or pocket of skin, the marsupium, covering the female's nipples. In kangaroos and phalangers, the pouch opens to the front; in others, to the rear.

At birth—the gestation period is only 12 days for the smallest and up to 33 days for the large kangaroos—young marsupials are tiny, hairless embryos, weighing less than an ounce. With no assistance from the mother, they crawl to the abdominal nipples. Once attached to a nipple, they do not let go for a number of months—until their development is completed.

Female marsupials mate a few days after giving birth. They have twin wombs and double vaginas. The testes in male are hung in front of the forked penis. Development of the fertilized egg stops if the pouch is occupied. It resumes after the young detach from the nipples or if they die or are lost. Marsupials have more teeth (as many as 52 in some species) than most mammals but only one set in a lifetime.

NEW WORLD OPOSSUMS   (FAMILIES DIDELPHIIDAE {OPOSSUMS} and CAENOLESTIDAE {RAT OPOSSUMS})

Opossums (11 genera, 60 species) and rat opossums (3 genera, 6 species) are the only marsupials occurring outside Australasia. The first marsupial described by a zoologist was collected in Brazil in 1500.

LARGE AMERICAN OPOSSUM *(Didelphis marsupialis virginiana)*, maximum body length about 20 in. and tail about the same length, weight 10 lbs.; but both

Murine opossum and young

length and weight vary over the animal's wide range. The large ears are almost naked, as is the prehensile tail. Young opossums ride on their mother's back, anchoring their tails to hers. The opossum is nocturnal, and though an excellent climber, it spends most of its time on the ground scavenging for food. Its principal defense is "playing possum," in which death is feigned in a state of self-induced temporary paralysis.

Prolific breeders, females may produce as many as three litters a year. They may give birth to 20–25 young at a time, but as they have only 13 nipples, about half of each litter dies of starvation. The high reproductive rate, adaptability to varied conditions and omnivorous diet account for the opossum's success. Though preyed on by larger animals and hunted by man for food and for the coarse fur, the opossum has continued to expand its range and is the only marsupial occurring in Canada. Individuals live only 2–3 years.

WOOLLY OPOSSUMS (*Caluromys*, 3 species), slightly smaller than the common opossum, live in tropical regions. Despite their thick coats, they become torpid when the temperature drops.

Woolly opossums are essentially arboreal—squirrel-like in appearance, habits and agility. They nest in the upper branches and eat fruits, insects and bird eggs. The rare black-shouldered opossum (*Caluromysiops irrupta*) (see illustration, p. 24) is larger and lives in the humid forests of Peru.

■ *Woolly opossum*　　■ *Large American opossum*

Four-eyed opossum   *Black-shouldered opossum (see text, p. 23)*

FOUR-EYED OPOSSUM *(Philander opossum)*, maximum length 20 in., weight I lb., favors forests along waterways and swamps. Its name comes from the white spot above each eye. The tail is half furred, half naked. This agile marsupial is equally at home on the ground or in trees. It can also swim well, its omnivorous diet including small aquatic animals. Its liking for fruit causes it to be ranked a pest in some areas.

RAT-TAILED OPOSSUM *(Metachirus nudicaudatus)* is similar in size, also "four-eyed" and likes fruit. But it is brown rather than gray, and its tail is naked.

Most abundant of the South American marsupials are the MURINE, or MOUSE, OPOSSUMS *(Marmosa,* 40 species), 6–12 in. long (see illustration, p. 23). These pouchless marsupials breed the year round in the tropics, three times a year in cooler regions. Most are arboreal, but some prefer open grasslands.

BARE-TAILED OPOSSUMS *(Monodelphis,* 11 species) are also small. One species inhabits dwellings like the house mouse. They are nocturnal and feed on rodents, insects and fruit. Glands on the neck and chest of the males produce a strong ordor. Young are born throughout the year and, since the pouch is poorly developed, cling to the nipples and flanks for the first two months.

RAT OPOSSUMS *(Caenolestes, Lestoros* and *Rhyncholestes)* are pouchless and shrewlike, mainly nocturnal and make runways in the grass. The tail is virtually hairless, and the soft, thick fur is gray to black, the underparts lighter. Some live near the timberline in Andean meadows, others at sea level.

■ *Four-eyed opossum*

Thick-tailed opossum

Yapok

YAPOK, or WATER OPOSSUM *(Chironectes minimus)*, maximum length 12 in. and tail 15 in., is the only aquatic marsupial. It is an excellent swimmer and diver. With its webbed feet, rounded head and short, dense fur, it reminds one of an otter. The wrist bone is enlarged into a sixth fingerlike projection on the forefoot; a thin webbing extends between it and the thumb. The tail is furred at the base and only partly prehensile.

The yapok is nocturnal, hunting for food—mainly crayfish—along and in waterways. It digs burrows above the waterline in the banks of streams, preferring those with clear, shallow, slow-moving water. The young are born in December and stay in the pouch until they are well furred. A strong muscle closes the female's pouch so tightly that it becomes waterproof. This permits her to continue her aquatic life—swimming and feeding—without danger of drowning the young attached inside. The male also has a pouch into which he retracts his scrotum.

The attractiveness of the yapok's fur led to intensive trapping of the animals during the 1920s and 1930s.

THICK-TAILED, or LITTLE WATER, OPOSSUM *(Lutreolina crassicaudata)*, maximum length 20 in., weight 1 lb., is an example of parallel development, for it occupies the same ecological niche as weasels. It looks like a weasel and has similar habits. Largely carnivorous, it lives in forests, plains and marshy areas. It climbs well, and its movements are quick and graceful. During the day, it hides in a hollow log or in a nest of leaves and grass.

■ *Yapok*   *Thick-tailed opossum*

25

Northern native cat

Tiger cat

NATIVE CATS, MARSUPIAL MICE AND KIN (FAMILY DASYURIDAE)

All the members of this large, diverse family are carnivorous, some eating insects and others attacking large animals. Included in the family are the smallest marsupials; others are about the size of dogs. Some are pouchless; in those that do have pouches, the opening is toward the rear.

NATIVE CATS, or DASYURE (subfamily Dasyurinae, 5 species), are not true cats but carnivorous marsupials. They measure about 2–3 ft. long, including the 1-ft. tail.

These lithe-bodied animals live in forests and are at home in trees, although the eastern and western species are believed to be terrestrial. Native cats have rough soles on their feet that greatly assist them when climbing. Nimble and fast on even the smallest branch, they feed on small mammals, lizards and insects.

Native cats have up to 24 young, but with only 8 teats in the simple pouch, a crescent-shaped fold of skin on the abdomen, many young are lost. They measure only ¼ inch at birth and grow to only 1¼ in. during the first month. They are weaned at 2 months and are independent at 5 months.

Once common, most native cats are now rare. The western native cat (*Dasyurinus geoffroyii*) lived in the eucalyptus groves and savannas of southern Australia but is now confined to isolated areas. The eastern native cat (*Dasyurus viverrinus*) is still widespread in Tasmania but rare on the mainland. There are two color phases, black with buff spots and brown with white spots. The smallest native cat is the northern species (*Satanellus hallucatus*), which prefers coastal grasslands. It is thought to be solitary and nocturnal. The largest dasyure is the tiger cat (*Dasyurops maculatus*) of eastern Australia and Tasmania.

Tasmanian devils

TASMANIAN DEVIL *(Sarcophilus harrisi)* once ranged over all of Australia but is now confined to remote regions of Tasmania, where it lives mainly along beaches and waterways. Stockily built, it is about 3 ft. long—including a l-ft.-long tail. Its forequarters are much more powerful than the hindquarters.

The innocuous Tasmanian devil resembles a small bear but is much more fierce in appearance. Its jet black coat interrupted by only a few white patches has contributed to its name of "devil," as has its eerie call—a loud growl that ends in a snarled spitting cough.

The Tasmanian devil's large head, powerful neck muscles, strong jaws and teeth enable it to overcome prey larger than itself. Small wallabies, birds and lizards form its usual diet. It tracks its prey relentlessly as it is not quick enough to run it down. Young animals can be tamed, becoming as playful and as affectionate as kittens.

Generally solitary and nocturnal, Tasmanian devils are found in open forests. Mating occurs in March or April. The three or four young are born in May and are carried in the mother's horseshoe-shaped pouch for only about a month. The mother then makes a nest for them, and they spend their time there until they are big enough to be independent.

The Tasmanian devil is the largest of the carnivorous marsupials—unless the slightly larger TASMANIAN WOLF *(Thylacinus cynocephalus)* still exists. Long ago the Tasmanian wolf, which has a distinctly doglike head, was also common in Australia. Like the Tasmanian devil, it made a last stand on Tasmania, where man became its worst foe. In the mid-1960s footprints and some hair were discovered, but the animal has not been seen for many years.

Narrow-footed
marsupial mouse

Mulgara marsupial mouse   Jerboa mouse

MARSUPIAL MICE, or PHASCOGALES (11 genera, about 39 species), are dasyurids (see p. 26), but as a group they are the smallest of the marsupials. Ingram's planigale (*Planigale ingrami*), about the size of a common mouse, is only 2–3 in. long, plus a 2-in. tail. Others, such as the black-tailed phascogale (*Phascogale tapoatafa*) and the kowar (*Dasyuroides byrnei*), are rat-sized—about 7 in. long, the tail slightly shorter (6 in.).

Marsupial mice have pointed, shrewlike muzzles with long whiskers. Their ears are large, the tail short. Instead of the two long incisors common to rodents, they have six to eight small incisors, more like those of insectivores.

Phascogales prey principally on insects and their larvae, which makes them valuable in pest control, but they also eat small mice and suck nectar. Some are burrowers, a few are arboreal. They are prolific breeders, even the smallest species having litters of 6–12 young. The different species occur from deserts to rain forests and from sea level to the tops of mountains.

The mulgara, or crested-tailed marsupial mouse (*Dasycercus cristicauda*), maximum length 8 in. plus a 5-in. tail, has a crest of stiff hairs at the tip of its tail. It inhabits some of the most arid regions of Australia, staying underground during the heat of the day. Most of its water needs are obtained from its food. Fat stored in its thick tail is used as a reserve when food is scarce. Its pouch is nearly absent; the young are protected by a ridge of skin.

The narrow-footed marsupial mouse (*Sminthopsis crassicaudata*) is one of about 11 species that are terrestrial and shrewlike in habits, hiding under rocks and logs when not actively hunting for food. Like others, it may eat more than its own weight in food daily.

Numbat

The rare, desert-dwelling jerboa marsupials *(Antechinomys*, 2 species) are mouse-sized but have long hind legs and a thin, tufted tail. They do not jump like true jerboas, however. Rather, they leapfrog, using their plumed tails as rudders. Jerboa marsupials are nocturnal.

Brush-tailed phascogales *(Phascogale*, 2 species) have long hairs tipping their tails. The hairs normally lie flat, but when lifted, the tail looks like a bottle brush. Both species are arboreal and squirrel-like in their agility as climbers.

Broad-footed marsupial mice, or dibblers *(Antechinus*, 13 species), are mainly terrestrial, but they are good climbers. Their grooved palms and sole pads give them a grip so firm that they can even run upside down on branches.

NUMBATS (FAMILY MYRMECOBIIDAE)

Two species comprise this family: the numbat, or banded anteater *(Myrmecobius fasciatus)*, and the rusty numbat *(M. rufus)*, which is not as well known. Both are about 10 in. long, the tail about 7 in. long.

Unlike most marsupials, the numbat is diurnal, sleeping in hollow logs at night. It feeds exclusively on termites. Like the true anteaters, it has a long tongue with which it picks up the insects exposed when it tears a nest apart with its long claws.

In its long muzzle the numbat has 52 teeth—more than in most mammals. The teeth are not used in eating, however, as insects are swallowed whole. The numbat is timid, inoffensive and slow-moving, an easy victim of predators.

Females lack a pouch. They give birth to four young that attach themselves to the nipples and cling to the mother's coarse fur.

Short-nosed bandicoot

30

Long-nosed bandicoot

BANDICOOTS (FAMILY PERAMELIDAE)

Bandicoots (9 genera, about 25 species) range through a variety of habitats, from lowland rain forests and cultivated lands to deserts and subalpine conditions at more than 10,000 feet. Bandicoots are found in Australia, Tasmania, New Guinea and neighboring islands. Several species have been greatly reduced in numbers, and some are near extinction. Bandicoots may damage lawns and gardens as they search for grubs and are hence killed as pests. They have also been victims of foxes, dogs and other introduced animals.

Most bandicoots are insectivorous, but they eat other small animals, roots and tubers. They are solitary and nocturnal; some are active at dawn and dusk. They spend the day resting in their "nest" of heaped vegetation on the surface of the ground.

In bandicoots, the pouch opens to the rear. Their scientific name, in fact, means "badger with a pouch." The face is pointed, the tail short. All have long, slim feet with long claws. The hind legs are large, and the animals hop about like rabbits. The front legs are used for digging. Bandicoots are extremely fleet, and when alarmed they may leap high in the air before running.

In eastern Australia, the long-nosed bandicoot (*Perameles nasuta*) is one of the most common species. In Tasmania, the barred bandicoot (*P. gunni*) is ubiquitous, along with short-nosed bandicoots (*Isoodon*, several species). Bilbies, or rabbit bandicoots (*Thylacomys*, several species), have long, rabbitlike ears. Several species are endangered, mainly due to foxes and human settlement. The pig-footed bandicoot (*Chaeropus ecaudatus*) was once common in the desert region but has not been seen since the 1920s.

Cuscus   Ring-tailed possum

AUSTRALIAN OPOSSUMS AND PHALANGERS
(FAMILY PHALANGERIDAE)

In this family (16 genera, 45 species), the pouch opens forward. Nearly all are arboreal, the big toe opposable so that the foot is used for grasping. The tail is long; in some, prehensile. Most are herbivorous, feeding on leaves, flowers and fruit, but some are insectivorous or omnivorous. They are nocturnal cr active in the twilight hours of dusk and dawn, and they nest in abandoned burrows, holes in trees, old bird nests or nests they build themselves in branches. Females bear one to three (usually two) young.

CUSCUSES (*Phalanger* and *Spilocuscus*) are superficially like monkeys but almost as slow-moving as sloths. All give off a foul odor when disturbed. They spend most of their day sleeping, typically in the fork of a tree; they feed at night on foliage and small mammals. The spotted cuscus (*Phalanger maculatus*) is about 3½ ft. long, its prehensile tail accounting for about half this length.

RING-TAILED POSSUM (*Pseudocheirus peregrinus*) is also nocturnal and arboreal, making a large leafy nest in a tree or living in a hole in a tree. Its name comes from its habit of keeping its long tail coiled in a ring when it is not in use, but the tail is prehensile and is used for grasping branches firmly when the animal is climbing. The thumb and index fingers are opposable, which facilitates climbing. The fur is dense and soft and woolly, and some species have lighter spots or stripes on the back and neck.

About a dozen species, all similar in appearance and habits, occur in Australia, Tasmania and New Guinea. Ring-tailed possums are usually slow. When cornered they do not fight but "freeze" and stare at the cause of alarm.

Pygmy possum   Brush-tailed possum

BRUSH-TAILED POSSUM *(Trichosurus vulpecula)*, one of several widely distributed species in its genus, is the size of a house cat and has a bushy tail, the tip bare on the underside for grasping. Its appearance suggested the name "foxlike opossum" to the naturalist who described the first one. Basically arboreal, it is also at home on the brushy plains where it lives in the abandoned burrows of rabbits. Though probably the most common small Australian marsupial, the brush-tailed possum is rarely seen because it is both nocturnal and secretive. Sometimes it takes up residence in buildings, having adapted well to living in and near human settlements.

The brush-tailed possum eats mainly insects, but its omnivorous diet includes fruit, leaves and buds of trees or occasionally even carrion. It mates between March and September, the female giving birth to one (rarely two) young, which are completely independent five months later.

The brush-tailed possum is hunted both for sport and for its thick, woolly fur. When, in 1920, it was no longer given protection, within three months over 100,000 were killed for the fur trade. It was introduced to New Zealand, where it became a serious pest of forest and orchard trees.

DORMOUSE POSSUM *(Cercartetus nanus)* is only about 4 in. long, plus a 3½-in. prehensile tail. Primarily insectivorous, it also eats spiders and other small animals. It is said to hibernate during part of the winter or during cold spells. These nocturnal possums sometimes use abandoned birds' nests for shelter.

LEADBEATTER'S POSSUM *(Gymnobelideus leadbeateri)* resembles a sugar glider without the gliding membranes. It was thought to be extinct but was rediscovered in 1961.

Lesser gliding possum

Greater gliding possum and young   *Pygmy gliding possum*

GLIDING POSSUMS, or FLYING PHALANGERS, are the marsupial counterparts of flying squirrels, with a gliding membrane between the front and hind legs. This extends fully when the legs are stretched, at other times lying in loose folds along the sides of the body. Gliders do not fly but make a gliding descent, using their membranes as a parachute. All are nocturnal, hence rarely seen.

The pygmy gliding possum (*Acrobates pygmaeus*) is the smallest, about 6 in. long. It is often abundant in wooded areas but rarely seen. During the day it stays in hiding in the hollows of trees, usually making a nest of shredded bark and eucalyptus leaves. The female has only four nipples in her pouch. She may give birth to many more young, but only the first four to attach themselves will survive.

The lesser gliding possum, or sugar glider (*Petaurus,* 3 species), is larger— about the size of a gray squirrel. It eats insects and also the leaves, buds and flowers of trees.

The female gives birth to one or two young. They are fully mature and ready to live independently within 60 days but may continue to use the same nest as their parents. Gliding possums use leaf nests that have a characteristic rank odor from the decomposing leaves.

The greater gliding possum (*Schoinobates volans*) is the size of a house cat, its bushy tail about 1½ ft. long. Mostly arboreal, it often glides 30–40 yards from tree to tree. Solitary and noctural, it feeds on eucalyptus leaves.

This large opossum is found in the mountain rain forests of Queensland. A single offspring is born in August and stays with the parents until fully grown. As with koalas, the weaning process onto eucalyptus leaves is difficult because youngsters dislike the pungent smell.

Koala and young

KOALA (FAMILY PHASCOLARCTIDAE)

The single species of this family is the koala (*Phascolarctos cinereus*), which is 2–2½ ft. long and lacks a visible external tail. It resembles a teddy bear.

Male koalas form a harem in August prior to the start of the breeding season, assiduously keeping other males away by striking out with their forepaws or chasing and biting them.

The female koala's pouch opens to the rear. She bears a single young after a gestation period of about 5 weeks. The newborn koala is less than an inch long, but by the time it is 2–3 months old, it is fully furred and ready to leave the pouch. At first it goes only as far as its mother's back. Until it is 12 months old, it remains quite helpless and does not become mature until it is 4 years old.

The arboreal koala has a highly specialized diet, eating only the leaves of various gum or eucalyptus trees. It seldom drinks: koala means "no drink" in Aborigine. The koala spends most of its life clinging to eucalyptus trees, moving from one to another only after stripping all the edible leaves and shoots. It can shuffle in a jerky manner along the ground at a surprising speed. A group of koalas is nearly invisible; when they are sleeping curled up in the forks of eucalyptus branches, their fur blends in with the background.

These once abundant animals, certainly among the most familiar and famous in Australia, were almost completely exterminated by pelt hunters. Timid and inoffensive, the koalas were easy victims, and in the 1920s millions of skins were exported every year. When the koala became rare, the government provided protection for those few remaining and also set aside preserves where the population is now increasing slowly.

Common wombat

Hairy-nosed wombat

WOMBATS (FAMILY PHASCOLOMIDAE)

These heavy-bodied, badgerlike marsupials are found in Australia and Tasmania. Like beavers and other rodents, they have two pairs of chisel-like incisors. They have only a stumpy tail, and their fur is coarse, almost wiry. The female gives birth to a single young that is carried in the pouch, opening to the rear, from the time of its birth in May or June until December.

Wombats dig extensive burrows—tunnels as much as 100 feet long in some instances. They spend the day resting in a nest of grass at the end of the burrow, coming out at night to forage on grass or other vegetation. Those that live in mountainous or rocky areas may dig shallower burrows or may settle for nesting in rocky crevices. Wombats are shy and wary animals, but they seem threatening with their sudden dashes, across roads, for example. When cornered, they kick backward and hiss like other marsupials. If food becomes scarce on the ground, wombats may cut down sizable trees, like beavers, to get the foliage. They use their forepaws like giant pandas to grasp and hold onto stems while they nibble the leaves.

The common wombat (*Vombatus ursinus*) is large—maximum length 4 ft., weight 80 lbs. It is still far from matching the size of ancestral types that were as big as hippopotamuses. The hairy-nosed wombat (*Lasiorhinus latifrons*) overlaps the common wombat in range but is considerably smaller, as is Barnard's hairy-nosed wombat (*L. barnardi*).

Wombats are hunted for sport and for food. Despite these inroads on their populations, naked-nosed wombats have so far survived in reasonably safe numbers.

Red kangaroo male   *Red kangaroo female and joey*

KANGAROOS, WALLABIES AND KIN (FAMILY MACROPODIDAE)

Most of the 15 genera and 55 species comprising this family occur only in Australia, a few inhabiting New Guinea, Tasmania and nearby islands.

Larger kangaroos occupy the same niche as antelopes in Africa. They usually feed and drink during the cool hours at dawn and dusk and rest in groups in the shade during the heat of the day. When the group is resting, one kangaroo always remains alert, ready to sound an alarm at the slightest sound or sight of danger. Kangaroos are usually silent. The young make squeaking noises and the adults soft clucking sounds, but when alarmed, they cough loudly and thump the ground with their hind feet. Once disturbed, a group may not settle again until it has moved several miles away.

Normally docile, kangaroos will attack if cornered. Balancing themselves on their tail they can deliver powerful, even fatal, kicks. Large males may wrestle or "box" with other males to establish dominance.

A newborn kangaroo is naked and minute, only about ¾ in. long and weighing about 1 gram. The mother licks the fur on her abdomen and the infant then makes its way unaided along a moist track to the pouch, where it fastens itself to a teat. It remains there for 8 months, by this time weighing about 10 pounds. It continues to suckle for another 6 months, after which it is reasonably independent but continues to use the pouch as a place of refuge.

A female kangaroo or wallaby becomes pregnant within a few days after she has given birth. If the young in her pouch grows without mishap, the fertilized egg remains dormant in her womb. If the young dies, the egg begins to develop within 2 days, and in about 30 days another young is born.

Gray kangaroos

As a general rule, a kangaroo's hind foot is more than 10 in. long; a wallaby's is less. Some wallabies are otherwise as large as kangaroos. Male kangaroos are called "boomers." Young females are called "flyers," the pouch young "joeys."

RED KANGAROO *(Macropus rufus)* is large, the males standing a maximum height of 6 ft. and weighing 200 lbs. Females are about 4 ft. tall and weigh about 65 lbs. It grazes on the plains, usually eating only green shoots and young leaves, and it generally travels in "mobs," which are groups of a dozen or so animals. The red kangaroo can run 30–35 miles per hour, with leaps of 25 feet. A closely pursued female may jettison the joey from her pouch.

Many kangaroos—and particularly the red kangaroo because it is common—have been killed for their supposed competition with domestic grazing animals. Kangaroos can actually subsist on much poorer pasturage than these animals and can also do without water for longer periods, thus thriving on lands worn out by the livestock.

GRAY KANGAROO *(Macropus giganteus)* is slightly larger than the red kangaroo, with males occasionally 7 ft. tall. It lives in open forests. The species is sometimes divided into two, the eastern gray kangaroo and the western gray kangaroo *(M. fuliginosus)*, which in addition to being most abundant in southwestern regions also tends to prefer dense scrub. The two do not compete for food and shelter. Both browse on leaves and twigs rather than graze like the red kangaroo.

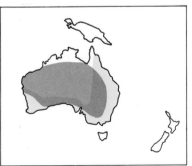

 Gray kangaroo   ■ Red kangaroo

Whiptail wallaby   *Red-necked wallaby and young*

EURO, or WALLAROO *(Macropus robustus)*, is another of the large kangaroos, almost as tall as the red kangaroo but more stockily built. It is easily distinguished from any other large kangaroo by its black nose and shaggy coat. Those animals living near human settlements have been exterminated, but euros still exist in wilderness areas. It lives in small groups on rock outcrops, usually near a water hole, coming down to graze at night.

Unlike other kangaroos, the more wary euro does not have the habit of running a short distance and then stopping to look back. This has spared it from hunters who depend on this trait of kangaroos to give them their killing shot. It does not adapt to captivity as readily as do other kangaroos and wallabies.

Other species are the black (actually brown) wallaroo *(M. bernardus)*, which lives in the granite hills of Arnhem Land, and the reddish antilopine kangaroo *(M. antilopinus)*, which favors woodland savannas.

ROCK WALLABIES *(Petrogale,* about 9 species*)* are small, none more than 3½ ft. tall. They live in open, rocky country. The soles of the feet are thickly padded and fringed with stiff hairs that help to prevent slipping on the rocks. In some species the long, slim tail is tufted at the tip.

The ring-tailed, or yellow-footed, rock wallaby *(P. xanthopus)* is easily distinguished from the others by its yellow ringed tail and by the yellow on the backs of its ears and on its feet. Like other wallabies, it eats grass and the leaves of shrubs at night.

HARE WALLABIES *(Lagorchestes,* 4 species*)*, smaller than rock wallabies, resemble hares both in appearance and habits and are very rare. They are fleet runners and may leap 8 feet high.

Pademelon wallaby   *Queensland rock wallaby*

NAIL-TAIL WALLABIES *(Onychogalea*, 3 species*)* are intermediate in size between hare and rock wallabies. The tail is tipped with a horny "nail," a feature shared among mammals only with the lion.

RED-NECKED WALLABY *(Wallabia rufogrisea)* is of medium size—maximum height 3½ ft. with a tail more than 2 ft. long. It is one of several closely related species of wallabies inhabiting principally brush country. Some members of the group range into New Guinea and Tasmania.

In markings, these are among the most handsome members of the kangaroo family. Shades of red, fawn and gray melt into each other, and the face and ears generally have black markings.

Swamp wallaby (*W. bicolor*) favors more forested habitat than the agile wallaby (*W. agilis*), which is found in open woodland. The whiptail wallaby (*W. parryi*) has a distinct white stripe on the side of its face and a long, slender tail. The dama wallaby (*W. eugenii*) is now extinct on the mainland but still abundant on Kangaroo Island. The black-striped wallaby *(W. dorsalis)* is the most numerous member of the kangaroo family. The smaller parma wallaby *(W. parma)* was once common in New South Wales but became extinct in 1930. Fortunately it had been introduced to New Zealand along with other wallabies. In 1958 it was discovered on an island north of Auckland and it has now been reintroduced to Australia, where its numbers are growing.

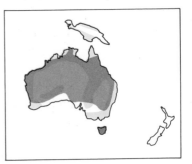

■ *Euro*   ▨ *Wallabies*

Potoroo

Brush-tailed rat kangaroo

RAT KANGAROOS *(Potorous, Bettongia* and others) are the smallest members of the kangaroo family, some only 20 in. long and weighing less than 1 lb. All have a long, hairy tail. The ears are small and rounded; and while the hind legs are much larger than the front legs, they are not as well adapted for jumping as are those of other members of the family. Rat kangaroos are strictly nocturnal. This fact and their size make them difficult to see in the wild.

The potoroo (*P. tridactylus*) is the size of a rabbit. Its sleek, grayish brown fur lacks distinctive markings. The tail is thickly furred at the base, the hairs more closely appressed and sparse toward the tip. It is distinctly ratlike in appearance. Females make a nest out of grass shortly before giving birth.

The brush-tailed rat kangaroo (*Bettongia penicillata cuniculus*) is one of several species in its genus, all similar in size to the potoroo. In all, the hind feet are longer than the head. The claws on both feet are larger than the potoroo's. The tail, more brushy than the potoroo's, is semi-prehensile. The tail is commonly wrapped around bundles of vegetation that are dragged to the nest, usually a hollow log or the crevice of a rock.

These small animals were among the victims of the introduction of the rabbit. The two are able to live together compatibly, even occupying the same burrows, but the rabbit is more aggressive in getting food. In seasons of food scarcity, it is the rat kangaroos that suffer. Their reproductive rate is much lower than the rabbit's so that their population does not recover as quickly when food is again abundant. Large numbers have also been exterminated by poisoning campaigns designed to eliminate rabbits. Some species are now probably extinct.

Bennett's tree kangaroo   Goodfellow's tree kangaroo

TREE KANGAROOS *(Dendrolagus*, 5 species) may stand 2–3 ft. tall. Adapted for an arboreal life, their hind legs are not as powerful for jumping as those of other kangaroos. To give them traction, however, they have thick, rough soles on their feet, and the claws are large and sharp. The front paws are sometimes used for grasping. The tail, more slender than in the ground-dwelling kangaroos, is used as a balancer and also as a rudder; it is not prehensile. Though they normally descend trees tail first, they may also make long leaps—30 feet or more—from tall trees to the ground.

During the day, tree kangaroos sleep in trees and forage in branches for leaves and tender shoots. If pressed, they can move through the branches with speed and agility. Much of their time is spent foraging for plants on the ground, especially at night, but they are always near trees into which they can run rapidly to escape. In New Guinea tree kangaroos are hunted as food. They are usually forced to jump from a tree and then are caught on the ground.

Two species occur in Australia: Bennett's tree kangaroo (*D. bennettianus*) and the pale Lumholtz's (*D. lumholtzi*). Two species live in New Guinea: Goodfellow's tree kangaroo (*D. goodfellowi*) and Matschie's tree kangaroo (*D. matschiei*). These are among the most brightly colored members of the kangaroo family. Although tree kangaroos are not rare, the inaccessibility of their forest habitat has made their study in the wild very difficult.

Solenodon

INSECTIVORES (ORDER INSECTIVORA)

Insectivores are small mammals with flattened skulls, small brains and low intelligence. They have poorly developed eyes; long, well-bristled snouts; primitive, unspecialized teeth; and five clawed toes on each foot.

Many insectivores are nocturnal, timid and comparatively defenseless. Some kinds have protective spines or special glands for emitting repellent odors. Others have poisonous saliva with which they can immobilize their prey.

The order is an excellent example of adaptive radiation, for while most are terrestrial, some have moved into trees, others have gone underground, and still others have become aquatic. They are widely distributed throughout the world, occurring on all major land masses except Australia, New Guinea, New Zealand and the polar regions, including northern Asia. Insectivores are believed to have originated close to the ancestral stock that gave rise to all placental mammals.

SOLENODONS (FAMILY SOLENODONTIDAE)

Two species comprise this primitive family: the Cuban solenodon (*Atopogale cubana*) and the Haitian, or Hispanolian, solenodon (*Solenodon paradoxus*).

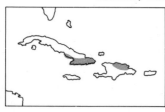

Both are rare, their decline attributed principally to the destruction or modification of their habitat by deforestation. Other contributing factors are their low reproductive rate (only one to three young per litter) and their elimination by the imported mongoose, cats and dogs. Both are ratlike, the body 12 in. long.

■ *Solenodons*

Giant otter shrew

OTTER SHREWS (FAMILY POTAMOGALIDAE)

Otter shrews (2 genera, 3 species) are closely related to tenrecs (see p. 44). The giant otter shrew (*Potamogale velox*) is one of the largest insectivores, its head and body reaching a maximum length of 12 in. and its tail of equal length.

Giant otter shrews resemble otters. They have a flat head, very powerful tail and soft, sleek, waterproof fur. The tail acts like a rudder. Excellent and agile swimmers, they hunt at night for fish and other aquatic animals. The entrance to their burrows is below the water level in the banks of streams or in wetlands. Though most common in forested regions, the giant otter shrew is found from sea level to about 6,000 feet, but it is rarely seen and little known.

GOLDEN MOLES (FAMILY CHRYSOCHLORIDAE)

Golden moles (5 genera, 15 species; see illustration, p.52) have habits like those of moles but are not closely related. Most species spend their life underground, emerging only if the worms or other invertebrates on which they feed are forced to the surface by flooding rains. They have a leathery pad on their muzzle which they use when excavating the soil; the nostrils are hidden under a flap which keeps them free from debris. Some species forage on the surface regularly at night, feeding on lizards and insects. Most golden moles are less than 5 in. long.

■ *Giant otter shrew*
■ *Golden moles*

44

Spiny tenrec

Hedgehog tenrec

TENRECS (FAMILY TENRECIDAE)

Tenrecs form a family of 10 genera and more than 20 species, all found exclusively on Madagascar and the Comoro Islands. Most species are solitary surface dwellers, spending the day rooting and probing for food in the forest litter. They eat mainly insects and other invertebrates but sometimes small vertebrates and plants. Their eyesight is poor, but their senses of smell, hearing and touch are highly developed. Some species are exceptionally prolific and mature rapidly. Some are active year round; others live off their fat at some seasons.

Tenrecs are preyed on by native carnivores, birds of prey and snakes, but their main enemies are the island natives, who regard tenrec meat as a delicacy.

Five of the genera (subfamily Oryzorictinae) have conventional fur. The remaining five (subfamily Tenrecinae) have spines or bristles.

FURRED TENRECS are represented most abundantly by the mouselike long-tailed tenrecs (*Microgale*), the genus containing more than half of all the living species. The tail is twice the length of the head and body, and they also have more vertebrae than any other mammals except pangolins. Long-tailed tenrecs are found mainly in the eastern rain forests and on the central plateau, occupying a niche comparable to that of shrews.

Rice tenrecs (*Oryzorictes*, 3 species) are also small, the body about 4 in. long and the tail 1½ in. Molelike in appearance and habits, they have short, velvety fur; and their front legs are modified for digging.

The web-footed tenrec (*Limnogale mergulus*) is semi-aquatic, with dense otterlike fur, a long flattened tail and webbed hind feet. It lives in swift-flowing streams at elevations of 2,000 to 6,500 feet.

Long-tailed tenrec

Striped tenrec

SPINY TENRECS include the large tenrec (*Tenrec ecaudatus*), the male reaching a maximum length of 14 in. and substantially larger than the female. It inhabits virtually all of Madagascar. Adults have an erectile crest of long hairs on the back of the head and a minute tail ½ in. long.

The tenrec is a prolific breeder, giving birth to as many as 32 in a single litter, after a gestation period of about 60 days. Within 3 weeks, the surviving young accompany their mother in search of food, and in about 8 weeks they are living independently. In winter the tenrec retires underground and hibernates.

The tenrec has been introduced to other islands of the Indian Ocean and appears to be thriving.

Hedgehog tenrecs *(Setifer setosus,* maximum length 7 in., and *Echinops telfairi,* maximum length 6 in.) resemble true hedgehogs. The upper parts of their bodies are covered with spines over a soft underfur. For defense, the spiny forehead is moved over the eyes like a visor, and the animal rolls into a ball.

Both species are essentially terrestrial but can climb well if necessary. Their burrows are about 2 feet long, ending in a grass-lined nest chamber. *Setifer* occurs over much of eastern Madagascar, preferring the central plateau to the rain forests. *Echinops* live in the arid southwestern region.

Striped tenrec *(Hemicentetes,* 2 species) is striped alternately with black and yellow (or white), with erectile spines most abundant in the yellow areas and on the crown. The spines have detachable barbed tips. For defense, the striped tenrec lunges at an intruder and tries to reach it with its spines.

Tenrecs produce high-frequency sounds by rapidly vibrating the quills on their backs. The sound helps keep contact or serves as a warning signal.

Moonrat

HEDGEHOGS AND GYMNURES (FAMILY ERINACEIDAE)

This Old World family is divided into two subfamiles: hairy hedgehogs, or gymnures (Echinosoricinae), and spiny hedgehogs (Erinaceinae).

GYMNURES, or MOONRATS, are a little-known group that has coarse hair rather than spines. The scaly tail is ratlike and almost naked. Largest and most common is the moonrat (*Echinosorex gymnurus*), body 16 in. and tail 8 in., which lives in mangrove swamps or similar wetlands and is the most aquatic member of this family. It feeds at night on snails, worms, insects and, sometimes, fish, crabs and frogs. During the day it retires to a burrow or crevice. The lesser gymnure (*Hylomys suillus*), body length 6 in. and tail 1 in., is a shrewlike forest dweller, probing for food in the litter. It is said to be a proficient climber.

The Mindanao gymnure (*Podogymnurus truei*) lives only in high mountains on Mindanao, a Philippine island. The shrew hedgehog (*Neotracus sinensis*) lives in mountain forests to 10,000 feet.

HEDGEHOGS (3 genera, 15 species) have a defensive covering of barbless spines on their back and sides. When the animal rolls into a ball, special skin muscles lift the spines and convert the animal into an impenetrable pincushion.

The common hedgehogs (*Erinaceus*, 10 species), maximum length 10 in., are forest dwellers. In Europe hedgehogs are partial to deciduous woodlands, feeding on worms, slugs, beetles and other small invertebrates. In cultivated areas they perform a valuable service in controlling insect pests.

■ *Gymnures*

Long-eared desert hedgehog   *Common hedgehog and newborn young*

In steppes and deserts the place of the common hedgehogs is taken by the long-eared desert hedgehog *(Hemiechinus,* 2 species) and the desert hedgehog *(Parechinus,* 3 species). Desert hedgehogs have adapted to their harsh environment by being able to go without food or water for up to 6 weeks.

Hedgehogs, like most insectivores, have poor eyesight but keen senses of smell and hearing. They are solitary and inquisitive, loudly sniffing and nosing under leaves as they scuffle through the undergrowth. They walk on the soles of their feet in a rolling gait, but can run very fast when pressed. Males mark territories with scent from their anal glands and possibly also with their droppings. They defend these territories, especially during the mating season.

Litters average four or five young, born after a gestation period of about 35 to 50 days. The spines remain under the skin until shortly after birth, when they grow from $1/16$ inch to $3/4$ inch in 5 hours. Within 4 weeks, the young are large enough to go with their mother on foraging trips.

Hedgehogs hibernate in winter. During this protracted sleep, the animal's body temperature drops, its heart beat is reduced to 10 percent of normal and breathing almost stops.

Because of their spiny protection, hedgehogs are immune to most predators. Some are killed for food by predators, but in developed regions thousands are run over by automobiles.

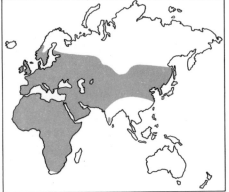

■ *Hedgehogs*

Four-toed elephant shrew

ELEPHANT SHREWS (FAMILY MACROSCELIDIDAE)

This is an exclusively African family (5 genera, 16 species) with features setting it apart from all other insectivores. Almost all elephant shrews are uniformly brownish gray; only a few bear spots. In general appearance, elephant shrews, whose hind legs are much larger and more powerful than their forelegs, resemble most closely the marsupial mice. They normally run on all four legs in sudden, swift, scurrying movements that enable them to cover distances at an astonishing speed. If hard pressed, they may jump, like jerboas, holding their tails high. The long tail is scaly, and in some species a special scent gland on the underside of the tail gives off a musky odor as the tail is dragged along the ground.

Compared to other insectivores, the elephant shrews, suited for their mainly diurnal existence, have large eyes and good eyesight. Despite their foraging in daylight hours, they are secretive in habits. All have a long, flexible snout that in most species resembles a miniature elephant's trunk. It has mobile vibrissae, or whiskers, along its sides. The ears are large.

The litter size is almost invariably one or two. The newborn are large in relation to their mother and are remarkably well developed. They are suckled for a brief period and become independent after a few days. Sexual maturity is reached in 6 weeks.

The smallest of the elephant shrews is the common or short-eared elephant shrew (*Macroscelides proboscideus*), maximum body length 4 in. and tail 4 in.; it lives in the thornbush plains of South Africa. Members of the genus *Nasilio* are the size of mice.

Checkered-back elephant shrew

Long-eared elephant shrew

The largest is the checkered-back elephant shrew (*Rhynchocyon cirnei*), which is as large as a rat—maximum body length 12 in. and tail 10 in. The black and white pattern of fur on the back is a conspicuous trait. It lives in the tropical forests along the Congo. Ants are a main source of food. Other species of *Rhynchocyon* inhabit the coastal regions of East Africa. Forest elephant shrews (*Petrodomus*) make runways in their habitat's dense undergrowth.

Most elephant shrews live in open and often arid country. Some favor grasslands or bush country. Others live in rocky outcroppings, where they commonly sun themselves on the rocks. They are ready in an instant to dash for shelter if there is a hint of danger, signifying alarm by thumping the ground with their hind feet. They are particularly vulnerable to attacks by hawks and other birds of prey.

Most elephant shrews live singly or in pairs, but some long-eared elephant shrews (*Elephantulus*), one of the most widely distributed genera, live in small colonies.

Elephant shrews are not equipped for digging, and so they frequently occupy the abandoned burrows of rodents. To these they add a bolt hole, usually vertical, for quick escapes. If an abandoned burrow cannot be found, they may live under rocks, in crevices or in vacated termite mounds.

Whatever their choice, there is invariably a series of regular surface runways that lead to their feeding grounds. The animals rarely move far from their burrows. Ants, termites and other insects are their principal food, but this diet is supplemented with berries, shoots, roots and, perhaps, eggs of birds. They appear to be able to live without water.

Arctic shrew

Least shrew

Short-tail shrew

SHREWS (FAMILY SORICIDAE)

True shrews form a large family of 20 genera and more than 200 species. All have small eyes, but their senses of smell and hearing are good. Some are believed capable of detecting ultrasonic sounds for echolocation, as do bats.

Shrews occur in a variety of habitats, from deciduous and coniferous forests to tundra, steppe and alpine conditions. They are common in cultivated areas. Most species prefer moist conditions, but some inhabit arid regions. Notable among these are the desert shrews (*Notiosorex*, 2 species) of the southwestern United States and northern Mexico and the piebald shrew (*Diplomesodon pulchellum*) of the deserts of Kazakhstan and Turkmenia. Some are highly localized in distribution. The Kenya mountain shrews (*Surdisorex norae* and *S. polulus*), for example, are found only on the moorlands of Mount Kenya and the Aberdares, at altitudes up to 10,500 feet.

Most species are roughly the size of mice. The smallest is the Etruscan shrew (*Suncus etruscus*) of the Mediterranean region; it is only about 1½ in. long, plus a 1-in. tail—the smallest living mammal. The pygmy shrew (*Microsorex hoyi*) of Canada and the United States is only slightly larger. The largest is the African forest shrew (*Praesorex goliath*), maximum body length 7 in. and tail 4 in.

Except briefly during the breeding season, shrews are solitary. Each defends vigorously a small territory crisscrossed with surface and subterranean runways. The mole shrew (*Anourosorex squamipes*), found from Szechwan in to China to North Vietnam, is molelike in habits and appearance. European water shrews (*Neomys*, 2 species), American water shrews (*Sorex*, 3 species) and Asiatic water shrews (*Chimarrogale*, 2 species) are semi-aquatic, with bristly hairs on their

European water shrew   European shrew

toes and tails that aid them in swimming. Some can run over the surface of the water. The Tibetan water shrew (*Nectogale elegans*) is the only shrew with webbed feet.

Voracious feeders, shrews regularly consume their own weight in food every day. They prey mainly on insects, spiders and other invertebrates.

Some shrews have glands that secrete a nerve-paralyzing venom into their saliva, enabling them to kill animals larger than themselves. Shrews go through periods of about three hours of intense nervous activity during which they chatter shrilly as they hunt for food. This is followed by a period of rest of similar duration. Their life span is short—averaging about 1½ years.

Females of most species do not breed until the spring following their birth. They produce as many as four litters before autumn, then die. The gestation period is 2–4 weeks, litters averaging 4–7 young.

Young of the white-toothed shrews (*Crocidura*) each grab the tail of the one in front and follow their mother in procession. Except for breeding, this is the only time when they are sociable.

Shrews give off a repellent odor from scent glands on their flanks. This prevents their predation by mammals, but owls, lacking a sense of smell, include shrews in their diet.

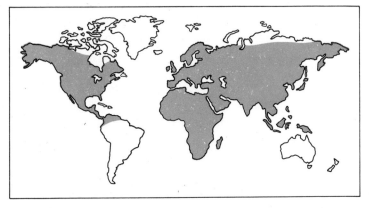

Pyrenean desman

Golden mole (see text, p. 43)

European mole

MOLES AND DESMANS (FAMILY TALPIDAE)

Moles are more completely adapted to a burrowing existence than are any other mammals. Old World moles (*Talpa,* 3 species) are so highly modified for a subterranean life that they have difficulty moving on the surface. They lack external ears, and their eyes are minute. Their fur is velvety and dense, the legs and tail short and the snout highly sensitive. The broad paws are tipped with heavy claws that are highly efficient digging tools.

Like most insectivores, moles are solitary except in areas of abundant food. Each occupies its own tunnel system, usually close to the surface but sometimes as much as 3 feet deep. The tunnels form the mole's territory, defended against others of its kind.

Like shrews, moles follow alternate 3- to 4-hour periods of activity and rest. Worms form the bulk of their diet. The worms may be immobilized with a bite, then stockpiled for eating later. Insects and their larvae are also eaten. Despite this pest-control service, moles are in disfavor because they upset tender plants in gardens and disfigure lawns with their near-surface runways.

Old World moles are about 5½ in. long, the tail about 1 in. long; females are smaller than males. Most females breed only once a year, bearing four young to a litter after a gestation period of 28 days. The nest, usually underground but sometimes just under a large mound at the surface, is lined with grass and leaves. Moles are safe from many predators because of their subterranean life and repellent glandular secretions.

American moles are similar to those of the Old World in appearance and habits, though some come to the surface regularly and may even climb small

Star-nosed mole

bushes. The common moles of North America belong to the genus *Scalopus*. The star-nosed mole (*Condylura cristata*), of the northeastern United States and southwestern Canada, has a rosette of fleshy protuberances at the tip of its snout. This highly sensitive organ of touch is used to help find food. The star-nosed mole is semi-aquatic.

DESMANS (*Desmana* and *Galemys*) are also semi-aquatic. They have webbed feet fringed with bristly hairs, a rudderlike tail and long guard hairs. Their long, mobile proboscis, like an elephant's trunk, serves as an organ of touch and smell. Valves at its tip keep out water when the desman is swimming.

The Russian desman (*D. moschata*), maximum body length 8 in. and tail another 8 in., is the largest member of the mole family. It lives in southern and central Russia. The Pyrenean desman (*G. pyrenaica*), maximum body length 5 in. and tail another 5 in., lives only in cold, swift, well-oxygenated streams in the Pyrenees and other mountains of the northwestern Iberian peninsula. Desmans are safe from almost all predators except man, who has hunted them intensively for their soft pelts. River pollution and construction of dams for water storage or for power are now taking a toll.

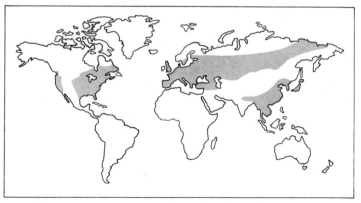

▦ *Moles*

Lesser
tree shrew

Mindanao tree shrew

Common tree shrew

TREE SHREWS (FAMILY TUPAIIDAE)

Tree shrews (5 genera, 18 species) look like squirrels with long snouts. Usually solitary in habit, they have a nervous disposition and are aggressive toward their own kind. They tame readily, however. Most kinds are diurnal, and all inhabit rain forests. They eat mainly insects and sometimes fruits or seeds.

The pen-tailed tree shrew (*Ptilocercus lowi*) differs from other tree shrews chiefly in being more like a rat than a squirrel; also, it is nocturnal. It has large membranous (as distinct from cartilaginous) ears.

Smooth-tailed tree shrews (*Dendrogale*, 2 species), the Indian tree shrew (*Anathana ellioti*) and the pen-tailed tree shrews are fully arboreal. Most of the common tree shrews (*Tupaia*, 13 species) are only partly arboreal. The large tree shrew (*T. tana*) and the Mindanao tree shrew (*Urogale everetti*) are almost totally terrestrial but are competent climbers.

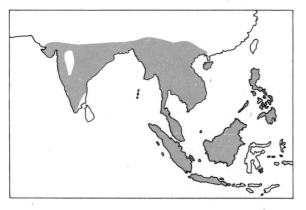

Females bear one to three young in a leaf- and moss-lined nest in a hole in the ground or in a tree. The gestation period is about 50 days. The nest is separate from the one the female retains for her personal use. The mother visits her young only about every 2 days to suckle them. Between times they must fend for themselves. They are weaned in about 6 weeks and become mature in 3–4 months.

Colugos and young

COLUGOS, OR FLYING LEMURS (ORDER DERMOPTERA)

Colugos, or flying lemurs (*Cynocephalus*, 2 species), superficially resemble lemurs. The Malayan flying lemur (*C. variegatus*) and the Philippine flying lemur (*C. volans*) are similar in size, the maximum body length 16 in. and the tail 10 in. A colugo's gliding membrane enfolds it like a furry cloak, reaching from neck to wrist, wrist to ankle and ankle to the tip of the tail. Only the claws extend beyond the membrane. Most gliders prefer relatively open woodlands, but colugos inhabit dense forests.

A colugo can glide remarkably long distances—more than 100 yards. For landing, it reduces its speed by lifting its head and tail and thrusting its feet forward. It rarely lands on the ground, but if it does, it lumbers to the nearest tree, climbing awkwardly—almost as if its limbs were hobbled. Even in trees its movements are ungainly, and it cannot stand erect.

Colugos become active at dusk and are largely nocturnal. During the day they roost in an upright position, either in a hole in a tree or in the fronds of a palm, or they may hang upside down from a branch. Their mottling is excellent camouflage in the sun-dappled forest. Much of their foraging is done upside down, like sloths, enabling them to reach leaves, shoots, buds, flowers and fruit on slender outer branches.

Mature females give birth to a single young (sometimes twins) after a gestation period of 2 months. The young may remain in the nest or cling to its mother's abdominal fur beneath the gliding membrane.

Malayan flying lemur ■ Philippine flying lemur

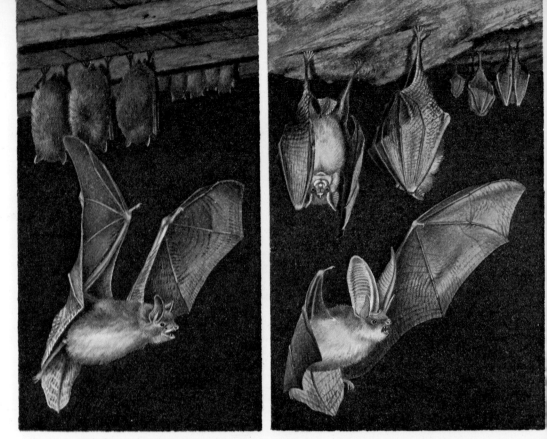

Little brown bat (see text, p. 58)   *Top: Horseshoe bats (see text, p. 59) Bottom: Long-eared b*

BATS (ORDER CHIROPTERA)

Bats are the only mammals capable of true flight. With 800 species in the order, they represent about 20 percent of all the mammals in the world, ranking next to rodents in abundance. They occur everywhere except in the Arctic and Antarctic but are most numerous and diverse in the tropics and subtropics.

The bones of a bat's forearm and hand, particularly the fingers but not the thumb, are elongated. They form the framework over which a thin membrane of skin, richly supplied with blood vessels, is stretched. The membrane is typically attached to the sides of the body. In the long-tailed fruit bats (*Notopteris macdonaldi*) and naked-backed bats (*Pteronotus*, 6 species), the wings are attached to the spine and cover the fur of the back.

The leading edge of each wing is supported by the index and middle fingers. The remaining two fingers spread to the trailing edge of the membrane, which extends from the tip of the little finger to the ankle. The calcar, a spur from the inner ankle, aids in spreading the tail membrane, and a claw on the thumb helps in locomotion after landing.

Fused bones in the wrists give the wing strength. The short hind legs are used with the wings in flight as the bat "swims" through the air. Curved claws on each of the five toes serve as hooks for hanging upside down when the bat rests. Suction cups of disc-winged bats (*Thyroptera*, 2 species) of Central and South America and the rare golden bat (*Myzopoda aurita*) of Madagascar replace the claws and enable the animals to move over smooth surfaces.

Most bats are grayish brown, but a few are brightly colored or have two color phases. The Honduran bat (*Ectophylla alba*) and the ghost bat (*Diclidurus albus*)

Noctule   Pipistrelle (see text, p. 58)

are white. Body covering varies from the dense, velvety fur of the New Zealand short-tailed bat (*Mystacina tuberculata*) to the Malayan naked bat (*Cheiromeles torquatus*), which is almost hairless.

Bats roost in caves, under ledges, in hollow trees, under eaves, in termite nests, in the burrows of rodents—in any dark place, including the hollow stems of bamboos or beneath the bark of trees. Some roost singly or in small family units, others in groups of thousands. Males and females of some species live together the year round. In others the sexes are segregated, females establishing maternity wards from which the males are barred. Some cave dwellers set up permanent roosts; others concentrate in caves only in winter.

Many tree-dwelling bats migrate to warmer regions in winter, often over distances of thousands of miles. Cave-dwelling forms generally hibernate in temperate regions, their body temperature dropping to low levels and the animals living on accumulated fat. The hibernation may be interrupted if the weather warms and resumed if it becomes cold again.

Tropical bats have no particular breeding season. Those of colder regions mate in autumn before the onset of hibernation, the sperm remaining viable in the female's reproductive tract and fertilization occuring the following spring.

Most bats give birth to a single young, but twins occur frequently in some species. The concentration of breeding females in special maternity caves raises the surrounding temperature enough to benefit the growing young. Still attached to the umbilical cord, the newborn young makes its way to its mother's nipples, located close to her armpits. At first it is carried by its mother, clinging to her by mouth, claws and wing hooks. When it becomes heavier, she leaves it hanging in the roost.

Fish-eating bats

INSECTIVOROUS BATS (FAMILY VESPERTILIONIDAE)

The most abundant and widely distributed of the bats belong to the genus *Myotis* (70 species). They are insectivorous and gregarious. Their slow and straight flight reaches speeds of 12.8 mph.

In North America the little brown bat (*Myotis lucifugus*) ranges over most of Canada and the United States. In winter it hibernates in caves, assembling by the thousands. In summer it roosts in hollow trees, attics, deserted buildings or similar places. A closely related species, the common mouse-eared bat (*Myotis myotis*), is widely distributed in western Europe.

Pipistrelles (*Pipistrellus*, 50 species) are also among the most widespread bats, occurring in Africa, Europe, Asia, Australia and North America.

FISH-EATING BATS (FAMILY NOCTILIONIDAE)

A single genus (*Noctilio*, 2 species) comprises this Central American family. Both species have a very wide mouth, sharp teeth and well-developed legs, feet and curved claws, all used for seizing fish out of the water.

FREE-TAILED BATS (FAMILY MOLOSSIDAE)

Free-tailed, or mastiff, bats have snubbed noses and at least half of their tail is free of the membrane. The Mexican free-tailed bat (*Tadarida mexicana*) is best known for the millions that roost in Carlsbad Caverns in New Mexico. A strong musky odor pervades their roost. Bat dung, or guano, was collected for 15 years from Carlsbad Caverns for fertilizer at the rate of 40–120 tons a day.

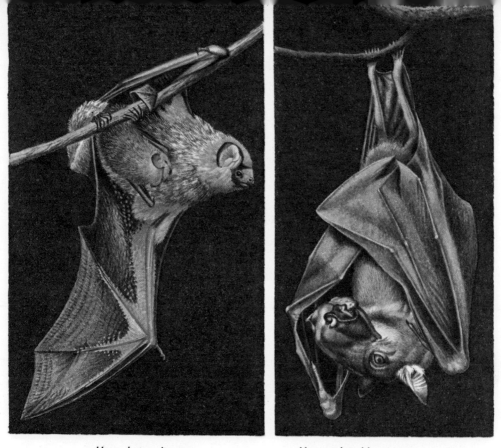

Hoary bat and young   *Hammerhead bat (see text, p. 62)*

LEAF-NOSED BATS (FAMILIES PHYLLOSTOMATIDAE {New World} AND HIPPOSIDERIDAE {Old World})

NEW WORLD LEAF-NOSED BATS (51 genera, 140 species) include both insect and fruit eaters. The false vampire (*Vampyrum spectrum*) and the javelin bat (*Phyllostomus hastatus*), both of South America, are carnivorous, preying on small mammals (even other bats), birds and lizards. The false vampire is the largest bat of the New World, its wingspan exceeding 3½ ft.

Most bats in this family have a simple nose leaf—the folds of skin on the nose that are important in the bat's echolocation system. In some, however, the nose leaf covers most of the long snout. All lack a tail, and the ears are large.

OLD WORLD LEAF-NOSED BATS (9 genera, 40 species) have a much more elaborate leaf-nose. In the Solomon Island flower-faced bat (*Anthops ornatus*) and the African triple nose-leaf bats (*Triaenops*, 5 species), the leaf-nose is arranged like flower petals.

HORSESHOE BATS (FAMILY RHINOLOPHIDAE)

Horseshoe bats (more than 50 species) are an Old World family. All have a complex nose leaf, consisting of a horseshoe-shaped appendage that surrounds the nostrils and upper lip. An erect lancet protrudes above this structure. At rest the wings are folded so that the head is almost completely hidden.

The greater horseshoe bat (*Rhinolophus ferrumequinum*) is widespread in Southern and Central Europe and Asia. It also ranges into North Africa. Its wingspan commonly exceeds 1 ft., but the body is only about 2½ in. long. The greater horseshoe bat hibernates in caves in winter.

Vampire bats

VAMPIRE BATS (FAMILY DESMODONTIDAE)

This exclusively New World family of bats (3 genera, 3 species) is restricted to the South American tropics and subtropics. It is the most highly specialized of all the bats. A vampire's diet consists wholly of fresh, warm blood. Its teeth are reduced to razor-sharp incisors for making minute incisions in the skin of its host, and the channel-shaped tongue fits into a special groove in the lower lip. This aids in directing the flow of blood from the bite wound into the bat's mouth. The blood is not sucked up but lapped from the wound with the tongue. An anticoagulant in the bat's saliva thins the blood so that it continues to flow.

Most astonishing, the sleeping host rarely detects the vampire's bite because of the stealthy approach of the bat and the neatness of the incision. Vampires fly low, about 3 feet above the ground, and use regular flight patterns. This habit allows them to be trapped in fine mesh nets strung across their path. International health organizations have supplied these "mist" nests to farmers in areas where vampire bats are abundant. They are also used to catch small birds and other bats—an unfortunate side effect.

The normal method of attack involves landing close to the sleeping host and then covering the final distance by crawling rapidly, using the feet and thumbs. Sometimes the vampire lands directly—and softly—on the victim. Usually, but not always, the amount of blood lost is insignificant, though the vampire itself may be so bloated after its meal that it can scarcely fly away. A vampire may feed for 15 minutes or longer before it gets its fill. After feeding, vampires return to their roost and spend the daylight hours digesting their meal.

Jamaican nectar-feeding bats　　　　　　　　Long-nosed bat

A vampire's bite is most dangerous because of diseases that may be contracted either directly or indirectly. Vampires, for example, are carriers of rabies in certain areas and have a remarkable tolerance to the disease themselves. Various secondary infections in the open wounds are another danger. Screwworm flies that gain entry through vampire bites cause heavy losses to livestock. In some areas of Latin America diseases brought by the vampire bats have made stock raising uneconomical.

The role of vampires as vectors of disease has understandably brought about their destruction whenever possible. It is unfortunate, however, that vampires have given all other bats a bad reputation. Most bats are not only harmless but also beneficial to man as checks on insect populations that would otherwise build up to prodigious numbers.

The most common and widespread of the species is the great vampire bat *(Desmodus rotundus)*, its head and body about 3 in. long. It ranges from northern Mexico to Uruguay and from sea level to 11,000 feet. Different races of these bats may become highly selective in their choice of hosts, preying only on particular kinds of mammals. Humans are seldom attacked. Dogs are also rarely bitten as they hear higher frequency sounds and detect the bat's presence in time. Livestock, particularly cows, are the most common victims. The bats choose hollow trees close to a herd as roosting sites and change roosts when the cows move on. Cows sleeping on the edge of the herd are the first to be bitten, and one cow can be bitten by several bats.

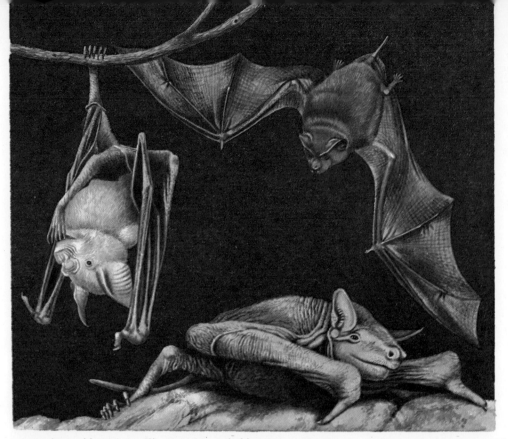

Left: Leaf-nosed bat (see p. 59)   Top: Free-tailed bat (see p. 58)   Bottom: Malayan naked bat (see p. 57)

FRUIT BATS (FAMILY PTEROPODIDAE)

Fruit bats (39 genera) are so distinct from all other bats that they are placed in a separate suborder, Megachiroptera, meaning "large bats." They measure 3 to 16 in., depending on the species. Most of them are large, with sharply pointed or foxlike snouts and simple ears—that is, no extra folds or nose leaves. They have large eyes, hence better sight than other bats, a claw on the index finger as well as on the thumb. The tail is short and hangs free of the membrane; some are tailless. Fruit bats have developed unusual color patterns, many with stripes and dots. Most are fruit eaters that suck juices from the pulp and discard the seeds. Others feed on pollen and nectar. Their teeth are small and not specialized.

The largest of the fruit bats are the so-called FLYING FOXES (*Pteropus*, 50 species), widely distributed in Australasia. The Indian flying fox (*P. giganteus*), its body rat-sized and its wings spanning up to 5 ft., is the largest of all the bats. Several others in the genus are nearly as large. It is not surprising that some of these big bats are used as food by local people. In many areas they are considered agricultural pests, and they may not be imported into the United States.

SHORT-NOSED FRUIT BATS (*Cynopterus*, 5 species) have a shorter, more rounded profile than do typical fruit bats. They prefer the juice, rather than the pulp, of fruit. By dropping the pulp and seeds while feeding in flight, they aid in the seed dispersal of date palms, figs, mangoes and other fruits. The African HAMMERHEAD BAT (*Hypsignathus monstrosus*) has a broad snout, giving it an almost horselike head. It also has a greatly enlarged larynx, highly developed vocal cords and inflatable air sacs, enabling it to make a wide range of loud croaking sounds. The hammerhead is a particularly noisy fruit bat.

Flying foxes

ROUSETTE FRUIT BATS (*Rousettus*, 11 species) are the only fruit bats thought to use echolocation during flight. They are fruit and nectar feeders. As they obtain nectar, pollen from the flower rubs off on their fur as they fly from one to another, thereby helping pollinate them like bees.

EPAULETTE BATS (*Epomophorus*, 7 species) of central and southern Africa are named for tufts of white hair on the male's shoulders.

During the day, fruit bats roost in trees, their "camps" sometimes containing thousands of individuals. These great hordes can devastate an orchard overnight, and the bats may fly long distances—to 25 or 30 miles—from their dormitory area to feeding grounds. Where fruit is available, the bats may establish permanent roost. Elsewhere they migrate seasonally.

LONG-TONGUED FRUIT BATS (*Macroglossus, Megaloglossus* and others) are also nectar and pollen feeders. They have flattened teeth, a modified lower jaw and a long, brush-tipped tongue that is thrust deep into flowers. The bats may hover in front of flowers like moths as they feed. Many night-blooming flowers of the tropics and subtropics are totally dependent on these bats for fertilization. These are the smallest of the fruit-bat group, their body no larger than that of a mouse and their wings spanning 12 in.

TUBE-NOSED BATS (*Nyctimene*, 7 species) include the lesser tube-nosed bat (*Paranyctimene raptor*) of Australia and New Guinea.

■ *Fruit bats*

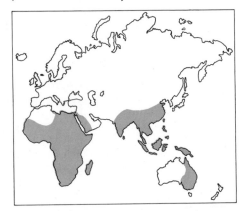

Ring-tailed lemurs   *Mongoose lemur*

PROSIMIANS (ORDER PRIMATES, SUBORDER PROSIMII)

Primates include the most intelligent of all mammals, distinguished by their large and well-developed brains. By ancestry, primates are linked most closely to insectivores, shown clearly in the prosimians—lemurs, galagos (bush babies), lorises and tarsiers, the most primitive members of the order.

Compared to higher primates, prosimians have a smaller brain, an elongated snout and a moist muzzle. The front teeth of the lower jaw form a "comb" that is used to scoop fruit from the peel and also in social grooming, as is the long claw on the second toe of each hind foot. Prosimians have a well-developed sense of smell, and scents play an important role in their social life. They have special glands to mark their territory. Other prosimians spread urine on branches instead.

LEMURS (FAMILY LEMURIDAE)

Lemurs (7 genera, 16 species) are confined to Madagascar, Comoro and nearby islands; despite protection, they are becoming increasingly rare, mainly due to habitat destruction. They move squirrel-like through trees. As a group they are omnivorous, though some are vegetarian and others insectivorous.

TRUE LEMURS (*Lemur*, 5 species) are gregarious, vocal and largely diurnal. The long tail is used for balance and provides anchorage when they rest in the branches. The largest is the ruffed lemur (*L. variegatus*), maximum length 30 in. The smallest is the mongoose lemur (*L. mongoz*), maximum body length 24 in. with a 12-in. tail. Intermediate in size are the ring-tailed lemur (*L. catta*), black

Black lemur, female and young   Ruffed lemur

lemur (*L. macaco*) and red-bellied lemur (*L. rubriventer*). All are arboreal, but the ring-tailed lemur lives in rocky country and spends much of its time on the ground.

The ring-tailed lemur runs its bushy tail through its hands and forearms, in the process smearing the tail with scent from glands on its wrists. The tail is then lifted vertically with its tip arched forward and vibrated to waft the scent toward a rival.

Females bear one or two (rarely three) young after a gestation period of 4½ months. For the first month the young clings to its mother's stomach in a horizontal position. Then it transfers to her back, where for about 6 months it rides jockey-style before becoming independent.

SMALL SPORTIVE LEMUR (*Lepilemur mustelinus*) occurs throughout Madagascar, with several subspecies occupying distinctive habitats such as rain and thorn forests. One is found only on the island of Nossi Bé. Essentially arboreal, the sportive lemur lives high in trees, leaping in an upright position from one trunk to another and moving along branches on all fours. When it descends to the ground, which is rare, the sportive lemur moves in a series of bipedal hops. Personal territories are small; small sportive lemurs are basically unsociable.

Births occur in a nest of twigs lined with leaves. The single young, born after 4½ months, remains in the nest or on a branch nearby while the mother searches for leaves, buds and fruit to feed it. The mother may carry the young in her mouth as she leaps from tree to tree. Young are weaned at 2½ months and become mature at 18 months.

Top: Greater dwarf lemur   *Left: Lesser mouse lemur*   *Right: Gray gentle lemur*

DWARF LEMURS *(Cheirogaleus,* 2 species) are solitary and nocturnal, spending the day asleep rolled into a ball in the hole of a tree or in a spherical nest, often high in trees. They move along branches on all 'fours, foraging for fruit, leaves and insects. Females normally give birth to twins or triplets after a gestation period of 70 days.

The greater dwarf lemur *(C. major)* is found only in the rain forests of eastern Madagascar; the fat-tailed lemur *(C. medius)* lives in the dry forests of the west and south.

GENTLE LEMURS *(Hapalemur,* 2 species) are represented by the gray gentle lemur *(H. griseus),* widely distributed in the bamboo forests of the east and west coasts, and the broad-nosed gentle lemur *(H. simus),* which is wholly adapted to a marshland existence and mainly eats reed shoots.

MOUSE LEMURS *(Microcebus,* 2 species) are among the smallest of all primates. The common and widespread lesser mouse lemur *(M. murinus)* is only about 12 in. long, including its tail.

Mouse lemurs are nocturnal. During the day they sleep rolled into a ball, often with the tail curled around a branch. Though primarily insectivorous, they may eat other small animals and fruit. Their call is a high pitched squeak. Mouse lemurs leap from tree to tree and run along branches like squirrels, using their long tails for balancing.

After a gestation period of 2 months, the female gives birth to twins or triplets in a nest either in a hole of a tree or in dense foliage. The young are weaned at 1½ months and live independently at 2 months. They are sexually mature at about 9 months. Mouse lemurs live in loosely knit colonies in which the individuals lead solitary lives. They are basically shy and retiring.

Indri   *Verreaux's sifakas*

INDRI and SIFAKAS (FAMILY INDRIIDAE)

These are the most monkeylike of the prosimians. They have long, narrow hands and powerful legs. The apposable big toe is almost as large as the remainder of the foot, the other toes partially webbed and the soles thickly padded. They rarely come to the ground, where they move with awkward hops. Even their tail-first descent is ungainly. In trees, however, they are agile and graceful; from a squatting position, they may jump 30 feet or more, one leap followed immediately by another. Sometimes they jump backward, turning in mid-air so that they land feet first.

Females bear a single young after a gestation period of 5 months. They usually associate in small bands or family units of about eight animals. The troop sleeps on a branch, often huddled together for warmth. They are strictly vegetarian. All are now rare or endangered, due to hunting and destruction of habitat.

INDRI (*Indri indri*), maximum height 3 ft. and with only a stumpy tail, lives in the rain forests of eastern Madagascar. Diurnal, the indri normally stays high in trees. Its voice, boosted by a laryngeal sac, is exceptionally powerful.

VERREAUX'S SIFAKA (*Propithecus verreauxi*) and diadem sifaka (*P. diadema*) are medium-sized, diurnal and distinctly marked. Sifakas live in small family units of six to eight individuals. A female leads the troop, while a male guards the rear.

The single young clings to its mother's stomach for the first month. Then it moves to her back and remains there for about 6 months. It is weaned at 3–4 months but keeps in close contact with the mother for about 2 years. When it is near sexual maturity, the dominant male in the troop chases it away.

Philippine tarsier   *Celebes tarsier*

AYE-AYE (FAMILY DAUBENTONIIDAE)

The aye-aye (*Daubentonia madagascariensis*), the only representative of its family, resembles a black squirrel. It lives in low-altitude rain forests along Madagascar's eastern seaboard.

The aye-aye has ever-growing, rodentlike incisors in its upper and lower jaws; it lacks canines. All digits have clawlike nails except the big toe, which has a flat nail. The hands are unusually long, the tip of the third finger especially long and hooklike. It is used to pick grubs from woody stems.

Solitary and nocturnal, aye-ayes sleep with the tail wrapped around the body. Females build a spherical nest of branches and line it with leaves; the entrance is at the side. A single young is the rule.

Aye-ayes are held sacred by natives who regard them as the reincarnation of their ancestors. As such they are not hunted, but because of habitat destruction, only a few dozen aye-ayes survive. The 1,286-acre Nossi Mangabé Island in the Bay of Antongil has been set aside as a special reserve.

TARSIERS (FAMILY TARSIIDAE)

Three species of tarsiers (*Tarsius*) inhabit coastal rain forests and bamboo thickets in the Philippines, Sumatra, Borneo, Celebes and nearby islands. Nocturnal and arboreal, a tarsier appears to be able to swivel its head nearly 360°, like an owl. This gives it a very wide field of vision. The unusually large and closely set eyes are prominent on the furry muzzle. Except for a few hairs at its tip, the ratlike tail is naked and longer (10 in.) than the head and body (6 in.). The large,

Slow loris (see text, p. 70)   *Slender loris and young (see text, p. 70)*

naked ears are mobile and constantly in motion, swiveling and flattening. The arms are short, but the legs and feet are greatly elongated.

The name "tarsier" is derived from "tarsus," a bone in the ankle, which is distinctly longer in this primate. The big toe is apposable, and both the second and third toes have claws used for grooming. All the digits have expanded or disc-shaped terminal pads.

A tarsier can spring from a vertical clinging posture to another branch with amazing speed, thrusting with its long legs and taking off backward. It turns in mid-air and lands feet first. The jumps commonly exceed 10 feet, and often the animal takes off again immediately. When moving horizontally, tarsiers also make frog-type leaps with their backs arched and their tails held up. When investigating an object they may walk slowly on all fours.

Like other small primates, such as the dwarf bush baby, tarsiers are highly territorial. A major portion of the male's waking hours is spent visiting the boundaries of his territory, which may overlap that of several females. Tarsiers are solitary or live in small groups, marking their territories with urine that is first deposited on the toe pads. Breeding may take place at any time, and courtship involves high-speed chases through the trees, during which the males emit high-pitched squeaks and trills.

A single young, born after a gestation period of 6 months, is well developed at birth and able to move independently. It clings to its mother's fur or is carried in her mouth. In about a month the young tarsier begins making leaps.

Tarsiers feed mainly on insects such as beetles and grasshoppers. Remaining immobile while watching its prey, a tarsier will suddenly leap forward and pin it down with its hands.

Top: Dwarf galago   Left: Thick-tailed galago   Right: Senegal galago

LORISES AND BUSH BABIES (FAMILY LORISIDAE)

All three species of lorises (see p. 69 for illustration) live in the rain forests of southwestern Asia. Arboreal and nocturnal, they spend the day asleep in holes in trees or among thick branches, curled into a ball with their heads between their thighs and their hands and feet holding onto a branch. They move slowly and deliberately, carefully placing each hand and foot and clamping it firmly in position before the next one is moved. They may crawl along the underside of a branch and hang from one or both legs, leaving the hands free. Their index finger is reduced to a vestige, and they lack a tail.

SLENDER LORIS (*Loris tardigradus*), maximum length 6 in., has long legs. It is pugnacious and not as sociable as the slow lorises.

A single young is born after a gestation period of 5½ months. Almost from birth, the young is left suspended from a branch. Within a month, it begins to move independently. It is weaned in 3–6 months but stays close to its mother for about 9 months.

SLOW LORIS (*Nycticebus coucang*), maximum body length 18 in, and the slightly smaller but rarer lesser slow loris (*N. pygmaeus*) are heavily built animals.

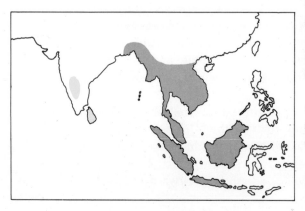

■ Slow loris

■ Slender loris

Potto   Angwantibo and young

BUSH BABIES , the potto and the angwantibo, are African counterparts of the lorises and belong to the same family. In contrast to the slow-moving potto and lorises, bush babies (*Galago*, 6 species) are extremely agile and swift, sometimes moving on all fours but usually with long leaps. The Senegal galago (*G. senegalensis*) can spring 7 feet vertically; the dwarf galago (*G. demidovii*), about 12 in. long, can jump 10 feet horizontally.

The bush babies, which inhabit tropical rain forests and savanna woodlands south of the Sahara, feed mainly on insects.

Females give birth to one or two young after a gestation period of 4½ months. At first the young is left in the nest. Then it is carried with the mother, clinging to her fur or held in her mouth. Young are weaned at 3–4 months and become sexually mature at 20 months.

POTTO (*Perodicticus potto*), maximum body length 16 in. plus a 3-in. tail, occurs from sea level to 6,000 feet in the lower branches of forests of West and Central Africa. The potto's protruding neck vertebrae, covered with skin and surrounded by long guard hairs, are used to ward off attackers. The potto lowers its head and thrusts its body forward to strike like a butting ram.

ANGWANTIBO (*Arctocebus calabarensis*), maximum body length 9 in. plus a 2-in. tail, inhabits canopy forests of Cameroon and Gabon and resembles a small potto without the protruding neck vertebrae.

▢ *Dwarf galago*
■ *Senegal galago*

White-fronted marmosets

NEW WORLD MONKEYS (ORDER PRIMATES)

Monkeys of the New World differ from those of the Old World in lacking cheek
pouches and in having nostrils that open to the side rather than down. The area
between the nostrils is wide and flat. Most have a long, prehensile tail and none
have callous pads on the buttocks.

MARMOSETS AND TAMARINS (FAMILY CALLITHRICIDAE)

Among the smallest of all primates, the squirrel-sized marmosets and tamarins
comprise a wholly South American family (5 genera, 16 species), whose distribution is centered in the Amazon Basin. They are the only primates with tactile
wrist hairs and with clawlike nails on all digits except the big toe, which has a flat
nail. The thumb is not apposable.

In many species the head is adorned with tufts, a beard, plumes, ruffs or
manes. The emperor tamarin, for example, has a mustache. Marmosets have
longer incisors but shorter canines than do tamarins. Marmosets use their
incisors as a "tooth comb," similar to the way lemurs do.

Both marosets and tamarins are arboreal and very active, diurnal and squirrel-
like in their movements. They live in family units consisting of adults and their
offspring, each marking its territory with a scent.

Marmosets groom their own pelts and those of their mates. They communicate with shrill birdlike twitters and high-pitched squeaks often beyond the
range of human hearing. Mainly insectivorous, they also eat plants.

Females give birth to one to three (normally two) young, with a gestation

Top (left to right): Mustached tamarin, cotton-top marmoset, pygmy marmoset, Geoffroy's tamarin
Bottom (left to right): Goeldi's marmoset, golden lion marmoset, silvery marmoset,
emperor tamarin, common marmoset

period of 4½–5 months. The male assists in rearing the young, carrying them much of the time but handing them to the female every few hours for suckling.

Large numbers of marmosets and tamarins have been captured and exported as pets and for research. They survive well in laboratories and zoos but make unsuitable pets.

MARMOSETS are mostly 7–10 in. long with an 8–10-in tail. Smallest is the pygmy marmoset (*Cebuella pygmaea*), maximum length 5 in. with an 8-in. tail. Females bear twins that are weaned and self-supporting in 3 months. Unlike other marmosets, the pygmy relies on hiding rather than flight for protection.

Marmosets move along branches on all fours. Usually they live in family units but sometimes form groups of 30–40.

The largest marmoset is the golden lion marmoset (*Leontopithecus rosalia*).One of the rarest mammals, these marmosets live only in small sections of the coastal forests of southeastern Brazil.

TAMARINS (*Saguinus*, 10 species and numerous subspecies) are slightly larger than marmosets, averaging 8–9 in. in body length and displaying a tail 13–14 in. long. Like the marmosets with which they are often classified, they move quickly when alarmed. Some are highly vocal and have shrill calls.

Tamarins are primarily rain-forest dwellers, but some range into open woodlands. They exist from sea level to an elevation of 3,000 feet. The evolution of the numerous species and subspecies has been a consequence of their isolation by impassable river barriers. Each species has distinctive color markings and facial tufts of plumes that vary with the locality.

Dusky titi   *Bald uakari*

CEBID MONKEYS (FAMILY CEBIDAE)

Nine genera and 23 species comprise this family, which includes all New World primates except marmosets and tamarins. In most species the long fingers and toes have true nails, but the big toe is apposable and the long tail is prehensile. Except for the douroucouli, all are arboreal, diurnal and vegetarian. A single young is the norm.

TITI MONKEYS (*Callicebus*, 3 species) live in the tropical rain forest—the collared titi or widow monkey (*C. torquatus*) mainly to the north of the Amazon, the dusky titi (*C. moloch*) to the south. They favor the forest canopy but descend lower or to the ground. They average 13 in. in body length and 16 in. in tail length. The tail is not prehensile. Male and female genitalia look almost alike. The head is round, the snout short and the ears large.

Family units defend their territories by gestures and vocalizations; the loud calls are complex and varied. A ritual dawn chorus occurs before the families move off to feed, and sometimes a communal call, which can carry over considerable distances, is given by all groups in an area.

Titis usually move on all fours, but they can also jump and leap, rising quickly from a hunched, relaxed position. The single young clings to a parent with hands, feet and entwined tail. The father carries the young except when it is being suckled. They eat fruit, buds and leaves.

■ *Titi monkeys*

Red howler monkey (see text, p. 79)   *White-faced saki monkey*

SAKI MONKEYS *(Pithecia,* 2 species; *Chiropotes,* 2 species) are about 14 in. long, the tail about 18 in. As with the titis, the tail is not prehensile and is used mainly for balancing. The arboreal sakis mostly inhabit the lower forest growth; and while they eat primarily fruit, they may also feed on leaves or even small animals.

The white-faced saki *(P. pithecia)* is noted for its sexual dimorphism—the males are black with a white face and the females brown with a dark face and white cheek stripes.

The monk saki *(P. monachus)* has a prominent coif that fringes its forehead and face, while the black or Humboldt's saki *(Chiropotes satanas)* is known for its black beard, the long hair on its head and its bushy tail. The white-nosed saki *(C. albinasa)* has white bristles over its reddish pink nose and upper lip.

UAKARIS *(Cacajao,* 3 species), about 16 in. long with a 5½-in. tail, are the only New World monkeys with short tails. Uakaris usually move on all fours but may run or walk on two legs, using their arms for balance. Males have a larger head then females, due to the prominent jaw muscles that give their face a square look. The bald uakari *(C. rubicundus* and *C. calvus)* has a bald head and a bright red face. The rare black-headed uakari *(C. melanocephalus)* has a black face and a prominent fringe of hair on its head. Uakaris are restricted to areas along rivers. Their numbers have been greatly reduced. They live in treetops and rarely descend to the ground. Like sakis, uakaris are generally quiet and can move silently through the forest, making them hard to spot from below. They subsist on fruit, flowers and insects.

               ■ *Saki monkeys* ■ *Uakaris*

Top right and left: Brown capuchins and young

Top left: White-fronted capuchin
Top right: White-throated capuchin
Bottom: Weeper capuchin

CAPUCHINS *(Cebus*, 4 species) have a body length of about 18 in. and a slightly longer semi-prehensile tail. Forest dwellers, they live in the canopy but descend to the ground to drink. They are found from sea level to 7,000 feet. Agile and active, they move on all fours, but sometimes walk on their hind legs. Capuchins show a high degree of intelligence in captivity; they have been observed using simple hand tools to break open nuts and performing tasks usually associated only with the great apes. Capuchins live in troops of two dozen or more. They are highly vocal and make use of a wide variety of calls, making them easy to see as they travel through the treetops. Females bear a single young after a gestation period of 6 months. Males are noticeably stockier than the females.

Largest of this genus is the tufted or brown capuchin *(C. apella)*, with horn-shaped tufts of hair above its forehead and a dark brown skullcap. The name

"capuchin" is derived from the resemblance of the cap to the cowl of the habit of the Franciscan monk *(capucin* in French).

The white-throated capuchin *(C. capucinus)*, the only species extending from South into Central America, has a white face, throat, shoulders and chest. It is the monkey commonly used by organ grinders.

The white-fronted capuchin *(C. albifrons)* has a yellowish forehead patch and a dark cap.

The weeper, or black-capped capuchin *(C. nigrivittatus)*, has a small light-colored forehead and a dark, V-shaped skullcap.

Douroucoulis and young

DOUROUCOULI *(Aotus trivirgatus)*, maximum body length 12 in. and tail about 14 in., is also called night monkey because it is the only nocturnal monkey. During the day, the douroucouli sleeps in a tree cavity, foraging mainly at dusk and dawn. It ranges from sea level to 9,000 feet and is found from the canopy almost to the forest floor.

The douroucouli's tail is not prehensile. Its large laryngeal sac gives resonance to its voice, which is further amplified by the use of its lips to form a "megaphone." Family units seldom intermingle, each marking its territory with urine. Territorial displays are usually silent, unlike those of howlers and capuchins. Douroucoulis face each other, arching their backs and jabbing with their hands. The victor may give a grunting roar as its rival retreats. The single young clings to its mother's abdominal fur for the first few days, after which it is carried by the father except when it is being suckled.

SQUIRREL MONKEY *(Saimiri sciurea)* has a body about 12 in. long and tail 16 in.; it is the most common South American monkey. It inhabits elevations from sea level to 5,000 feet and from the forest canopy to the floor. Troops may contain a hundred or more individuals. The single young, born after 6 months of gestation, clings to either parent, though the mother is not especially attentive. Each year many thousands are captured for the pet trade and for research laboratories.

Douroucouli

Squirrel monkey

Black spider monkeys

SPIDER MONKEYS (*Ateles*, 1 species; *Brachyteles*, 1 species). The body is about 20 in. long and tail about 29 in. A very prehensile tail with a hairless strip on the underside near the tip functions as a fifth limb. The legs are long and slender, and the thumb is not apposable.

Spider monkeys live in the upper strata of lowlands and along the edges of forests. They are highly selective in their diet and eat only fruit. They spend their days in small groups, but many congregate in units of a hundred or more at night, huddling together in tight groups. Extremely agile, they swing from branch to branch, often making lengthy downward jumps. They also move on all fours and sometimes walk upright. Males are dominant and are aggressive toward other males, particularly in the presence of females.

A single young is born after a gestation period of 4½ months. It clings to its mother's abdomen for about 4 months; then it moves to her back.

The black spider monkey (*Ateles paniscus*) is widely distributed and occurs in a number of races, all very slenderly built. The rare woolly spider monkey (*Brachyteles arachnoides*) is more stockily built and has smaller incisors than the other spider-monkey species. It occurs only in southeastern Brazil.

WOOLLY MONKEYS (*Lagothrix*, 2 species) have a body about 19 in. long and tail 25 in.; they have dense woolly fur, a muscular prehensile tail and a hairless tip like that of spider monkeys.

Woolly monkeys live in the upper strata of rain forests, from low levels to mountains. They eat mainly fruit and leaves, often gorging themselves. Little is known about their social structure and behavior except that they sometimes live in troops of 50 or more.

Squirrel monkeys (see text, p. 77)   *Humboldt's woolly monkeys and young*

HOWLER MONKEYS *(Alouatta,* 5 species) (see illustration, p. 75) have a body length about 24 in. and tail about 24 in.; they are the largest New World monkeys. The thick tail is strongly prehensile, and the larynx is enlarged, particularly in the male. Both male and female genitalia are conspicuous.

Howlers are wholly arboreal—swinging from branch to branch, moving on all fours and occasionally leaping. Mainly leaf eaters, they inhabit the upper strata of rain forests as well as drier deciduous forests.

Howlers live in bands of up to 30, with several mature males always present. When the group is active, the males utter the loud booming calls that give howlers their name and announce their claim of a territory. These calls can be heard 2 miles away. After this dawn chorus, the others join in before all going off to forage. Howlers may also call at dusk and during the night.

Both males and females assist in caring for the single young, which is suckled for a year and matures slowly. The infant clings to its mother's abdomen and, when older, moves to her back, where it rides as the mother leaps through the trees.

Species differ in size, color and capacity to howl as well as in geographical distribution. They are the red *(A. seniculus),* brown *(A. fuscus),* red-banded *(A. belzebul),* mantled *(A. villosa)* and black *(A. caraya).*

■ *Spider monkeys*

Woolly monkeys

Woolly spider monkey

▨ *Howler monkeys*

Talapoin

Mustached guenon

Vervet

OLD WORLD MONKEYS (FAMILY CERCOPITHECIDAE)

All monkeys native to the Old World belong to this family, which comprises 13 genera and 71 species. All are diurnal, and some are terrestrial.

In Old World monkeys, the muzzle protrudes and the jaws are heavy. The 32 teeth include molars for grinding and, in males, long, tusklike canines used for cutting and shearing. Many members of this family have cheek pouches for temporary storage of food. The ears are rounded, and the nostrils are set close together, facing forward and downward.

Both the hands and the feet are adapted for grasping, the big toe partly or wholly apposable. All digits have flat nails. The tail is almost never prehensile; some species are tailless. Callous pads on the buttocks are often bright and, in the case of the females in heat, swollen.

GUENONS (4 genera, 19 species) occupy a variety of habitats—from equatorial forests to savannas and semideserts; from sea level to 10,000 feet. Most species live at the edges of stratified forests.

Guenons are small (they average 20 in., plus the tail) with rounded heads and small teeth. The arms are a bit longer than the legs, and the long tail may be slightly prehensile. Most guenons have striking multicolored markings. The callous pads on the buttocks are small and do not swell when the females are in heat, except in Allen's guenon and the talapoin monkey.

A single young is born after 6–7 months and is weaned at 6 months. Normally 3–12 females live in single-male harems, but some species form groups of 50–100 or more.

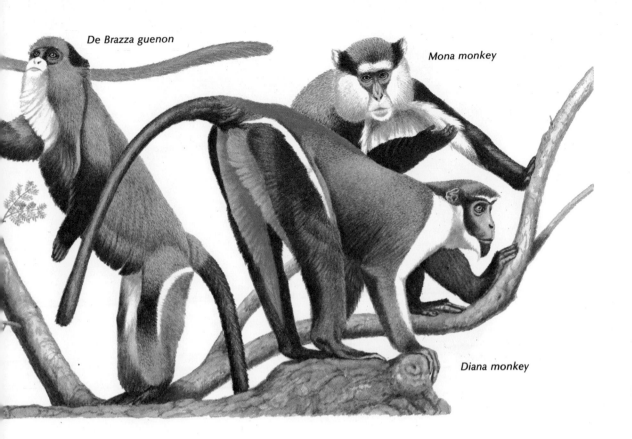

De Brazza guenon

Mona monkey

Diana monkey

Guenons communicate through a wide variety of calls, ranging from birdlike twitters to hisses, clicks and sharp barks. In addition to serving as warnings, these cries keep the troop in contact; louder, booming calls are used when a territory is defended against a neighboring group.

Guenons can move faster through the trees than a man can run on the ground. Some species are known to swim. The Diana monkey (*Cercopithecus diana*) is reported to eat leaves and fruit; others supplement their diet with insects, bird eggs and, possibly, even small vertebrates. Some raid crops.

Vervet, or green, monkeys *(C. aethiops)* are the most common of the African primates, living in large troops in savanna woodlands and grasslands. Most of the other 15 species in this genus are arboreal. Many are localized in distribution, and some, such as the Diana monkey, are now rare.

The rufous Patas monkey *(Erythrocebus patas)* is tall (maximum length 30 in.) and almost wholly terrestrial (see illustration, p. 88). It can run on the ground faster than any other monkey, living in open savannas and acacia woodlands and ranging far into the Sahara. Allen's monkey *(Allenopithecus nigroviridis)* is a short-legged swamp dweller. Another swamp dweller is the talapoin *(Miopithecus talapoin)*, which reaches a maximum length of 12 in. and is the smallest of the guenons. It has adapted to life near river settlements, even stealing cassava roots left at the river's edge to soak overnight.

■ *Guenons*

Japanese macaque

Celebes black ape   *Pig-tailed macaque*

MACAQUES *(Macaca*, 12 species*)* are stockily built monkeys, averaging about 20 in. in body length with a slightly longer tail. The front and hind legs are about equal in length, and the thumb is fully apposable. The low brow forms a ridge.

Macaques have the widest distribution of any genus of monkeys. They occur, too, in a great variety of habitats—from grassland savannas to mangrove swamps, from deciduous to evergreen forests; in climates ranging from tropical to temperate and humid to dry and from coastal regions to 13,000 feet.

Most macaques spend the day on the ground, but they usually retire to trees to sleep. In some areas they use rocky cliffs rather than trees. Some are wholly arboreal. Macaques move mainly on all fours, but they may walk or run on their hind legs, particularly if their hands are being used for some other purpose, such as carrying food.

Highly gregarious, macaques live in groups of ten to several hundred. A number of subgroups with male leaders are in turn controlled by a single dominant male. Each group occupies a specific range, but these are not clearly marked and often overlap. Subordinate groups relinquish their position to a dominant group readily; serious fights are rare and of short duration.

Communication is by a variety of sounds and postures including lip-smacking, teeth-baring, eyebrow-raising and other expressions. Grooming is an important social activity which takes up a large part of the macaque's day.

A single young, with a gestation period of 5½–7 months, is normal. It is suckled for 1 year and becomes sexually mature in 4 years, though males may not reach full growth until they are 10 years old. Macaques have a life span of about 30 years.

Lion-tailed macaque

Crab-eating macaque   Rhesus monkey   Stump-tailed macaque

Macaques are among the most intensely studied of all primates. The extensive use of the rhesus monkey, crab-eating macaque and Barbary ape in medical research has severely depleted the wild population.

Common species are the red-faced toque, or bonnet monkey (*M. sinica*); the rarer lion-tailed macaque (*M. silenus*), with gray ruff and beard; the pig-tailed macaque (*M. nemestrina*), distinguished by its short, curled tail; the crab-eating monkey (*M. fascicularis*), an inhabitant of mangrove swamps; and the rhesus monkey (*M. mulatta*), the common monkey of India. The Assam macaque (*M. assamensis*) resembles the rhesus but has a longer coat and a shorter tail. The rare Taiwan macaque (*M. cyclopsis*) looks like the rhesus but occurs only on Taiwan.

The Southeast Asian stump-tailed macaque (*M. arctoides*) and Japanese macaque (*M. fuscata*) have very short tails (1–2 in.). Others are the moor macaque (*M. maura*) and the black "ape" (*M. nigra*), both of the Celebes and nearby islands. The misnamed black "ape" (a monkey, not an ape) sports a prominent crest of long black hair.

The Barbary "ape," or magot (*M. sylvana*), is geographically isolated from all other Asian members, being the only species ranging into Europe (Gibraltar) and North Africa. An old superstition predicts that when the Barbary apes desert Gibraltar, British rule on this tiny peninsular colony will end.

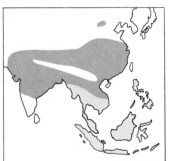

■ Rhesus monkey   ▢ Crab-eating monkey

Olive baboons

BABOONS *(Papio,* 5 species, 11 subspecies) are found solely in Africa. Included in the baboon group are the mandrill and the drill (see p. 86).

Baboons are large, powerful monkeys. Some males stand almost 3½ ft. tall, twice as large as the females. They have a doglike head; and the long, pointed, naked muzzle has a prominent bony structure on each side, with the nostrils at its extreme tip. The jaws are powerful, the canine teeth especially large. The eyes are deep-set beneath prominent brow ridges. Long hair on the neck and shoulders form a heavy mane particularly prominent in the hamadryas, or sacred baboon *(P. hamadryas),* but lacking in the yellow baboon *(P. cynocephalus).* The tail is short to moderate in length; in some species there is an unusual bend near the base. The callous pads on the buttocks are conspicuous, red to flesh-colored in the hamadryas, gray in the olive baboon *(P. anubis).* Baboons have keen eyesight and hearing.

Baboons are mostly terrestrial, spending their days on the ground but sleeping at night in trees. This varies somewhat with the subspecies. The hamadryas baboon, for example, inhabits open savannas and is almost wholly terrestrial. It sleeps on cliffs and rock faces rather than in trees. At the opposite extreme, the yellow baboon is highly arboreal. Baboons usually walk on all fours.

Baboons are gregarious and live in troops that commonly contain more than a hundred animals. Each group, which includes both males and females, is dominated by one mature male. The group occupies an extensive territory that surrounds its sleeping area. They travel in a loose formation as they forage, with young males stationed at the edge of the group to act as sentinels. Females and their young stay at the center. The dominant male stays with his harem.

As the population of the group builds through natural increase, the food resources of the territory are outgrown. Part of the group then moves away and becomes an independent group with its own territory.

Females are almost invariably mated by the dominant male. Subordinate males do not get an opportunity to copulate until after the female has passed her sexual peak. Normally a single young is born after a gestation period of 6 months. It is weaned in 6–8 months. The mother attends to the rearing and training of the young, which rides on its mother's back, and the male may discipline the young when it is unruly. Females become full-grown in 4–5 years, males in 7–10 years. The life span is 30–40 years.

Baboons often associate with herds of impalas, kobs or gazelles. They benefit from the superior sense of smell and hearing of the grazing animals, which in turn get the advantage of the baboons' fighting ability. Adult male baboons can intimidate most carnivores. Only lions and leopards are generally feared. Chimpanzees may occasionally kill and eat young baboons in certain areas, but the baboons do not avoid contact with the apes. On the contrary, they continue to live and feed in close proximity in the forest.

Baboons normally eat plants, insects and small animals, which may include hares, small monkeys, newborn gazelles or almost any other animal available when they are hungry. They make themselves pests by raiding crops, and they carry away far more than they eat by filling their cheek pouches. Baboons are also used in great numbers in research but remain abundant in the wild. They have been studied intensively in the field.

Drills

Mandrills

MANDRILLS *(Papio sphinx)*, maximum length 30 in., and drills *(P. leuco-phaeus)*, maximum length 27 in., inhabit rain forests—the mandrill in coastal forests from north of the Congo River to Cameroon and the drill farther inland to Nigeria and the island of Fernando Po.

The callous pads on the buttocks of the male mandrill are especially striking because of their vivid color—red infused with lilac and mauve. The crimson nose and nostrils stand out in sharp contrast against the blue ridges and the purple grooves of the muzzle flutings. These colors are further accentuated by the orange-yellow beard, white cheek tufts and whiskers, the crest of dark hair and mane. The genitalia are also brightly colored, the female's less so.

The drill is not only smaller but also more subdued in color. Its black face is surrounded by a white ruff.

Both the mandrill and the drill are forest dwellers and largely terrestrial. They prefer rocky glades, however. They sleep in trees and may also forage there. Like other baboons, they are omnivorous, feeding on either plants or animals and becoming pests when they raid croplands. Like the baboons, they can be beneficial when they feed on locusts.

While much is known about the baboons through field studies, the natural history and ecology of the mandrill and the drill are not well known. They bear a single young, but the gestation period is longer—as much as 8 months. They travel in groups and communicate by barking and growling to give warning and to keep in contact.

Geladas   Mandrills and drills

Geladas

GELADAS *(Theropithecus gelada)* are the only living representatives of a group of ground-dwelling primates that was once widely distributed in Africa but now occurs only in northern and central Ethiopia. Geladas inhabit largely treeless highlands up to 15,000 feet.

A large, baboonlike monkey, maximum length 28 in., the gelada has a short, rounded muzzle. The jaws are bulbous and the cheeks fluted, with long tufts of light hair on the upper cheeks. The brow ridges are prominent, and the tail is long and tufted. Callous pads on the buttocks are dark, and there are conspicuous red chest patches in both sexes, those of the female surrounded by warty tubercles that become swollen and flushed with color when she is in heat.

The shift of the erogenous zone from the buttocks to the chest may be an adaptation to the gelada's sedentary existence. Special features include its cushionlike rump pads, exceptionally long thumb, small canines and short legs. Geladas gather their food in a sitting or squatting position. Baboons, in contrast, forage while on the move.

The gelada is almost wholly terrestrial. Cliffs and rock faces replace trees as resting places and refuges. Even when foraging, a group does not stray far from the security of a cliff. The females and young stay closest, the males sometimes moving far off. A troop is subdivided into harems of 5–30 females under a dominant male. There are also bachelor and juvenile units in the herd.

A marked social hierarchy is evident, however, among females as well as males. Dominance is asserted by symbolic mounting and submission, by various postures and by such facial expressions as rolling back the lips to expose the teeth and gums.

Gray-cheeked mangabey

White-collared mangabey   *Patas monkey (see text, p. 81)*

MANGABEYS (*Cercocebus*, 5 species) are large monkeys, the head and body about 22 in. long and the tail 30–34 in. long. They are closely related to baboons.

Slenderly built, mangabeys have long arms and legs and an apposable thumb. The muzzle is long, and the cheek pouches are large. The eyelids are white, accenting their facial expressions. The long tail is not prehensile and is usually carried arched over the back. Mangabeys are diurnal, most active at dawn and dusk. They usually move slowly and deliberately, but they are agile and capable of considerable speed. They eat principally fruit, nuts, seeds and green plants, occasionally supplemented by small animals. The ample cheek pouches are used to store food.

Mangabeys live in closely knit groups that have a strict hierarchy. The dominant male's powerful call notifies neighboring groups of his whereabouts so that intruders into a territory can avoid contacting him. Females regularly groom the males and each other, but males seldom groom the females.

Mangabeys often live in association with guenons, and because they differ in habits, the species do not compete or conflict. Mangabeys feed on fruit with thick peels that they tear with their strong teeth; guenons are unable to do this. Mangabeys are active at dawn, midday and dusk when the guenons are resting. Their presence may even be mutually beneficial: Guenons respond to the mangabeys' alarm calls and vice versa.

Mangabeys are divided into two natural groups: crested and uncrested.

Crested mangabeys have long fur, with a prominent cap on the crown of the head. Wholly arboreal, they live in the upper strata of the forest and rarely descend to the ground. They are shy and retiring, shunning contact with hu-

Black mangabey *Golden-bellied mangabey*

mans and preferring the more remote jungle areas along rivers. Crested mangabeys live in small units of 4–12 individuals under a dominant male.

Two species belong to the crested and arboreal mangabey group. The gray-cheeked mangabey (*C. albigena*), which is predominantly black with a flowing mane and a long head crest, ranges north of the Congo River from Cameroon to Uganda and just across the Tanzania border. It prefers humid forests and is often found near rivers, where it lives in small troops with a single dominant male. The male's special throat sac adds resonance to his territorial calls. The black mangabey (*C. aterrimus*) is also dark but has distinctive side whiskers and a pointed skullcap that looks much like a half of a coconut. It lives south of the Congo River and in Angola.

Uncrested mangabeys have short fur. They frequent the lower strata of the forest and are partly terrestrial, thus closer in habits to the baboons. Also, they come near human settlements and may raid crops regularly. They live in groups of 10–24 individuals, sometimes more.

Three species form the uncrested group of mangabeys. The white-collared mangabey (*C. torquatus*) has white cheek flashes, a white band around the neck and a fox-red skullcap. It lives in swampy areas between the lower Niger and the Congo rivers. The sooty mangabey (*C. atys*) has charcoal-colored fur, a dark-brown cap and prominent cheek tufts. It occurs from Senegal to Dahomey. The agile mangabey (*C. galeritus*), which is light gray tinged with olive, is found north of the Congo River from Gabon to eastern Zaire. A relict race (*C. g. galeritus*) lives in the gallery forests of the lower Tana River in Kenya.

Black colobus

King colobus

Zanzibar red colobus

COLOBUS MONKEYS (*Colobus*, 4 species; and *Procolobus*, 1 species) are leaf eaters, corresponding to the langurs of Asia (see p. 92). They differ from langurs in having no thumb or only a vestige and in lacking cheek pouches. The septum of the nose extends to the upper lip. Their complex stomach structure is adapted to digest leaves.

Black-and-white colobus (*C. guereza* and *C. polykomos*), head and body a maximum length of 20 in., are slenderly built and attractive. More than 20 races are recognized. They inhabit tropical rain forests from lowlands to 11,000 feet, occupying the middle and upper strata and seldom descending to the ground. Troops are composed of 15–20 animals, each claiming a small territory through which the animals move on a regular route from their sleeping trees to where they feed and spend most of the day.

Claim to a territory is made by the male's distinctive call. This is chorused almost immediately by the entire troop and then answered by neighboring troops, quickly mounting in a reverberating crescendo. It is one of the most distinctive sounds of the African forest.

In a territorial confrontation, two males face each other, click tongues and wave tails, but do not make contact. The male whose territory is invaded bobs up and down and roars. A series of roars may last 20 minutes and be heard a mile away. He climbs high into a tree, then drops down from one branch to another in a ritualized display. Eventually one of the troops moves off, the male bringing up the rear.

Black-and-white colobus have been subjected to heavy hunting for their pelts. Their population continues to decline due to habitat-destroying settlement and deforestation.

Abyssinian coiobus and young   Red colobus   Abyssinian colobus

The red colobus (*C. badius*), head and body maximum length 20 in. and tail 25 in., occurs in numerous color combinations—from mahogany to various shades of red or orange, brown, gray and black. It is more slenderly built than the black-and-white species. Three relict races (in Zanzibar, Tanzania and Kenya) are rare and endangered.

The red colobus also inhabits a variety of forest types but is never far from water. It favors the upper strata of the forest but may descend to lower levels to feed. The troops, larger than those of the black-and-white species, sometimes contain 50 or more animals. The red colobus has declined in numbers.

The olive colobus (*Procolobus verus*), head and body maximum length 18 in. and tail 20 in., is olive green to gray and unpatterned and untufted except for a small frontal head crest. It spends its day foraging in the lower strata but sleeps in the middle strata, living in troops of 15–20 animals that include several males. They often associate with guenons. When threatened, a colobus normally sits quite still in the foliage, where its drab color serves as camouflage. Olive colobus do not have the noisy territorial displays of the black-and-white. Little is known about the olive colobus's social habits but it has a unique trait. The female may carry her newborn in her mouth for the first week; then she transfers it to her abdominal fur, where it clings by itself.

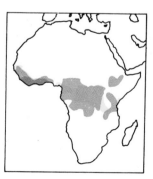

■ Red colobus

■ Olive colobus

■ Black and white colobus

Capped langur

LANGURS *(Presbytis*, 14 species; 3 other genera) are a large and diverse group of Asian leaf-eating monkeys. A few species have been studied, but the group as a whole is poorly known. They are large, the head and body 15–30 in. long and the tail 20–43 in. All are slender in build, with long arms and legs. The round head is frequently capped or crested, and the face is either black or gray, with bushy eyebrows and a short nose. The hands are long, the thumb apposable.

Langurs occur in mangrove swamps and tropical forests; others live in snow-covered mountains to 12,000 feet. Some live in arid regions, others in monsoon areas that have the highest rainfall in the world. As a group they are arboreal, the silver langur *(P. cristatus)* rarely descending to the ground. But at the opposite extreme, the sacred langur *(P. entellus)* is largely terrestrial.

Most langurs belong to the genus *Presbytis*, and largest of these is the sacred langur *(P. entellus)*, maximum length 30 in. with a tail 39 in. long. It is common and venerated by the Hindus even though it raids crops.

Their principal diet is leaves, supplemented with fruit, buds and other plant parts. Normally they move on all fours, but they sometimes run along branches on their hind legs. They appear to follow regular routes through the forests, making long leaps from one tree to another and covering up to 15 feet in a horizontal direction and even a greater distance at an oblique angle.

The size of the groups varies from small, single-male family units in the arboreal forms to a hundred or more in terrestrial species. Territories are established, but intrusions are tolerated. Similarly, shifts in dominance from one male to another take place without violence. The dominant male also shows little concern when other males copulate with members of his harem.

Proboscis monkey, male   *Douc langur and young*

A single young is normal, the gestation period 5½ months. The young is weaned at about 12 months and gradually becomes more independent. The mother rejects the young the following year when she has another baby. Langurs are sexually mature at 3–4 years but may not become full-grown until they are 6–7 years old.

Two species comprise the genus *Nasalis*. The pig-tailed langur (*N. concolor*), maximum length 20 in., is noted for its short (7-in.) tail, naked except for the tip. The proboscis monkey (*N. larvatus*), maximum length 26 in. with a 27-in. tail, has a protruding, bulbous nose on its flesh-colored face. In older males the nose can become pendulous and hang down below its chin. Air emitted through the nose as the monkey makes its characteristic honking noise distends the nose momentarily like a balloon. The proboscis monkey is very agile, swinging by its arms, leaping and even plunging into the water from a considerable height. It is an excellent swimmer and has been found far from land.

The rarest langurs are the snub-nosed langurs (*Rhinopithecus*, 3 species) of China, Tibet and Assam.

The douc langur (*Pygathrix nemaeus*) is found in Indochinese forests and is now rare. The douc langur population has decreased since the Vietnam war, due mostly to the use of defoliants that destroyed both its food and habitat.

Until recently, langurs had the reputation of not adjusting to captivity. Now zoos have learned that these leaf eaters require large quantities of fresh leaves all year and must be kept in well-adjusted family groups in order to thrive.

Siamangs

GIBBONS (FAMILY HYLOBATIDAE)

Gibbons (*Hylobates*, 6 species) are the smallest of the anthropoid apes and are sometimes included in the family Pongidae (see p. 96). They are the least advanced of the higher primates. Gibbons are thickly furred and tailless, with prominent callous pads on the buttocks. Long arms enable gibbons to swing hand over hand (a process called brachiation) through the trees at great speed. They can also reach far out on a limb to get fruit, their principal food. They scoop water from tree hollows and then suck it from their hands. On the ground they walk on their hind legs.

Gibbons are well known for their remarkable calls—a series of musical "woops" rising in a crescendo, then dying down as they call back and forth across the treetops at sunrise. Their powerful voice is amplified by an inflatable laryngeal sac present in both sexes in some species (e.g., the siamang and the concolor), only in females in others (white-handed gibbon). All gibbons are extremely noisy, giving howls, barks and cries.

Males and females differ in color in some species. Capped or pileated gibbons (*H. pileatus*), for example, are white at birth but become fawn within a few weeks. Gradually they develop a black cap and a breast patch, the males turning progressively darker until they are totally black except for their white hands, feet, facial markings and groin tufts. The females remain basically fawn, though they acquire various black markings. In the white-handed gibbon (*H. lar*), both dark and light color phases occur and are not sex-linked or related to age.

White-handed gibbons   Top: Hoolock gibbon, male   Right: Capped gibbon, male
Left: Concolor gibbon, male

Wholly arboreal, gibbons occupy the highest strata in the rain forests, from sea level to 7,000 feet. They rarely descend to the ground and sleep in the foliage without building a nest or shelter. They live in small family units consisting of a mated pair and their young. They are strongly territorial. Males announce their territorial claim to an intruder by protracted calls, sometimes accompanied by agitated movements and posturing. The invader gives counter calls. The male dashes at the intruder and chases him a short distance back into his own territory and may even attack before withdrawing.

Females give birth only every 2 years. A single young, born after a gestation period of 7 months, is invariably white and changes color gradually. For the first few months it clings tightly to its mother as she swings through the trees. It stays with her for about 2 years. Then the adults become increasingly aggressive until they drive the young away. Most species of gibbons are sexually mature in about 5–7 years; others take longer.

Largest of the gibbons is the siamang (*H. syndactylus*), maximum height 3 ft., weight 15–20 lbs. Smallest is the island-dwelling dwarf siamang (*Symphalangus klossi*), maximum height 2 ft. The hoolock, or white-browed gibbon (*H. hoolock*), has a bold white stripe across its forehead. The capped or pileated gibbon *(H. pileatus)* from Thailand has a black cap.

Deforestation and hunting have reduced the population of gibbons. In Thailand, demands of the pet and laboratory trade have been devastating; to obtain a gibbon the mother is shot and only her young is taken.

■ Dwarf siamang   ▨ Capped gibbon   ▨ Siamang gibbon
■ Concolor gibbon   ▨ White-handed gibbon

96

Gorillas

GREAT APES (FAMILY PONGIDAE)

The great apes, the 5 living genera confined to Old World tropical forests, are the most advanced of the nonhuman primates. Their brains are highly developed, and they are the closest living relatives of man. Typically, both the long arms and the legs are used in walking, the animals leaning on their knuckles. The fingers are long, the thumb apposable. They have no tail. All are active during the day and are principally vegetarian.

GORILLAS *(Gorilla gorilla)* live in the rain forests of equatorial Africa, to elevations of 10,000 feet. Destruction of habitat is one of the greatest threats to the species, hunting being another. Males stand 6 ft. tall, have an arm spread of 8 ft. and may weigh 400 lbs.; females are about half this size. The head is massive, with a prominent crest and heavy ridges over the eyes. The thickset body is covered with short, dense, blackish hair, absent from the face, hands, feet and upper chest. Mature males become increasingly gray and are called silverbacks.

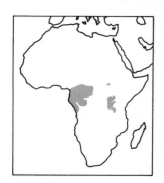

Gorillas forage during the day. Females and young may sleep in trees; silverbacks prefer the ground. They live in groups of 10 to 20 with one dominant silverback. When two troops meet, the silverback may hoot and beat its chest, a sign that he wishes to avoid a fight. If the confrontation persists, he may roar and charge, but attacks are very rare. Gorillas are the gentle giants of the forest.

Females become sexually mature at 6–7 years, males at 9–10. Females usually reproduce every fourth year, more frequently if the young dies (the infant mortality rate is 40–50 percent). Babies remain with the mother for 3 years.

Chimpanzees

CHIMPANZEE *(Pan troglodytes)* males stand about 5 ft. tall and weigh up to 175 lbs.; females are smaller. The muzzle protrudes, the nose is small, the ears are prominent. Adults become gray on the back and thighs. The young have pink faces, which darken with age. The pygmy chimpanzee (*P. paniscus*) is smaller, more lightly built and very dark.

Chimpanzees occur from Sierra Leone to western Uganda and Lake Tanganyika, at elevations to 9,000 feet; the pygmy chimpanzee is found only between the Congo and Lualaba rivers. An open canopy forest is preferred, but woodland savannas may be inhabited. These sociable animals normally live in unstable groups that vary in size and formation from day to day.

Chimps climb well but spend most of their time on the ground. They are mainly vegetarian, but their diet also includes termites, various larvae and, occasionally, monkeys or other small mammals. Chimps build nests each evening and sleep in them overnight.

The single young, born after a gestation of 225 days, is suckled for as long as 4 years. Even after it is weaned, the young stays with its mother until well into adolescence. Females become sexually mature at about 8–9 years but do not breed until 11–12 years. Males achieve full social maturity at about 15 years.

Chimpanzees are extremely intelligent. They make and use tools regularly in the wild, adapting a twig to remove termites from a nest and using a wad of leaves as a sponge. Chimps have 32 sounds in their vocal repertoire. Some laboratory specimens have been taught to communicate in sign language.

Orangutans

ORANGUTAN *(Pongo pygmaeus)* lives in the jungles of Borneo and Sumatra. Gibbons and orangutans are the only apes to occur outside central Africa. The males may stand 4½ ft. tall and commonly weigh more than 150 lbs. in the wild. Those kept in captivity have exceeded 400 lbs. The females are much smaller.

Orangutans have relatively short legs, but their arms are exceptionally long and powerful. In males they may have a span of more than 7 feet. The reddish brown hair covering the body becomes increasingly darker as the animals get older and is especially long in males. The orangutan has 12 pairs of ribs and 12 thoracic vertebrae, the only great ape sharing these features with man.

Orangutan is a Malayan word meaning "man of the woods." The forehead is high, the ears small and hairless and the nostrils large. Both the face and the palms are naked. The cheeks are pouchy, particularly in old males. Males also develop pouchlike throat swellings, like goiters. Older males make loud roars with these laryngeal sacs when they are disturbed by other males.

The orangutan is largely arboreal, deliberate in its movements but swinging from branch to branch with ease. On the ground, it sometimes walks on its hind legs, its gait clumsy and its arms held over its head. To move more rapidly, it clenches its fists and then uses its long arms as crutches, swinging its body between them. The orangutan feeds mainly on fruits, particularly the pungent durian, but it varies this diet with other plants and also eats shellfish, bird eggs and insects or other small animals.

Orangs generally live singly, in pairs and rarely in small groups up to four animals. The old males are usually solitary except during

Man

brief mating encounters. Females and younger males sleep in trees, typically making a platform of branches in a fork and then curling up on their sides with their arms pillowing their head. If it is cool or raining, they may cover themselves with leaves or branches. They rarely use the same nest for more than a day.

The reproductive rate of orangs is low. Females give birth to a single young every 4 years, and the mortality rate of the infants is as great as 40 percent. The gestation period is about 275 days. The young are suckled for about 18 months. They become mature at 10 years, and their life span is about 25 years.

Captive orangutans are usually friendly, but as the males mature, they are often unpredictable and aggressive. Orangs are among the world's most endangered animals. Partly this is due to the extensive destruction of their habitat, for the forests are being cut for timber. Until strict legislation was enforced, large numbers were captured for use either in research or for exhibit. Unfortunately, a mother is generally killed in order to capture her young, and most of the young die before ever reaching their destination. It is believed that fewer than 5,000 orangutans still exist in the wild—most of these in Borneo. Several biological stations have been set up there and in Sumatra to reintroduce confiscated pets and smuggled orangs back to the wild.

MAN (*Homo sapiens*) occupies all the world except parts of Anarctica. He is the most numerous and widespread primate, totaling over 4 billion individuals. The extraordinary development of his brain has allowed him to completely modify, control, even destroy his environment. A single offspring is the norm after a gestation of 9 months, and the period of dependence on the mother is longer than that of any other mammal.

Giant anteater and young

EDENTATES (ORDER EDENTATA)

Edentates are natives of the New World, ranging from the Amazon Basin northward into the southern United States and southward to Patagonia. Edentate means "toothless," but only anteaters are toothless. Sloths and armadillos lack canine and incisor teeth. There are two groups: hairy edentates (anteaters and sloths) and armored edentates (armadillos).

Edentates have specialized to such a high degree that they are removed from competition with most advanced forms. They are remnants of a much larger group that evolved and flourished in South America when that continent was isolated. They could not compete with more recent mammals such as the prairie dogs and gophers that spread their range southward. Some edentates extended their distribution northward; one—the nine-banded armadillo—reached the United States.

ANTEATERS (FAMILY MYRMECOPHAGIDAE)

Anteaters have a tubular snout, with a small mouth at the tip, and a long, whiplike tongue coated with sticky saliva for picking up ants and termites, their principal food. They have no teeth. The claws on the front legs—particularly on the middle finger—are large and powerful. They are so long and thick that the animals must walk on the sides of their knuckles, the claws turned under and inward. These powerful claws are used to rip apart ant and termite nests, and they are also effective weapons for defense. Anteaters are basically but not exclusively nocturnal. Their sense of smell is better than their hearing or vision.

Tamandua

GIANT ANTEATER (*Myrmecophaga tridactyla*), maximum length more than 6 ft. including the bushy tail, has a much longer muzzle than other anteaters, and its tongue may be 2 ft. long. It lives in grasslands and savannas, roaming widely in search of food. Usually traveling alone, the anteater goes from one termite hill to the next, probing with its snout into holes at the base, sometimes enlarging them with a sweep of its claws. When alarmed it will raise its nose to test the air and may gallop a short distance to elude a pursuer. At rest, it puts its head between its paws and spreads its tail like a fan over its head and body. To defend itself, the giant anteater stands on its hind legs and lashes out with its front feet. The long, coarse hair on the giant anteater's body has no commercial value, but the animal is nevertheless killed by ranchers. It has been eliminated from much of its original range, the pampas regions of South America.

TAMANDUAS (*Tamandua*, 2 species), head and body 2 ft. long, have a prehensile tail almost as long as the rest of the body. The tail is hairless on the underside and scaly at the tip. Tamanduas live in dense tropical forests. They are both terrestrial and arboreal in habits. Their short, coarse fur has no value, and because they are nocturnal, they are generally not seen.

DWARF, or SILKY, ANTEATER (*Cyclopes didactylus*) is about the size of a squirrel, the head and body 6½ in. long and the prehensile tail 7½ in. long. It has only two functional toes on each front foot. These have large, curved claws useful to the animals in climbing. Each hind foot has four toes and an apposable "thumb" used for grasping as it moves sluggishly along branches. Almost wholly arboreal, it feeds on ants and termites that nest in trees in the tropical forests. Both dwarf anteaters and tamanduas can hang by their tails.

Hairy armadillos

ARMADILLOS (FAMILY DASYPODIDAE)

Armadillos (9 genera, 21 species) are the most widely distributed edentates. Their most distinctive feature is their horny skin, which resembles hardened leather. The armor plates cover the upper surfaces and sides, and each is linked to the next by flexible skin. In most species the top half is almost completely encased, but the shape and arrangement of the armor varies with the species. In some, the underparts are covered with hair that projects from beneath the armor and sometimes between the plates.

Timid and inoffensive, the armadillo's first defense is dashing to the safety of its burrow. Or, if the soil permits, it will dig very quickly into the ground. Some draw in their legs and tail, then lower their carapace until its edges rest on the ground. Others roll into an armored ball. Armadillos have large, powerful claws for digging, and these may be used also for defense when necessary. The giant armadillo's sickle-shaped middle claw can measure 7 in. around the outer curve.

Strictly terrestrial, most species prefer grasslands and savannas, but some inhabit forests. Because they lack fur, armadillos are not able to tolerate cold and are restricted to warm lowlands. Most armadillos are solitary in habit, occasionally gathering in small groups. Nine-banded armadillos are the most gregarious, several often sharing one burrow. They eat insects and their larvae. Several feed on ants and termites. They locate their prey mainly by scent, using their nose like a plow. They eat plants and occasionally small vertebrates and carrion.

Armadillos usually bear several identical young of the same sex. They are born with a leathery skin that hardens gradually.

Three-banded armadillo curled up   *Nine-banded armadillo*

Armadillos dig a series of burrows, building a nest of grass or leaves in one of them. Because they are mostly nocturnal and burrowers, their status is difficult to assess. Some are now believed to be rare. The THREE-BANDED ARMADILLO *(Tolypeutes tricinctus)* may be extinct.

GIANT ARMADILLO *(Priodontes giganteus)* can be 5 ft. long including its 2-ft. tail and weigh up to 120 lbs. It possesses more teeth than any other land mammal—over 100 small peglike projections that are shed in the adult. It is extremely powerful and deceptively agile. The smallest armadillo is the FAIRY ARMADILLO, or lesser pichiego *(Chlamyphorus truncatus)*, less than 6 in. long. The armor plates of the shy and little-known fairy armadillo, which favors arid areas, are not attached to the body except at the crown of the head and down the midline of the back. A separate back plate, fused to the pelvis, is used by the animal to plug the entrance to its burrow. The body is covered with silky hairs.

HAIRY ARMADILLO *(Chaetophractus villosus)* has eight movable bands, while the closely related SIX-BANDED ARMADILLO *(Euphractus sexcinctus)* has six to eight.

NINE-BANDED ARMADILLO *(Dasypus novemcinctus)*, maximum length 3 ft. including its 1-ft. tail, has been expanding its range steadily over the past century. It is the only armadillo occurring in the United States.

Giant armadillo	Fairy armadillo
Nine-banded armadillo	Three-banded armadillo

Two-toed sloth

Three-toed sloth and young

SLOTHS (FAMILY BRADYPODIDAE)

A sloth's fingers, fused for most of their length, are tipped with large, curved claws, used mainly to hook onto branches as the animal hangs upside down from all four legs and crawls along slowly. They seldom descend to the ground, where they move with difficulty. The sloth's exclusive diet is leaves and buds. Its spherical head can be rotated about 270°, and its body temperature fluctuates between 76° and 96° F.

Sloths live in rainy jungles in South America north of Argentina. A layer of green algae commonly grows on their long, dense fur, helping to camouflage them. Also, they have thick, loose skin, and they can roll into a tight ball. They will use their powerful claws for protection only if necessary. In its normal sleeping position a sloth squats in the fork of a tree with its back against the trunk or branch and its head bent forward as it holds onto the branch overhead with its front legs.

THREE-TOED SLOTHS (*Bradypus*, 5 species) maximum length 20 in., have three toes on all feet, and their arms are longer than their legs. They have nine neck vertebrae, two more than most mammals. The tail is a short stump. They are fond of the leaves of the Cecropia trees that grow along rivers.

TWO-TOED SLOTHS (*Choloepus*, 2 species) have only two toes on the front feet, and the arms and legs are about equal in length. One species has only six neck vertebrae, the other seven. Their diet is less restricted, hence they are more widely distributed.

Sloths bear only a single young after a gestation period of 4–6 months. It clings to its mother's back.

Top left: Long-tailed pangolin   Top right: Small-scaled tree pangolin   Bottom: Indian pangolin

PANGOLINS (ORDER PHOLIDOTA)

Pangolins, or scaly anteaters, have evolved similary to edentates, sharing features and habits. They are covered with sharp-edged scales attached to the skin like a pine cone. When threatened, they roll into a ball and lift their scales to expose the sharp edges. The long tail can be wielded like a mace, and the animals can release a repellent secretion from anal glands.

Four of the seven species are from Africa, south of the Sahara. Largest is the giant pangolin (*Manis gigantea*), maximum length 32 in. plus a 26-in. tail. The small-scaled tree pangolin (*M. tricuspis*) is 18 in. long plus a 20-in. tail; the long-tailed pangolin (*M. tetradactyla*), maximum length 14 in. with a 28-in. tail, is also distinguished by having 46–47 vertebrae, more than any other mammal. The Cape pangolin (*M. temmincki*) is intermediate in size, as are the three Asiatic pangolins: Chinese (*M. pentadactyla*), Indian (*M. crassicaudata*) and Malayan (*M. javanica*). Males are generally larger than females.

The giant and Cape pangolins are terrestrial burrowers, inhabiting forests, savannas and relatively arid areas. The long-tailed and small-scaled species are arboreal, their tails prehensile. Asiatic pangolins are partly terrestrial, partly arboreal. Terrestrial pangolins run on their hind legs with the tail slightly raised for balance. Arboreal species are solitary, the others live in pairs. All are nocturnal and feed on ants, termites and larvae with their long sticky tongue. The nostrils and ears can be closed at will to ward against ant stings.

African pangolins give birth to a single young; Asiatic species may have twins or even triplets. The young rides perched on the mother's back just above the base of her tail.

Pikas

LAGOMORPHS (ORDER LAGOMORPHA)

This highly sucessful order, including rabbits, hares and pikas, has colonized all land areas except Antarctica and Madagascar. Rabbits were not native to Australia or New Zealand but were introduced there. As a group, lagomorphs are adapted to all habitat conditions, from sea level to the snow line, from deserts to the Arctic and from grasslands to forests. Most species prefer grasslands, as grasses are their principal food. In open country, their good eyesight and hearing warn them of danger, and they can use their speed to escape.

Lagomorphs differ from rodents in having two pairs of incisors in the upper jaw, one pair located behind the other and not functional. The front incisors grow throughout the animal's life, as in rodents. In rare cases they do not meet and become grotesquely curved; with its jaws locked shut, the animal starves. Another difference is the hard enamel on both sides of the incisors, which therefore do not become chisel-sharp.

PIKAS, OR CONIES (FAMILY OCHOTONIDAE)

All pikas are small—about the size of guinea pigs—with small, round ears and a very short tail. The single genus, *Ochotona*, contains 14 species, all inhabitants of rocky areas at high mountainous elevations in Asia and North America. The soles of the feet are hairy, giving them traction for running over rocks.

The gregarious pikas are diurnal. They do not hibernate. They spend their days collecting grass and other plants, which they place in the sun to dry, later storing this "hay" under rock ledges for winter use. They give sharp, whistling calls, similar to the European marmot's.

European hares

Antelope jackrabbit

HARES AND RABBITS (FAMILY LEPORIDAE)

HARES (*Lepus*, 30 species) are larger than rabbits, have longer ears and are strong runners with larger feet. Their young are born with their eyes open and fully furred; newborn rabbits are naked, or nearly so, and their eyes are shut.

Hares have three or four young after a gestation period of 47 days. Rabbits are born after 28 days. Hares do not breed until the season following their birth; in some species, not until the second year. During the spring mating season, male hares or "jacks" cavort and spar. Immediately after giving birth, the mother takes each young, called a "leveret," to a different part of her territory. A young hare instinctively remains absolutely still when danger threatens. It lacks a scent, and so a predator can come close without detecting it.

Hares are usually solitary, do not burrow and are active mainly at night. During the day, they rest in "forms"—shallow depressions in grass or other vegetation.

The Arctic hare (*L. arcticus*), maximum length 30 in., occurs in Greenland, Alaska and northern Canada. In the northern part of its range it is white all year; elsewhere it is gray in summer.

The varying hare, or snowshoe rabbit (*L. americanus*), maximum length 18 in., lives in North American forests. Its population goes through cycles of abundance and scarcity, causing similar fluctuations in the populations of its predators. The blue, or mountain, hare (*L. timidus*), maximum length 20 in., inhabits European forests. The common European brown hare (*L. europaeus*), maximum length 25 in., inhabits opens lands, as do white-tailed (*L. townsendii*), black-tailed (*L. californicus*), antelope (*L. alleni*) and other jackrabbits of western North America. Africa and Asia each have about half a dozen species of hares.

Varying hare (see text, p. 107)   *Arctic hare, summer coat (see text, p. 107)*

EUROPEAN RABBITS *(Oryctolagus cuniculus)*, maximum length 18 in., live in the grasslands and open woods of southern Europe, the British Isles and North Africa. Very gregarious, they live in underground warrens, often with intricate mazes of tunnels that accommodate hundreds of animals. They are mainly nocturnal.

Notoriously prolific,females become sexually mature at 3–4 months and produce litters of 4–6 young with only 4 weeks' gestation. The naked, blind young may be suckled for 3 weeks. A female mates a few hours after giving birth, thus producing litters at monthly intervals. This high reproductive rate is sustained only during the spring and summer breeding seasons. During the remainder of the year, breeding is less intensive and resorption of embryos is common.

Rabbits rarely go far from their warrens. When alarmed, they dash for their burrows after sounding a warning by stamping the ground with their hind feet.

As an aid to digesting the coarse plants they eat, rabbits produce soft droppings of partly digested food and then eat them. This also provides them with vitamin B they do not obtain from their diet.The second droppings are hard pellets.

Where rabbits are abundant, they may damage crops, girdle trees and thus become serious pests. They were introduced in Australia and spread over the continent within a few decades. The rabbits destroyed the vegetation and drank the water—needed by native animals and livestock.

In the early 1950s a man-caused epidemic of myxomatosis eradicated rabbits over much of their range. There has been partial recovery in some areas, but the population is generally lower than in former years.

European rabbits

COTTONTAILS *(Sylvilagus*, 13 species), most species 12–15 in. long, are the native rabbits of North America, living mainly in grasslands and open woods. Cottontails do not dig burrows but may occupy the burrows of other animals. An exception is the pygmy rabbit (*S. idahoensis*), a desert dweller that digs burrows to escape the hot sun. All cottontails, including the pygmy, make their nests on the surface.

The most common and widespread is the eastern cottontail (*S. floridanus*), occurring over all of eastern North America to the Rockies and southward into Central America. The swamp rabbit (*S. aquaticus*) and marsh rabbit (*S. palustris*) are darker species that live in wetlands of the southern United States. Both are adept at swimming. Slightly smaller are the pale desert cottontail (*S. auduboni*), the brush rabbit (*S. bachmani*) and the Mexican cottontail (*S. cunicularis*). The forest rabbit (*S. brasiliensis*) lives in the forests of South America.

The rare VOLCANO RABBIT (*Romerolagus diazi*) has short ears and no tail. It lives in grassy pinelands only on the south side of the Valley of Mexico at elevations of 9,000 to 10,500 feet. RED or ROCK HARES (*Pronolagus*, 4 species) live in southern and eastern Africa, where they occupy rocky outcroppings much like the rock hyraxes. They are very vocal, which is unusual for lagomorphs, but are seldom seen. Their presence is best known by their accumulated droppings, also called dunghills.

Rabbits and hares are heavily hunted wherever they occur near human settlements. They are an important source of food, and their low-quality fur is used to make felt. They survive because of their high reproductive rate and because their natural predators are usually eliminated from these areas.

Mountain beaver

RODENTS (ORDER RODENTIA)

Rodents are gnawers. A rodent's large incisors grow throughout the animal's life; and because the enamel in front is more resistant than the dentine at the back, the two sides wear away unevenly. The teeth are thus self-sharpening. The incisors are separated from the teeth at the rear by a space, dividing the mouth into two compartments.

To bring the upper and lower incisors together for gnawing, the lower jaw is slid forward slightly. This movement plus a contraction of the cheek muscles closes off the rear part of the mouth so that the animal does not swallow unwanted material as it is gnawing. When the jaws are moved backward for chewing, the incisors no longer fit together. Thus the two sets of teeth work independently of each other and without unnecessary wear. This arrangement is a major factor in the success of rodents as a group.

More than a third of all living species of mammals are rodents. They are adapted for running, burrowing, climbing, gliding and swimming and occupy all basic habitats, their diversity occurring even within a single genus. In numbers of species and individuals, geographical distribution and range of environmental tolerance, including the ability to adapt to man, rodents rank among the most successful of all mammals. They live virtually throughout the world except in Antarctica.

MOUNTAIN BEAVER, or SEWELLEL (*Aplodontia rufa*), the most primitive rodent, lives in northwestern North America. It is not closely related to beavers or any other existing rodent family. Thick-set, measuring 15 in. long, mountain beavers are burrowers and live in colonies. Their extensive burrows run parallel to the surface and include chambers where food is stored during the winter.

Eurasian red squirrel   *Gray squirrel*

SQUIRRELS (FAMILY SCIURIDAE)

With 47 genera and about 250 species, squirrels comprise one of the largest families of rodents. They are worldwide in distribution, except for Australia, Madagascar and Antarctica. Their bushy tail, usually carried arched over the back, is as long as the head and body combined.

Some squirrels are burrowers, and others can "fly" or glide. Most are climbers. Except for flying squirrels, they are diurnal. Squirrels are primarily vegetarian, but some are at least partly carnivorous, and a few are almost wholly insectivorous.

Tree squirrels are abundant in the subtropics and tropics but are not well known because they live in the upper strata in or near the canopy. Those of temperate regions do not hibernate; they bury acorns for winter food.

EURASIAN RED SQUIRREL *(Sciurus vulgaris)*, maximum length 16 in. including a 7-in. tail, occurs from Great Britain (the only native species) across Europe and Asia to Japan. It prefers mature woodlands, feeding on nuts and fruits supplemented with insects, small birds and eggs. In winter, it relies on caches of food. It may also feed on buds, often damaging trees. In Great Britain, the red squirrel is being replaced by the introduced gray squirrel.

GRAY SQUIRREL *(S. carolinensis)*, maximum length 18 in. including a 10-in. tail, is more restricted to deciduous forests, but its diet is similar to the red squirrel's. In North America it is most abundant in woodlands east of the Great Plains. A slightly larger race, lacking reddish marks on the head and sides, occurs in western woodlands. A black color phase is not uncommon.

The average litter is four, the gestation period about 6 weeks. The young are weaned and leave the nest about 6 weeks after birth.

African fire-footed striped squirrel   *African red-legged sun squirrel*

AMERICAN TREE SQUIRRELS *(Sciurus)* include the abundant gray squirrel plus several other species. Largest is the fox squirrel (*S. niger*), maximum length 2½ ft. including the tail. The fox squirrel is generally less abundant than the gray squirrel, though a local area may have more of this species.

Fox squirrels live in open woods or at their edges. In cool regions or in winter, they live in the hollows of trees; in warm regions or in summer, they make bulky nests of leaves and branches. Two litters per year are usual, one in late winter or early spring and the other in midsummer. The 2–5 young are born after a gestation period of 40–45 days.

Red squirrels (*Tamiasciurus*, 2 species) are the smallest North American diurnal tree squirrels, only 14 in. long including the tail. The red, or pine, squirrel (*T. hudsonicus*) is widely distributed in coniferous forests of Canada, eastern United States and the Rockies. The chickaree, or Douglas squirrel (*T. douglasii*), is found only in pine forests of the Pacific Northwest.

Smallest of the American tree squirrels is the pygmy squirrel (*S. pusillus*), body 4 in. and tail 4 in., which lives in the canopy of the jungles of the Amazon Basin and the Guianas. Dwarf squirrels (*Microsciurus*), ranging from Peru to Nicaragua and from lowlands to 6,000 feet, are only slightly larger.

Tufted-eared squirrels—the Kaibab *(S. kaibabensis)* and Abert's *(S. aberti)* both measure up to about 20 in. long, including the tail—are rare squirrels that live in the pine forests of the southwestern United States. The Kaibab is found only north of the Grand Canyon; Abert's only to the south. Kaibabs have a completely white tail; Abert's tail is black or gray above.

ASIATIC TREE SQUIRRELS include the largest of all squirrels—the giant squirrels (*Ratufa*, 4 species), more than 3 ft. long including the tail. They range from

Bottom: Finlayson's squirrel   Top left: Indian giant squirrel   Top right: Prevost's squirrel

Nepal, India and Ceylon through Southeast Asia to Sumatra, Java and Borneo. They live in the upper strata of the forest and move rapidly from tree to tree. Despite their size and bright colors, they are difficult to see. They are noisy, and so are often heard.

Asiatic tricolor squirrels (*Callosciurus*, 25 species) are the most brightly colored of all the tree squirrels. Distributed throughout Southeast Asia, Indonesia, Taiwan and the Philippines, they are similar in appearance and habits to the various species of *Sciurus*.

Asiatic palm squirrels (*Funambulus*, 5 species) inhabit peninsular India and Ceylon, from the rain forests to the arid plains. The five-striped palm squirrel (*F. pennanti*) is almost a commensal of man, frequenting fields, gardens, even houses.

AFRICAN TREE SQUIRRELS are most abundantly represented by bush squirrels (*Paraxerus*, 11 species) of eastern and southern Africa, where they are common in woodland savannas. Striped squirrels (*Funisciurus*, 14 species) have one or more conspicuous stripes running the length of their body. Sun squirrels (*Heliosciurus*, 12 species), highly variable in color and behavior, inhabit equatorial Africa from rain forests to grasslands.

The African giant squirrel (*Protoxerus stangeri*), found from the west coast to Angola and East Africa, usually has a mottled olive coat that is sometimes almost black. Easily distinguished by its large size (maximum length nearly 3 ft.), it has a bushy tail sometimes ringed with black and white. Smallest is the African pygmy squirrel (*Myosciurus pumilio*), maximum body length 3 in. It is restricted to the jungles of the Cameroon and Gabon. Rarest are the palm squirrels (*Epixerus*, 2 species) of West Africa.

Giant flying squirrel   *North American flying squirrels*

FLYING SQUIRRELS can glide for long distances, as can phalangers (see p. 31). They have a membrane of skin between their front and hind legs; and when they stretch out their legs, the membrane is pulled tight between them. The body and featherlike tail are flattened.

Some of the large Asiatic flying squirrels are said to glide for as much as a quarter of a mile. They land on a tree trunk and immediately dash around to the other side to elude possible pursuers.

Flying squirrels are nocturnal. Their eyes are very large, the ears small and rounded. During the day, they sleep in a hollow tree. Because they live in the forest canopy, they are rarely seen. Most of the 14 genera (37 species) live in Southeast Asia. Two species occur in North America and one in Eurasia.

In size Asiatic flying squirrels range from the giant flying squirrels (*Petaurista*, 5 species), with maximum head and body length 18 in. and tail 18 in., to the smaller flying squirrels (*Pteromys*, 2 species), with head and body of 3 in. Asiatic flying squirrels tend to be richly colored (some with red patches), and their fur is thick and soft. Those that live in temperate regions do not hibernate.

The European flying squirrel (*Pteromys volans*) resembles the North American flying squirrel and is about the same size. It ranges over northern Europe and Asia, from Sweden to northern China and Japan. American flying squirrels (*Glaucomys*, 2 species), body 8 in. and tail 4 in., are abundant but seldom seen.

Females give birth to 2–6 young after a gestation period of about 6 weeks. Their eyes open in about 30 days, and they are weaned at 2 months. Before they are 3 months old, they are capable of gliding like the adults, but they stay with their mother until the following spring.

Scaly-tailed
flying squirrel

Springhaas

True flying squirrels are not found in South America, Australia or Africa. In western and central Africa, however, there are 4 genera (8 species) of scaly-tailed flying squirrels (such as *Pinomalurus*), members of an entirely different family (Anomaluridae). The species of *Anomalurus* and *Anomalurops* are large—from 1–2½ ft. including the tail. Species of *Idiurus* and *Zenkerella* are small—maximum length about 8 in. including the tail. The species of *Zenkerella* do not have a flying membrane. The tail is bushy, as in squirrels, but on the underside near the base are two rows of sharp, horny scales that are probably used to help give anchorage in climbing.

SPRINGHAAS (FAMILY PEDETIDAE)

The springhaas, or Cape jumping hare (*Pedestes capensis*), maximum length 16 in. and with a black-tufted tail of the same length, is not closely related to any other rodent and is the only species in its family.

The springhaas resembles either an overgrown jerboa or a rat kangaroo. The short front legs have curved claws for digging. The tail is long.

Inhabiting sandy semi-arid lands from Kenya through eastern, southern and southwestern Africa, a pair of springhaas digs a system of burrows and may alternate between them. Half a dozen or more pairs form a loosely knit colony.

The springhaas leaves its burrow after dusk and can sometimes be seen by moonlight, squatting on its haunches and using its tail for support or moving along slowly on all fours as it forages. Its usual food is roots and tubers. If alarmed, it makes for its burrow with quick leaps that cover up to 15 yards.

Breeding is believed to occur only once a year.

116

Left: African ground squirrel   Top right: Least chipmunk   Bottom right: 13-lined ground squirrel

GROUND SQUIRRELS (several genera) resemble tree squirrels but have smaller ears, shorter legs and more powerful claws. The tail is usually less bushy. They have large cheek pouches in which they stuff seeds, their principal food, for carrying to storage places.

Most ground squirrels dig burrows (some 10 feet deep), bringing large amounts of subsoil to the surface while at the same time carrying leaves, their droppings and other organic matter below. Ground squirrels are strictly diurnal. Most are also gregarious, their colonies containing up to thousands of individuals. Much of their time is spent on the surface feeding or sunning near their burrows. Inquisitive and alert, they often sit on their hind legs to get a full view of their surroundings. If danger threatens, they give a warning whistle and dive into their burrows, soon reappearing to see what is happening. In contrast to tree squirrels, they hibernate in winter or estivate during hot, dry periods.

In North America ground squirrels are represented most abundantly by the more than half a dozen species of *Citellus*. The 13-lined ground squirrel (*C. tridecimlineatus*), maximum length 12 in., is typical of the group widely distributed in the prairies.

In Africa ground squirrels of the genus *Xerus* live in grasslands and savannas south of the Sahara. The Barbary ground squirrel (*Atlantoxerus getulus*) of northwestern Africa is the only representative north of the Sahara.

Some ground squirrels do not burrow. Striped ground squirrels (*Laricus*, 2 species), of Sumatra, Java and Borneo, nest in cavities of fallen trees. In the same region, Oriental pygmy squirrels (*Nannosciurus*, 7 species) live in dense forests. The Bornean mountain squirrel (*Dremomys eversetti*) lives at elevations to 11,000 feet; Chinese rock squirrels (*Sciurotamias*, 2 species), among rocks on

Black-tailed prairie dogs (see text, p. 118)

cliff faces. The long-clawed ground squirrel (*Spermophilopsis leptodactylus*) inhabits extremely arid regions in Turkmenia, northern Iran and Afghanistan. It has stronger claws, thickly furred feet and special "whiskers," or vibrissae, on its underparts. The long-nosed ground squirrel (*Rhinosciurus laticaudatus*), of Sumatra, Borneo and the lower Malayan peninsula, has a long muzzle and tongue, adaptations for its specialized diet of ants, termites and fruit.

CHIPMUNKS (*Tamias* and *Eutamias*, 16 species) are both arboreal like tree squirrels and terrestrial like gophers. The Siberian chipmunk (*E. sibiricus*) ranges across Eurasia from northern Russia to China and Japan. All other chipmunks are North American. The eastern chipmunk (*T. striatus*), maximum body length 10 in. with a 4-in. tail, is widely distributed in the woodlands of eastern North America. The others, similar in size and most with stripes down the back, occur mostly in western woodlands, some at high altitudes in the mountains. All are good climbers but spend most of their time on the ground. Because of their attractiveness, alert movements and constant chatter, they are among the best known of all American animals.

Chipmunks nest underground, some species breeding more than once in a season. Young are born after a month's gestation, and litter size is four to six. All have sizable cheek pouches used for carrying food. Up to four nuts can be held in each cheek pouch and a fifth between the teeth. They do not go into deep hibernation as true ground squirrels do; their winter sleep is often interrupted for feeding from their cache, accumulated during the more clement months. Hoards of hundreds of nuts have been reported. Foxes, lynxes, owls, weasels and snakes prey on chipmunks. When alarmed they give a call and dash to the safety of their burrow, but snakes and weasels can follow them inside.

Steppe marmots

Woodchuck

MARMOTS and PRAIRIE DOGS are terrestrial squirrels. Marmots *(Marmota,* 8 species) occur in temperate regions of Eurasia and North America. Prairie dogs *(Cynomys,* 5 species) (see illustration, p. 117) are found only in North America. Prairie dogs are sociable, marmots are not.

Marmots are all similar in size—24–30 in. including the tail; prairie dogs are smaller, averaging about 15 in. in total length. All are animals of open country, found from lowland plains to alpine meadows. An exception is the woodchuck *(M. monax),* which lives in woodlands in eastern North America.

Marmots and prairie dogs breed in the spring, with two to four young the usual litter. The gestation period is 6 weeks. The young mature slowly and do not breed until they are 2–3 years old.

Prairie dogs live in colonies of many thousands in a well-organized hierarchy of dominant males. Their name comes from their cry, which sounds like a sharp bark. Prairie dog "towns" were once widespread on the Great Plains. The rodents compete with grazing livestock for food, and their burrows can be a hazard. They have been eradicated over most of their original range.

The steppe marmot *(M. bobak)* of Eurasia has been similarly eliminated from the lowland portions of its range. The alpine marmot *(M. marmota)* lives largely above the tree line and out of conflict with human activity.

Marmots differ from other terrestrial squirrels in their heavier build and their lack of cheek pouches. They do not store food for winter, and their diet is mainly green plants. In autumn they accumulate fat, then hibernate through the cold months. Prairie dogs go into partial hibernation, which is interrupted whenever the weather warms. The yellow-bellied marmot *(M. flaviventris)* of the western United States may estivate in summer to escape intense heat and dryness.

Plains pocket gopher   *Kangaroo rat (see text, p. 129)*

POCKET GOPHERS *(Geomys, Thomomys* and other species in the family Geomyidae) inhabit the prairies and mountains of western North America down to Panama. Their 10- to 12-inch body is molelike, with large claws and short legs. The naked tail serves as a sensory organ when the animals move backward in their burrows. A gopher can run backward as fast as it can forward, a distinct advantage in one-way tunnel systems.

Gophers have several adaptations for their subterranean life. Fur-lined cheek pouches help carry quantities of food from the surface down to deep storage chambers. Tear glands exude a thick fluid to remove dirt from their eyes. A strong muscle closes the lips behind the incisors so that dirt will not enter the mouth while the gopher is burrowing with its teeth. Unlike marmots, gophers do not hibernate; they feed on their stored food during winter.

Two types of burrows are dug—long, winding ones close to the surface to obtain roots and tubers; and deep ones, where small dens for storage, sleeping and even lavatory facilities are found. Solitary for most of the year, gophers fight viciously with other gophers, both male and female.

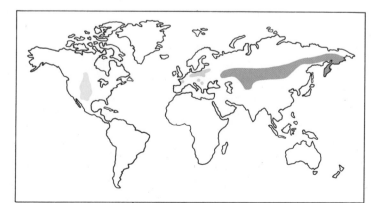

■ *Steppe marmot*

■ *Prairie dogs.*   ■ *Alpine marmot*

North American beavers

BEAVERS (FAMILY CASTORIDAE) AND MUSKRAT (FAMILY CRICETIDAE)

The European beaver (*Castor fiber*) and the North American beaver (*C. canadensis*) both reach a maximum length of about 42 in. including a 12-in. tail; they are so closely related that some authorities consider them to be the same species. They are the largest rodents in the Northern Hemisphere.

Excellent swimmers, beavers can remain submerged for considerable lengths of time. Their soft, dense underfur is waterproof and is surrounded by long, protective guard hairs. The hind feet are webbed, the tail broad and paddlelike. The tail is used as a rudder in swimming and to slap the surface of the water as a warning signal. The large incisors, used to gnaw through trees 6 inches or more in diameter, are bright orange.

Beavers live in colonies made up of family units. Adults pair for life. Their territories, marked with secretions from scent glands at the base of the tail, are defended against intrusion by other beavers. The young, normally three, are born in spring and remain under parental care until the following year. Adult males will usually fight with adolescent males, who then leave the group.

Beavers may live in a burrow in a river bank, the entrance dug a little below the surface of the water. If this is not possible, the beavers modify their enviroment by building a dam of timbers, branches and stones plugged with vegetation and plastered with mud. Sometimes the dam may be hundreds of feet long. The pond formed behind the dam becomes a protective moat around the lodge. Inside is an above-water dry chamber in which the beavers rest. Frequent maintenance of the dam is necessary to keep the water level constant so that the submerged entrances to the lodge are not exposed during droughts.

Muskrat   *Beavers*

A system of interconnecting canals make safe passageways to feeding grounds. Beavers eat aquatic plants and other green food when available, but their principal diet is the inner bark of young poplar and willow trees. Piles of food are accumulated underwater near the lodge for winter when the pond is frozen over.

The beaver long ago became rare in Europe. In North America trapping for beaver pelts contributed to the continent's early development. Uncontrolled trapping made the beaver extinct over much of its range, but now protection has resulted in restoration of populations in many areas.

MUSKRAT *(Ondatra zibethica)* , maximum length 25 in. including a 10-in. tail, is also an aquatic rodent but is most closely related to voles (see p. 126). The long, sparsely haired tail is flattened from side to side, the hind feet webbed. Muskrats live in burrows in river banks or in nests above water in marshes. They are sometimes "farmed" for their valuable fur and were accidentally introduced in Europe when they escaped from captivity. They are prolific, producing several litters a year with about six young per litter.

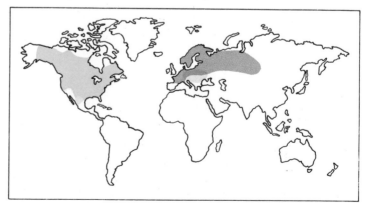

North American beaver ■ European beaver ■ Muskrat

Deer mouse (see text, p. 124)

House mouse

Harvest mouse

RATS AND MICE (FAMILIES MURIDAE, CRICETIDAE AND OTHERS)

The largest and most important of the several families of rats and mice are Cricetidae (New World) and Muridae (Old World). They differ in tooth structure. A number of other small rodents in different families bear the generalized and nonspecific name of rat or mouse.

The two principal families contain more than 200 genera and about 1,200 species. Together they form the largest, most widely distributed and one of the most successful of all groups of mammals. None can fly or glide, but they occupy all other ecological niches.

The success of rats and mice can be attributed not only to their adaptability but also to their exceptional reproductive rate. They become sexually mature within 1–3 months of birth and produce large litters with a gestation period of only 3–4 weeks. They breed throughout the year.

OLD WORLD RATS AND MICE (FAMILY MURIDAE)

Among the best known of all rodents are the BLACK RAT (*Rattus rattus*), maximum body length 7 in. with a scaly tail slightly longer than the body, and the BROWN, or NORWAY, RAT (*R. norvegicus*), maximum body length 10 in. or more with a tail about the same length as the body. Both were originally native to Southeast Asia but were long ago spread throughout the world by man. Both have become virtual commensals of man. They are mainly nocturnal but may also be active by day. The black rat is the better climber, the brown rat the better swimmer. The brown rat ranges farther north.

African climbing mouse

Striped grass mouse

European wood mouse

Golden spring mouse

The ubiquitous HOUSE MOUSE (*Mus musculus*), maximum body length 5 in. with a 3- to 4-in. tail, is found wherever man lives. It thrives near and in human habitations but lives outdoors. House mice are omnivorous but prefer grain. Along with the black and brown rats, they are a symbol of vermin, not only because of their destructiveness but also as carriers of disease. They soon multiply to pest proportions wherever food is readily available.

One of the smallest members of the Old World group is the EURASIAN HARVEST MOUSE (*Micromys minutus*), less than 2½ in. long. Its tail, about the same length as the body, is prehensile. It ranges over most of Europe and Asia.

Similar in appearance but slightly larger and without a prehensile tail are the FIELD MICE (*Apodemus*, 5 species). The hind legs are notably larger than the front legs. They are not as skilled at climbing but can run swiftly and leap. Field mice occur over Europe, Asia and northern Africa.

GIANT POUCHED RAT (*Cricetomys gambianus*), maximum body length about 16 in. with a tail of equal length, occurs in tropical Africa. It has capacious cheek pouches in which it carries seeds. It is hunted not as a pest but for food.

BUSHY-TAILED CLOUD RAT (*Crateromys schadenbergi*), maximum length 3 ft., is a Philippine species adapted for life in trees. The closely related slender tail cloud rat (*Phloemys cumingi*) has apposable digits for grasping and semi-prehensile tails that give support when wrapped around branches.

STICK-NEST RAT (*Leporillus conditor*), maximum body length 9 in. with a 6-in. tail, is one of three closely related Australian rats that live in deserts. Stick-nest rats build huge nests of sticks over their burrows as a protection from the searing heat. The pile of sticks is often anchored with stones on top.

Brown rat (see text, p. 122)

Black rat (see text, p. 122)

Giant pouched rat (see text, p. 123)

NEW WORLD RATS AND MICE (FAMILY CRICETIDAE)

The rats and mice in this family differ from those in the Old World family (see p. 122) in the structure of their cheek teeth, which have two rows of cusps or bumps rather than three. Like their Old World relatives, however, they have adapted to a wide range of habitats, from amphibious to burrowing and tree dwelling. None of the species has reached worldwide distribution, but some are pests locally. Over 100 genera of cricetid rodents are spread worldwide.

PACK, or WOOD, RATS (*Neotoma*, 20 species) are about the same size as brown rats but are more attractive, with a hairy tail and white underparts. Widely distributed, they are most abundant in the western deserts and mountains of North America.

These rats are best known for their habit of collecting and hoarding all sorts of unusual objects in their nests. They are attracted to bright or shiny objects, and many tales have been told of their thievery around camps. Their nests are huge mounds of sticks and litter. Those that live in deserts build their nests under cacti and then surround them with impenetrable barriers of spines.

The most attractive of the New World mice are the WHITE-FOOTED and DEER MICE (*Peromyscus*, more than a dozen species). They range throughout North and Central America. Some are gray, others fawn and still others reddish or gold—but all have snow-white underparts and feet. Some live in woodlands, others in grassy meadows. One species inhabits deserts. Only occasionally do these handsome mice invade dwellings, though it is not uncommon for a white-footed mouse to cohabit with campers. They are friendly and quickly become tame enough to feed from the hand.

Bushy-tailed pack rat

Bushy-tailed cloud rat (see text, p. 123)

125

Australian water rat

GRASSHOPPER MICE (*Onychomys*, 2 species), maximum length 7 in. including a 2½-in. tail, feed almost exclusively on grasshoppers and other insects. Both species are North American, one living in the plains and the other in the desert.

RICE RATS (*Oryzomys*, several dozen species) range through the southern United States, Central and South America. About 12 in. long including a 5-in. tail, they live in marshes, both fresh and salt, and feed on a variety of plants. They nest above the waterline or burrow in drier habitats.

COTTON RATS (*Sigmodon*, several species) occur in the same range as rice rats but inhabit dry or upland areas. Omnivorous, they eat vegetation, insects and invertebrates. They breed year round. Up to 12 young are born after 27 days of gestation. They leave the nest after 7 days to breed 5 weeks later.

NEW WORLD HARVEST MICE (*Reithrodontomys*, several species) are the size of house mice and resemble them. They live in grasslands throughout most of the United States, Mexico and Central America. Harvest mice build a ball-shaped or spherical nest of grass on the ground or anchored in bushes or tall grass. Harvest mice eat mainly seeds.

Arboreal rats and mice of the New World include the VESPER RATS (*Nyctomys* and *Otonyctomys)* of Central America. These mice were formerly found with such regularity in shipments of bananas from Central America that in Europe and the United States they became known as banana mice.

FISH-EATING RATS (*Ichthyomys*, 7 species), from northwestern South America, are 6–8 in. long with a tail equally long. Their toes are partly webbed and are fringed with hair. The hair on their body is dense and close-pressed. Semi-aquatic, they feed on fish and water vegetation.

Common hamster   Norwegian lemming

HAMSTERS are members of the family Cricetidae (see p. 121), but all 14 species in 5 genera are natives of Eurasia. All have large cheek pouches in which they carry food for winter storage in their nests. They do not hibernate but do become semidormant. The pouches are also puffed with air to threaten adversaries and to give the animals buoyance when swimming.

Hamsters are normally solitary. Their burrows usually have many chambers and may be near the burrows of another, but each is clearly marked with scent.

The common hamster (*Cricetus cricetus*), maximum length 10 in., has a stubby tail. The golden hamster (*Mesocricetus auratus*), popular as a pet and as a research animal, came from a single female and her 12 young caught in Syria in 1930. None has since been found in the wild.

VOLES and LEMMINGS are most abundant in cool temperate and subarctic regions. The muskrat (see p. 121) is the largest member of this group.

Most famous are the lemmings. The collared lemmings (*Dicrostonyx*, 4 species) range northward close to the North Pole. In winter, they not only get a white coat but also special "ice claws" on their front paws. Both lemmings and voles mature very early and are prodigious breeders. They may breed within 4–5 weeks of birth and two or more times a year thereafter. The gestation period is only 3 weeks, and each female produces 4–8 young. As a result, lemming populations build to large numbers. Great fluctuations occur in their populations, however, usually in 4-year cycles. In optimum conditions, their numbers soon exceed the carrying capacity. Exhaustion of the food supply combined with the physiological stress of crowding results in large numbers dying of starvation and a drastic decline in numbers.

Rough-tailed gerbil (see text, p. 129)

Water vole   Short-tailed vole

In exceptional circumstances, mass movements of lemmings occur. These immense hordes wander in search of more favorable conditions. The movements of the Norwegian lemming (*Lemmus lemmus*) are legendary; but they are not, despite the stories, always suicidal trips to the sea. All lemmings take these journeys in search for food at their population peaks.

Voles and lemmings are the most abundant animals (and the only rodents) inhabiting the tundra. They are key prey species in food chains of Arctic predators, such as the Arctic fox and the snowy owl, and hence are critical to their survival. The common field or meadow mice ((*Microtus*, about a dozen species) are voles. All are similar in size—5–6 in. including the tail—with rounded bodies, small ears and small, black eyes. Active day and night, they inhabit grasslands, each eating its own weight in grass and other plant foods daily. Like other voles, they make clearly defined runways under grass or burrow in open terrain.

The red-backed vole (*Clethrionomys gapperi*), maximum length 6 in. including a 1½-in. tail, is mainly a woodland species, occurring in northern United States and Canada. The bank vole (*C. glareolus*), slightly smaller, inhabits Great Britain, Europe and central Asia. Their individual range size is affected by the amount of food available.

The water vole *(Arvicola amphibius)*, maximum length 7 in. plus a 4-in. tail, lives along the banks of streams in the British Isles. It is semi-aquatic, feeding on both plants and small animals. Other species in the same genus, some of them molelike in habits, range over most of Europe. Tree voles *(Phenacomys*, several species) build nests high in the branches of trees.

Common dormouse   Fat dormouse

DORMICE (FAMILIES GLIRIDAE, PLATACANTHOMYIDAE AND SELEVINIIDAE)

In appearance, behavior and dentition, the true dormice of the family Gliridae show close affinity to squirrels. Except African dormice (*Graphiurus*, 20 species), all are confined to Eurasia and mainly to temperate regions. Most are arboreal and nocturnal. All except the terrestrial mouse-tailed dormouse (*Myomimus personatus*) have bushy tails. The fat or edible dormouse (*Glis glis*) occupies the upper strata of the forest; the small hazel or common dormouse (*Muscardinus avellanarius*) favors dense undergrowth and lower branches. Garden dormice (*Eliomys*, 2 species) occur in marshlands and woodlands and from rocky areas to cultivated land; the Japanese dormouse (*Glirulus japonicus*) inhabits mountain forests to 9,000 feet. The tree dormouse (*Dryomys nitedula*) is found in Eurasian forests. They are quite aggressive and will suddenly leap into the air and spit if they are disturbed.

Arboreal dormice make spherical nests of grass, twigs, leaves or bark lined with moss in the hollow of a tree or on a branch. Some construct several nests—for living, for bearing and rearing young and for winter, usually on or under the ground when they go into a deep sleep with a substantially lowered body temperature, heartbeat and respiration. This may be interrupted periodically for feeding on the hoarded food. Dormice eat mainly nuts, berries and fruit and may become pests. Dormice have one litter of 2 to 9 young a year.

Based on their dentition, the two species in the family Platacanthomyidae are linked most closely to mice. The Malabar spiny dormouse (*Platacanthomys lasiurus*) lives in woodlands in southern India, the Chinese pygmy dormouse (*Typhlomys cinereus*) lives in mountain forests in China and North Vietnam.

Meadow jumping mouse

Naked mole rat   Four-toed jerboa

JUMPING RODENTS, which live mainly in arid regions, are unrelated groups that have evolved along similar paths, even on different continents.

Gerbils (12 genera, 100 species—family Cricetidae) are about the size of rats and mice and resemble them in general appearance; they differ in having long hind feet and furry, tufted tails. Occurring in Africa and Asia, principally in sandy plains but also in open and woodland savannas, they are industrious burrowers, constantly cleaning, renovating and extending their tunnels.They move to alternate warrens to avoid flooding or when there is a scarcity of food. Gerbils normally run on all fours, but when alarmed they jump—often spanning 4 or 5 feet.

Jerboas (10 genera, 25 species—family Dipodidae) live mainly in sandy deserts in Asia and North Africa. Their leaps may cover as much as 10 feet. Like many deserts dwellers, they can subsist on metabolic water. Impoverishment of the Eurasian steppes has actually favored some species.

Many species of gerbils and jerboas become dormant several months of the year. Gerbils hoard food for the period; Jerboas do not. Fat-tailed jerboas (*Pygeretmus*, 2 species) from Turkmenia and the fat-tailed gerbil (*Pachyuromys duprasi*) from North Africa store food in their tails, like marsupial mice and the fat-tailed lemur.

Other jumping rodents include the Australian hopping mice (*Notomys*, 9 species—family Muridae), the North American kangaroo rats (*Dipodomys*, 22 species—family Heteromyidae) (see illustration, p. 119) and kangaroo mice (*Microdipodops*, 2 species— family Heteromyidae). Some Eurasian and North American jumping mice inhabit moist grasslands.

Tree porcupine   Canadian porcupine

PORCUPINES (FAMILIES HYSTRICIDAE AND ERETHIZONTIDAE)

Whether these two families are related or are another instance of convergent evolution remains an open question.

The Old World crested porcupines (*Hystrix*, 8 species) may be 3 ft. long and weigh 50 lbs. Their well-developed quills are hollow, sharp-pointed and detachable, and may be as much as 12 in. long. When alarmed, a porcupine lifts its quills and crest, thereby greatly increasing its apparent size. It will also rattle its tail quills ominously. If this does not intimidate the intruder, the porcupine turns around and backs up to impale the attacker with the quills. The quills are never hurled. African species also have a crest of bristles on the head and nape.

Crested porcupines are strictly terrestrial. They inhabit relatively dry country throughout the Middle East (except the southern portion of Arabia), India and southern Asia and have been introduced to southern Europe. They normally live in pairs or family units in deep burrows or crevices. Their twin or triplet litters are born in the spring after a gestation period of 3–4 months. The young are well developed at birth, but their quills are soft. The young remain in the den until their quills harden, usually in about 10 days.

Brush-tailed porcupines (*Atherurus* 4 species) of the equatorial rain forests in Africa and southeastern Asia are substantially smaller, the head and body as long as 18 in. and the long tail bristle-tipped. The Bornean long-tailed porcupine (*Trichys lipura*) is similar but lacks quills.

Old World porcupines are nocturnal and herbivorous, feeding on roots, tubers, fruits and berries. They are also addicted to gnawing on bones, even elephant tusks. In cold weather they are sometimes inactive.

African brush-tailed porcupine

Crested porcupine

In the New World the Canadian porcupine (*Erethizon dorsatum*) may be 3½ ft. long, including a 6-in. tail, and may weigh 40 lbs. It is a forest dweller, and in the northern part of its range its hair grows so long in winter that the quills, as much as 4 in. long, are almost hidden. It uses its quills in the same manner as the crested porcupine: When threatened, it will gnash its teeth, pause, then leap around to present its bristling and thrashing tail. The quills have barbed points and are easily detached when they come in contact with an adversary. Porcupines swim readily, their hollow quills giving added buoyancy.

Canadian porcupines feed mainly on the bark and buds of trees. They are more arboreal than their European counterparts but less so than the South American species. They have an affinity for salt, hence they will seek out and gnaw on ax handles or other items coated with human sweat. During courtship, the male sprays the female with urine. The 7-month gestation period is long for a rodent; a single, well-developed offspring is born in the spring.

Tree porcupines (*Coendu*, 8 species) live in the tropical forests of Central America and northern South America. They have short, barbed spines, almost completely hidden in fur in some species, and a long, prehensile tail that is bare on the upper side and is curled under rather than over a branch. The long, curved claws are used for gripping and climbing. Nocturnal, tree porcupines shelter in hollow logs and burrow during the day.

Tree porcupine
Canadian porcupine

Chinchilla (see text, p. 134)

Degu

Wild guinea pig, or cavy

CAVIES (FAMILY CAVIIDAE)

Most familiar of the cavies is the guinea pig (*Cavia porcellus*), domesticated for so long that its wild ancestry is not known. About 20 species of *Cavia*, 10–12 in. long, are known in the wild. All are tailless, large-headed and short-legged. Mainly creatures of grasslands and open savannas, they are vegetarian, nocturnal and highly sociable. They breed the year around; the young (usually in litters of two or three) sexually mature at about 2½ months.

The rock cavy (*Kerodon rupestris*) lives in dry, rocky country, a niche comparable to that of African hyraxes.

The mara, or Patagonian cavy (*Dolichotis patagonum*) (see illustration, p. 134), maximum length 2½ ft., has hooflike claws. It runs like an antelope and looks and acts like a hare. The mara is diurnal, sheltering in burrows at night.

The capybara (*Hydrochoerus hydrochaeris*) (see illustration, p. 135) is the largest of all rodents; it may be as much as 4 ft. long and weigh 100 lbs. Inoffensive and gregarious, it lives in or near swamps along large rivers, in a semi-aquatic niche akin to that of a hippoptamus. Though it grazes and suns on land, it takes refuge in the water, emerging with only its eyes, ears and nostrils above the surface. The capybara breeds once a year, producing four or five young.

Capybaras are the principal prey of jaguars, pumas and other large predators. Hunted extensively by man for its delicious meat, capybaras have been exterminated in many areas.

■ *Capybara* ▨ *Rock cavy* ■ *Cavy* ■ *Mara*

Paca

Agouti

PACAS, AGOUTIS AND ACOUCHIS (FAMILY DASYPROCTIDAE)

Like cavies, these herbivorous rodents are among the ungulate (hoofed mammal) group and have hooflike claws on their hind feet. All live in South America.

PACAS (*Cuniculus*, 2 species) are normally solitary and nocturnal, inhabiting equatorial rain forests through which they move on trails and runways. Though less aquatic than the capybara, they are good swimmers and will take to the water if pursued. They prefer small streams. One species lives high in the Andes.

AGOUTIS (*Dasyprocta*, 13 species) have erectile rump hairs that are lifted for display or fighting. They are solitary rain-forest animals, preferring clearings near water. In undisturbed conditions, agoutis are diurnal, but constant persecution has forced them to become crepuscular. When danger threatens, they run rapidly and disappear in the undergrowth.

ACOUCHIS (*Myoprocta*, 2 species) resemble the agoutis but are smaller, maximum length 15 in., and have longer tails.

Both the agoutis and the pacas are much hunted for their flesh by the natives of their regions. This constant pressure plus the widespread deforestation of their habitat has resulted in their becoming increasingly rare. Both breed twice a year, the agoutis bearing two to four young and the pacas a single offspring.

The slow-moving, rarer PACARANA, or FALSE PACA (*Dinomys branickii*), maximum length 2½ ft. plus a 6-in. tail, is a rain-forest animal of the Andean foothills. In a distinct family (*Dinomyidae*), it is believed near extinction.

■ *Agoutis and pacas*

Maras (see text, p. 132)

Plains viscacha

Tucotuco

VISCACHAS AND CHINCHILLA (FAMILY CHINCHILLIDAE)

All three species in this family are herbivorous and highly gregarious.

PLAINS VISCACHA (*Lagostomus maximus*), maximum length 20 in., inhabits the Argentine pampas, its warrens resembling prairie dog "towns." It breeds once a year, with a gestation period of 5 months.

MOUNTAIN VISCACHAS (*Lagidium*, 4 species), maximum length 14 in., are sparsely distributed in the Andes. They have been heavily hunted, mainly for their fur. They breed twice a year, and the gestation period is 3 months.

CHINCHILLA (*Chinchilla laniger*), maximum length 10 in., is native to the Andes (see illustration, p. 132). Severely hunted for its fur, now supplied by commercial breeders, it survives only in Bolivia and northern Chile. Chinchillas breed twice a year, the gestation period being 3½ months.

TUCOTUCOS (FAMILY CTENOMYIDAE)

Tucotucos (*Ctenomys*, 27 species), the only representatives in this family, range from Peru and Brazil southward to the tip of the South American continent. These small rodents share the same habits as North American pocket gophers but lack cheek pouches. They favor sandy soils, each pair digging its own system of burrows. Their name comes from the sound of their call.

Tucotucos are crepuscular, rarely going far from their burrow entrance. Roots and tubers are stored in the burrows for winter use, and water requirements are met from the vegetation they eat. Because they conflict with grazing and agriculture, tucotucos have been greatly reduced in numbers, some to extinction.

Coypu   *Capybara (see text, p. 132)*

HUTIAS AND COYPU (FAMILY CAPROMYIDAE)

LONG-TAILED HUTIAS (*Capromys*, 4 species) are confined to Cuba and the Isle of Pines. They are arboreal, except for the rare rat-sized dwarf hutia (*C. nana*) that lives in Zapata Swamp on small, dry, bush-covered islands.

SHORT-TAILED HUTIAS (*Geocapromys*, 2 species) are terrestrial. Except for bats, a hutia (*G. browni*) is the only surviving native mammal in Jamaica. The other species (*G. ingrahami*) occurs only on East Plana Cay, an almost waterless coral island in the Bahamas.

DOMINICAN HUTIA (*Plagiodontia hylaeum*) lives in a small forested area of the Dominican Republic; Cuvier's hutia (*P. aedum*) in the Dominican Republic and Haiti. These basically terrestrial rodents are rare, their decline in numbers due to hunting, predation by the mongoose and destruction of habitat.

Hutias have a low reproductive rate and litters of one to three. They live in pairs. Long-tailed forms are diurnal, the others nocturnal. All are vegetarian.

COYPU (*Myocastor coypu*), maximum length 2 ft. plus a 1½-ft. bare, ratlike tail, lives in wetlands and near rivers in southern South America. The coypu feeds mainly on aquatic plants. It has long and powerful orange incisors and webbed hind feet. Solitary and mainly nocturnal, it digs burrows in river banks but usually nests in a heap of vegetation on the surface like a muskrat.

Coypu fur farms exist in North America and Eurasia, where escaped coypus have proliferated and become a threat to agriculture. In some areas of the southern United States they have displaced muskrats.

The female coypu's mammary glands (6 pairs) are on her flanks, enabling the young to suckle as the mother swims. Litters average four to six.

136

Sperm whale (see text, p. 138)

Greenland right whale

WHALES, DOLPHINS AND PORPOISES
(ORDER CETACEA)

All members of this order are aquatic, and nearly all are marine. They never leave the water, though they must surface from time to time to breathe. Their bodies are streamlined or fishlike, the hind legs totally absent and the forelegs paddlelike flippers. The tail is flattened horizontally and broadened into flukes. The single or double nostril, called a blowhole, is located on top of the head.

A layer of fat, or blubber, just under the hairless skin serves as an insulator and may account for a third of the animal's weight. The eyes are small, the sense of sight enhanced by acute hearing (the ears are invisible). Dolphins, like bats, use a system of echolocation enabling them to hunt and to maintain contact even in conditions of poor visibility. Other, louder sounds emitted from the blowhole are used in communication.

There are two broad groups: whalebone whales (suborder Mysticeti) and toothed whales (suborder Odontoceti).

WHALEBONE WHALES are toothless. The head and mouth are disproportionately large—as much as a third their total length. Hanging down on either side in the mouth are numerous long plates of whalebone, or baleen. In feeding, the whale swims through the water with its mouth open. When it closes its jaws and at the same time raises its huge tongue toward the roof of its mouth, water is forced through the baleen and out the sides of the mouth. Shrimplike krill or other plankton remain in the mouth, adhering to the hairy tendrils on the plates. In the nearly extinct Greenland right whale (*Balaena mysticetus*), the largest right whale, the plates may be 10 ft. long, and the tongue may weigh 4 tons.

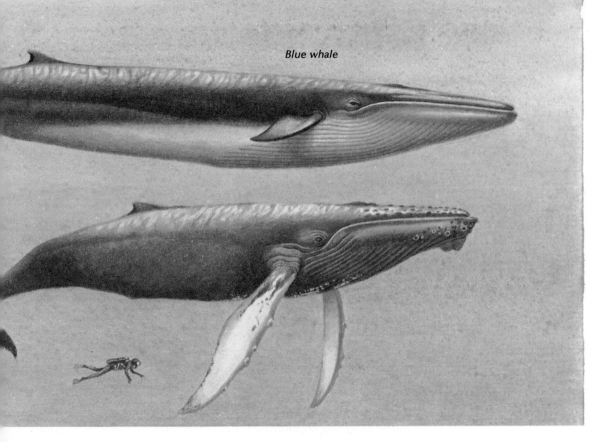

Blue whale

Humpback whale

The gray whale (*Eschrichtius gibbosus*), maximum length 45 ft., exists in two populations, one off California and Mexico, the other off Korea.

Six species of rorqual, or finback whales, are distinguished by a series of grooves on the throat and chest, allowing the skin to expand and thus increasing the capacity of the mouth. They include the 100-ft. blue whale (*Balaenoptera musculus*), the largest animal that has ever lived. It may weigh 130 tons. It is estimated that fewer than 8,000 blue whales are alive today.

Other rorquals are the razorback, or finback whale (*B. physalus*), maximum length 80 ft.; the sei whale (*B. borealis*), maximum 60 ft., the lesser rorqual, or minke (*B. acutorostrata*), maximum 30 ft.; Bryde's whale (*B. brydei*), maximum 40 ft.; and the humpback whale (*Megaptera novaeangliae*), maximum 50 ft.

Most rorquals are gregarious, living in schools of up to a hundred. The blue whale, however, is solitary. Rorquals spend their summers in Arctic and Antarctic waters where plankton crustaceans are most abundant. In winter they move toward the equator, where they breed and bear their young. Because calves have no protective blubber, they must start life in warm waters. Whale milk is about 50 percent butterfat, and so a layer of fat is quickly acquired.

The gestation period varies from 9–12 months for the blue, 10 for the razorback and 12 for the humpback and the gray. The single calf is usually about a third as long as the mother. It is born tail first underwater and must move to the surface immediately to get its first breath.

All whalebone whales except the pygmy have been heavily exploited by man. Several have been reduced to near extinction. Some were first given protection when their numbers were so reduced that hunting was no longer profitable.

White whale

Killer whale (see text, p. 140)

TOOTHED WHALES have teeth instead of baleen and eat fish rather than plankton. Some toothed whales are in fact toothless and feed on cuttlefish. Because they are not dependent on plankton-rich waters, the toothed whales are more widely distributed, occurring most abundantly in tropical and subtropical seas. They have a single nostril, or "blowhole," on top of the head; whalebone whales have two.

The narwhal (*Monodon monoceros*), maximum length 15 ft., is toothless except for a single, greatly enlarged upper incisor that projects as a spiral-shaped tusk as much as 8 ft. long. It is present only in males and usually only on the left side. (Less commonly it is on the right side; and in rare cases, on both sides.) The function of the tusk is not clear. It is not a "tool" for spearing fish, but is most probably a secondary sexual characteristic that serves no known purpose. The narwhal has been hunted for these ivorylike tusks. The narwhal occurs only in Arctic waters and usually travels in herds of about a dozen or more individuals.

The white whale, or beluga (*Delphinapterus leucas*), maximum length 17 ft., also inhabits Arctic waters but roams over a much wider area, frequently entering shallow coastal waters and even ascending tidal rivers in its search for fish. The white whale's attractive skin is sold as "porpoise hide."

The sperm whale (*Physeter catodon*), maximum length 60 ft., is the largest of the toothed whales (see illustration, p. 136). It has numerous teeth, but in the lower jaw only. The sperm whale's preferred food is the giant squid. The whale dives to 1,000 feet and has been recorded at depths of 3,000 feet. It may remain submerged for over an hour and can swim at more than 15 miles per hour.

Pilot whale (see text, p. 141)

Narwhal

The sperm whale's head accounts for about a third of its total length. Its blunt snout projects beyond the mouth. The boxlike cavity contains a thin, transparent oil that once was the main oil burned in lamps. Sperm whales provide still another valued item of commerce: ambergris. This blackish, foul-smelling solid from the intestines is sometimes found along beaches, generally in small amounts, but sometimes the deposits weigh hundreds of pounds. Ambergris is used in the perfume industry because of its capacity to retain the desirable odors of expensive perfumes. The widespread pygmy sperm whale (*Kogia breviceps*), maximum length 12 ft., is similar to the sperm whale but has a proportionately smaller head.

Beaked whales (family Ziphiidae) are small- to medium-size toothed whales that have only a few teeth. Their snout is sharply defined. Beaked whales prefer colder water than most toothed whales. They are most abundantly represented by the genus *Mesoplodon*, which contains about a dozen species that have only one pair of teeth—in the lower jaw. These are among the rarest whales, though they are widely distributed.

The bottle-nosed whale (*Hyperoodon rostratus*), maximum length 30 ft., is relatively common and distinct because of its bulbous forehead. This bulge becomes increasingly larger as the whale gets older. As in sperm whales, the bulge is an oil reservoir. Cuvier's beaked whale (*Ziphius cavirostris*), maximum length 20 ft., goes also by the name of goosebeak whale because of its flat, projected snout. It travels in schools of 40 or more, swimming and diving in search of squid. Beaked whales give birth in the spring after a year's gestation— the calf measures one third the adult length at birth. It suckles for a year.

Common dolphins

Pacific white-sided dolphins

DOLPHINS and PORPOISES are small toothed whales. Dolphins (family Delphinidae) are generally larger, their mouths extending into a prominent beak-like muzzle. They are noted for leaping from the water and for their high intelligence. Porpoises (family Phocaenidae) are smaller; few species exceed 6 ft. in length. Their body is more rotund, the forehead bulbous in most species. As a group, they are more timid than the dolphins and do not leap from the water. Both dolphins and porpoises normally give birth to a single calf.

The common dolphin (*Delphinus delphis*), maximum length 8 ft., can swim 30 miles per hour and cruises at about 10 miles per hour. It lives in warm and temperate seas throughout the world, sometimes in schools of thousands, feeding on fish. Like other dolphins and porpoises, the common dolphin is regularly caught in the nets of commercial fishermen. This has severely depleted their total numbers.

The bottlenose dolphin (*Tursiops truncatus*), maximum length 12 ft., is an Atlantic species well known because it is frequently exhibited at marine attractions. It prefers shallow coastal waters.

Risso's dolphin (*Grampus griseus*), maximum length 12 ft., lives in schools of only about a dozen animals. It is widely distributed in warm seas.

The Pacific white-sided, or striped, dolphin (*Lagenorhynchus oliquideus*), maximum length 10 ft., is regularly seen in marine exhibits. It is one of more than half a dozen species in its genus, including Wilson's hourglass dolphin (*L. wilsoni*), that is restricted to the Antarctic pack ice.

The killer whale (*Orcinus orca*), maximum length 25 ft., is a large dolphin, found throughout the world but most common in cool seas. It has evolved into a

Amazon dolphin

Ganges River dolphin

highly efficient predator. It hunts in packs sometimes containing several dozen individuals and attacks fish, penguins, seals, even large whales.

The pilot whale, or blackfish (*Globicephala melaena*), maximum length 28 ft., has a swollen or bulbous head. It lives in the North Atlantic, but related species occur in other seas. They travel in schools, following a leader, or "pilot." The schools are sometimes stranded on shore, where the heavy animals suffocate because their chest cavities are compressed by the weight of their bodies.

The common porpoise (*Phocaena phocaena*), maximum length 6 ft., is a North Atlantic species, common along shore and often going far up rivers. It feeds mainly on schooling fish such as herring.

Many of the toothed whales live in rivers and adjoining coastal waters. Among these are the Irawaddy dolphin (*Orcaella brevirostris*) maximum length 7 ft.; the Amazon white dolphin (*Sotalia fluviatilis*), maximum 3½ ft.; the Chinese white dolphin (*S. sinensis*), maximum 3½ ft.; the finless black porpoise (*Neomeris phocaenoides*), maximum 4½ ft.

River dolphins (family Platanistidae) are specially adapted to the freshwater environment. They tend to be solitary. The Ganges River dolphin (*Platanista gangetica*), maximum length 8 ft., occurs in the Indus, Ganges and Brahmaputra rivers. The white flag, or Chinese river dolphin (*Lipotes vexillifer*), maximum length 7 ft., is known only in the Tung Ling Lake and adjacent parts of the Yangtze River, 600 miles from the sea. The Amazon dolphin (*Inia geoffrensis*), maximum length 8 ft., lives in the upper Amazon and Orinoco rivers, 1,000 miles from the sea. The La Plata dolphin (*Stenodelphis blainvillei*), maximum length 5 ft., lives in the broad estuary of the River Plate and the coastal waters.

Timber wolves

CARNIVORES (ORDER CARNIVORA)

Carnivores are basically flesh eaters; but some, such as bears and raccoons, eat large amounts of fruits and other plant materials, and one, pandas, thrives on bamboo.

Carnivores are found throughout the world except for the Antarctic. They range in size from the least weasel, measuring 3½ in., to the grizzly bear, 10 ft. long and weighing up to 1,700 lbs. The brain of carnivores is well developed—a predator must use his wits to find and catch his prey. Carnivores include terrestrial species like bears and arboreal ones like civets. Sea otters are the only carnivore to have adapted to a marine life.

All carnivores have clawed toes, and most have five toes on each foot. Each jaw contains three incisors for shearing, a large canine tooth for holding and several premolars and molars for grinding.

WOLVES, WILD DOGS AND FOXES (FAMILY CANIDAE)

These typical carnivores all resemble dogs, with long muzzles and powerful canine teeth. The ears are erect. The tail, usually bushy, is shorter than the body.

Nearly all eat flesh, including insects and carrion. Some form pairs that stay together only while the female is in estrus. Males help rear the young.

WOLF *(Canis lupus)* , maximum height 31 in. at the shoulders, 4½ ft. long and weighing as much as 150 lbs., is the largest member of the dog family. The wolf lives in both grasslands and open woods but is now confined in North America to forests and tundra lands, a last stronghold. Its valuable fur and its infringe-

ment on man's interests, particularly livestock, has brought about the wolf's extermination over most of its range.

A wolf is powerful enough to attack and overcome animals as large as musk ox and caribou but prefers to prey on smaller animals like deer, wild sheep and goats. Typically it hunts in family packs consisting of a male and a female and their pups—from the previous as well as the current year. When food is plentiful, several families may band together, forming packs of a dozen or more animals. Packs define their territories with scent-marking. Howling also warns neighboring packs that a territory is occupied. A strict social order is maintained by both signs and sounds.

Dens are usually underground or in a cave, rocky crevice or thicket. The usual litter size is five or six, produced after a gestation of 2 months. Both parents care for the pups, which are weaned in about 6 weeks but are not sexually mature for 2 years. Wolves normally mate for life.

The wolf is not responsible for depleting wildlife populations. Rather, it helps maintain healthy populations by eliminating the weak and the sick.

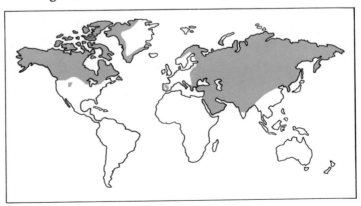

■ *Wolf, original range*

Black-backed jackal

JACKALS, maximum body length about 2½ ft., prey on small animals and scavenge on the remains of larger animals. They may group together to attack large prey but do not form packs. They live alone, in pairs or in small families.

The black-backed jackal (*Canis mesomelas*) has a conspicuous dark patch streaked with silver along the full length of the back. Primarily nocturnal, it is sometimes seen during the day, alone or in small family units, and is very vocal—yapping, barking and howling. Though often a scavenger, it may prey on animals as large as small antelopes. Main foods are mice, insects and lizards.

The side-striped jackal (*C. adustus*) has an ill-defined pale stripe sometimes edged with black and a dark, white-tipped bushy tail. Almost wholly nocturnal, more retiring and less vocal than the black-backed variety, it is not commonly seen. Essentially a scavenger, it feeds on the remains of lion kills and on other small mammals.

The golden jackal (*C. aureus*), with no clearly defined pattern on the back, inhabits open savannas and bush country. It scavenges when it can but usually feeds on rodents, insects and fruit. It sometimes ventures into villages to get its meals. Despite heavy hunting and poisoning—because man fears it transmits rabies and because the jackal preys on poultry—this jackal survives in surprisingly large numbers.

Jackals normally bear four or five pups in a burrow; the gestation period is about 2 months. Pups begin accompanying the adults at about 2 months and are independent by 6 months.

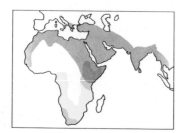

Black-backed jackal   *Side-striped jackal*   *Golden jackal*

Coyotes

COYOTE *(C. latrans)*, maximum length 3 ft., is more slenderly built and less bold than the wolf. The coyote was originally confined to the prairies of North America, where it preyed primarily on the prairie dog, though it also attacked deer and pronghorns. When the Great Plains became untenable for the coyote as a result of intensive development, it spread into new regions. It is, in fact, one of the few carnivores that has extended its range. Over the years, too, the coyote changed from being a primary predator to a semiscavenger, its role now comparable to that of the Old World jackals. In addition to preying on small animals and eating carrion, it will make its meals of fruits, tubers or other plants when very hungry. The coyote is cunning and versatile in evading traps and snares set by farmers who wrongly fear for their livestock. Massive poisoned-bait campaigns in the United States have not only reduced coyote numbers but affected other predators like lynxes and small carnivores in the process.

Coyotes usually live alone or in pairs, but they sometimes form small and temporary bands to hunt prey. They are perhaps best known for their eerie howling, which is one means of communicating and also a method of demarcating territories. Their yaps and barks are different from those of wolves.

Mating occurs in late winter or early spring. The gestation period is about 2 months, the litters averaging 1–7 pups but occasionally containing as many as 10 or 12. The pups are weaned at 6 weeks. Both parents, constantly on the move in search of prey or carrion, help rear the young.

African wild dogs

AFRICAN WILD, or CAPE HUNTING, DOGS *(Lycaon pictus)*, maximum length 3½ ft., live in grasslands and open savannas south of the Sahara from sea level to alpine meadows. Their mottled coat shows wide variation in color patterns, but the head is usually dark and the tail tip white. They travel in packs of about a dozen animals, sometimes numbering up to 60. The packs commonly roam over wide areas.

The cooperative hunting of African wild dogs requires intelligence, coordination, efficiency. A pack will single out an animal from a herd and give chase, running at speeds up to 30 miles an hour, cutting corners to gain ground. They will hunt zebra, warthog, gazelle and wildebeest. Once the prey has been cornered, the dog disembowels it quickly. Hunting dogs will move to another area when food sources are no longer available. In the packs, the dominant females maintain a loose but effective discipline. Communication is by a variety of barks and whimpers. Food is shared. Partly digested meat is regurgitated to feed nursing females, young and the ill when the pack returns from hunting.

Wild dogs are diurnal, active mainly in early morning and evening hours. There is apparently no specific breeding season. The young, usually six to eight in a litter, are born in an abandoned aardvark hole, under rocks or in similar den locations. The gestation period is 70 days.

The wild dog has come into conflict with man and, like the wolf, has been wrongly accused of depleting wildlife populations. Its numbers have been substantially reduced even in some national parks, so that it is now uncommon. Like other predators, wild dogs help maintain a balance in prey populations and should be preserved as an integral part of the ecological community.

Dholes

DHOLE, or ASIATIC WILD DOG *(Cuon alpinus)*, maximum length 3 ft., is primarily a forest dweller but also ranges onto the steppes. It usually hunts in the morning and in the same style as the African wild dog. Packs roam widely. Dholes have a distinctive fox-red coat with a white-tailed tip.

Litters average 4–6 but may contain as many as 10; the gestation period is 63 days. Several females may rear their young communally. Dholes communicate by whistles, cries, yaps, howls, barks and whimpers.

DINGO *(Canis dingo)*, maximum length 4 ft., is the wild dog of Australia, where it was apparently introduced by aboriginal man. Because of the livestock industry, the dingo was systematically eradicated from most areas.

RACCOON DOG *(Nyctereutes procyonoides)* (see illustration, p. 149), maximum length 2½ ft., occurs in China, Japan and the Soviet Far East. It has been widely introduced in some of the coniferous forests of Europe. Colored like a raccoon, it normally lives in warm temperate and subtropical forests, along rivers or in marshy areas.

The raccoon dog is nocturnal. Mated pairs establish well-marked territories. Its diet includes fish and frogs as well as rodents. Acorns are also a favorite. In autumn it accumulates fat and, unlike most members of the dog family, becomes semidormant in winter. Although it is heavily hunted for its hide and meat, it is thriving and even expanding its range.

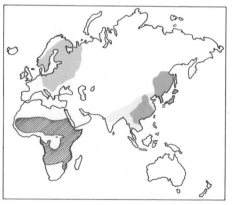

///. African hunting dog   ▪ Raccoon dog, introduced range   ▪ Raccoon dog, natural range   ▫ Dhole

Red fox

Arctic fox

FOXES are smaller than wild dogs, and, unlike them, the foxes hunt alone and mainly at night. They rely on their nose and ears rather than on their eyes and on cunning and stealth more than speed. Their craftiness is legendary. Varying in range from deserts to the Arctic, foxes are among the most adaptable mammals.

The red fox (*Vulpes vulpes*), maximum body length 2 ft., has been heavily hunted but persists even in settled regions. It lives in habitats ranging from semi-arid to alpine and has been introduced to South America, Australia and New Zealand. It has also been reared on "farms" to supply pelts for the fur industry. The red fox is regarded as a menace to man when it preys on poultry and game birds, but it is helpful in controlling rodents.

Females, or vixens, bear litters of four to six pups, with a gestation period of about 50 days. The red fox occurs in several color variations—black, cross (red with black stripes on the shoulders and underparts) and silver (black with white tips on the hairs). In each, however, the tip of the tail is white.

The kit fox (*V. velox*), as large as 2 ft. but often smaller, inhabits desert lands in western North America. Like most desert-dwelling mammals, it has very large ears that pick up the slightest sounds and warn against enemies. The ears also act as "radiators" to help get rid of excess heat. Shy and seldom seen, this once-common species has been greatly reduced in numbers. Some races have been exterminated. It has been heavily hunted for its valuable pelt, but the greatest losses have resulted from poisoning campaigns to eliminate coyotes and rodents.

About half a dozen similar species in this genus live in the arid regions of Africa and Eurasia.

Kit fox   Raccoon dog (see text, p. 147)

The North American gray fox (*Urocyon cinereoargenteus*), maximum length 2 ft., prefers woodlands and warmer conditions than the red fox. It is the only fox that regularly climbs trees. Like the red fox, it has adapted well to the pressures of civilization and may even live within large cities. The gray fox is nocturnal; and though it eats mainly rodents and other small animals, it may feed on fruits from time to time.

The Arctic fox (*Alopex lagopus*), maximum length 2½ ft., lives on the tundra, but it may travel far out onto the pack ice to scavenge polar-bear kills. In winter it commonly moves southward where food is more easily found. The relationship of the Arctic fox to the polar bear is comparable to that of the jackal and the lion. Keeping a respectable distance, the Arctic fox often accompanies the polar bear in hopes of getting the remains of the bear's kill. The Arctic fox subsists mainly on voles and lemmings, however, its population fluctuating with the cyclic abundance and scarcity of the rodents.

Despite heavy trapping for its valuable pelt, the Arctic fox—a bluish gray form is called the blue fox—appears to be maintaining its numbers. Females may bear two litters a year if the first is unsuccessful.

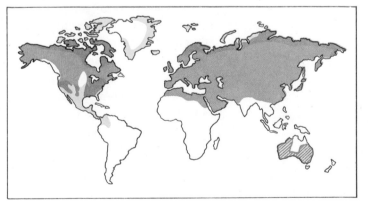

▪ *Arctic fox*   ▪ *Gray fox*   ▪ *Red fox, natural range*   ▨ *Red fox, introduced range*

Bat-eared foxes

BAT-EARED FOX *(Otocyon megalotis)*, maximum length 2 ft., has exceptionally long ears, though not as long proportionately as the fennec's. Largely nocturnal, the bat-eared fox lives on the open savannas and short-grass plains. It feeds principally on insects, especially dung beetles, but also eats rodents and other small animals, supplementing these with fruits from time to time. Its largely insectivorous diet is reflected by the number of teeth it bears—a total of 48, or 6 more than any other member of the dog family.

More sociable than other foxes, the bat-eared fox lives in small family groups and sleeps communally. Females bear three to five young from Nonember to March after an approximately 70-day gestation period. This species is very localized in southern Africa, and though not rare, it is becoming increasingly uncommon. Outbreaks of distemper, introduced by domestic dogs, periodically reduce the bat-eared fox population in a given area to only a few individuals, and it takes several years for them to build up again.

Crab-eating fox *(Cerdocyon thous)*, maximum length 28 in. with a bushy tail about 12 in., is one of several South American foxes that fill the niche occupied in other countries by wild dogs, jackals and hyenas. In social organization, behavior and hunting techniques, they are more like dogs than foxes. The crab-eating fox's diet consists of land crabs, crayfish, frogs, insects and rodents. Sometimes the bulk of its diet may consist only of fruit, seeds and even corn. It is often seen as a pet in native villages, but its habits in the wild are not well known.

　■ *Bat-eared fox*　　■ *Fennec*

Fennec foxes

FENNEC *(Fennecus zerda)*, smaller and much paler, is the smallest fox, measuring only 1–1½ ft. long. Its ears may be more than 4 in. long, about a fourth the body length. The fennec, strictly a desert dweller, lives in small colonies in sand dunes. All its water needs are satisfied from the mice, lizards, birds and insects on which it generally feeds. The hairy soles on its feet enable it to run over the loose sand with ease; it can also burrow into the sand rapidly, melting out of sight in a matter of seconds. Escaping the heat of day by staying underground, the fennec comes out at night to feed. It breeds during January, giving birth to two to five cubs 50 days later. Fennecs are playful and very social; the French foreign legionnaires often adopted them as pets.

The Culpeó fox, or Andean wild dog *(Dusicyon culpaeus)*, is the largest South American fox, its body as much as 36 in. long and the tail 16 in. It occurs from the foothills to 15,000 feet in the Andes. Though normally solitary, it sometimes hunts in small packs and is much bolder than most foxes. Pairs form in August during the breeding season, and the cubs are born in November. Both parents rear the cubs, and food is cached near the underground den.

Smaller relatives include the Peruvian fox *(D. sechurae)*, confined to the western slopes of the Andes and often living on the sea cliffs. The pampas fox *(D. griseus)* lives in the grasslands and coastal beaches of Chile and Argentina. Its population was first greatly reduced by excessive hunting, and then much of its range was taken over by the more aggressive and adaptable red fox.

■ *South American foxes (Dusicyon species)*   *Crab-eating fox*

Maned wolf

MANED WOLF *(Chrysocyon brachyurus),* maximum body length 4 ft. and with a distinct crest of long hair from the nape of the neck to the shoulders, is the largest member of the dog family in South America. It looks like a fox both in the shape of its head and in general color but has exceptionally long slender legs, an adaptation for its life in the open grasslands and savannas. It is called "fox-on-stilts" by the natives and is very conspicous when seen wandering among the termite hills on the pampas. Maned wolves are curious, often pausing to look back at an intruder, which gives hunters a killing shot. It preys mainly on rodents and other small mammals, but it also eats birds, reptiles, insects and, occasionally, fruit. Excess food is buried for later use.

The maned wolf hunts like a fox. It either surprises its prey and pounces on it before it can get away or digs its quarry from their burrows. It does not run down its prey like a timber wolf.

Solitary and nocturnal, males and females live alone except for a brief period for mating in spring. Individuals scent-mark their territories with urine, using landmarks such as termite hills, then give notice of occupancy with a special bark, usually at dusk and after dark. Intruders are met by a threatening display which includes growling, erection of the mane and lifting of the tail. Serious fighting is rare, however.

The now very rare maned wolf has apparently never been abundant and is unable to live in proximity to man. Females give birth to twin or triplet pups after a gestation period of 65 days. The males do not help rear the cubs.

Bush dogs

BUSH DOG *(Speothos venaticus),* maximum body length 25 in. and tail about 6 in., is a squat, short-legged forest dweller, opposite in appearance and habits to the maned wolf. The bush dog lives in dense undergrowth, usually along rivers. It is an excellent swimmer and will enter the water in pursuit of agoutis and other rodents.

Because of its inaccessible habitat, its nocturnal habits and its rarity, the bush dog is seldom seen. It is known to be sociable, living in packs of about a dozen animals controlled by a dominant male. The bush dog is believed to spend most of its day underground, often occupying an abandoned armadillo burrow. It emerges at dusk to begin hunting. Unlike most wild canids, the female comes into heat twice a year. She heralds the fact by depositing scent on tree trunks, using an unusual handstand posture. Males cock their legs like dogs.

Though it is a small animal, the bush dog has a reputation for ferocity. It tames easily, however, and is often kept as a pet by Amazonian Indians. This explains its appearance in zoos though it does not breed well in captivity.

SMALL-EARED DOG, or ZORRO *(Atelocynus microtis),* is a foxlike wild dog of the Amazon Basin. Very dark and with exceptionally short ears, it is known for the grace and lightness of its movements and for the musky odor of the males anal glands. Females are substantially larger and appear to be more aggressive, but the male dominates the pair. This is a rare and sparsely distributed species.

▧ *Bush dog*
▨ *Small-eared dog*

Spotted hyena

Striped hyena

HYENAS (FAMILY HYAENIDAE)

Hyenas are superficially doglike in appearance but are more closely related to cats. They have large heads, broad snouts and heavy forequarters, which are noticeably higher than the hindquarters. The bushy tail and the hind legs are short. Hyenas' scent glands have a structure similiar to that of civets.

Hyenas are scavengers, capable of crushing large bones with their powerful jaws and teeth, as well as predators. They have an undeserved reputation for being cowardly, for they can be aggressive toward lions and dogs.

Mainly but not exclusively nocturnal, hyenas hunt by sight. They spend the day in a den or burrow, coming out at night. They usually inhabit open country but may live in and along the fringes of forests.

Mature females have a annual litter of pups, usually one to four. The gestation period is 90–110 days.

SPOTTED HYENA *(Crocuta crocuta),* the largest of the hyenas—body 3–3½ ft. long and weighing up to 175 lbs.—is a powerful animal. Skulking only in appearance, it has been known to drive lions from their kill and steal the carcass. By day, the spotted hyena is a scavenger; by night, a hunter.

The spotted hyena has a well-developed sense of smell, good sight and hearing. When it finds food or is alarmed, it emits a "laugh"—a series of maniacal cries, cackles, howls, hoots and barks that is often heard across the African plains.

The basic social unit is the clan, consisting of 10 to 60 hyenas.

■ *Spotted hyena*

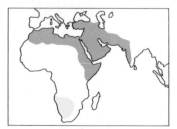

■ *Brown hyena*   ■ *Striped hyena*

Aardwolf

Clan members may be scattered like lion prides. Clan size is adapted to the availability of food, with large clans hunting zebras, smaller ones scavenging kills from other predators. They can trot tirelessly, wandering over great distances to find food.

STRIPED HYENA (*Hyaena hyaena*), maximum length 2½ ft., weight 100 lbs, is less aggressive, less of a predator and less noisy. The mane or crest of long hair along its back is distinctive. Nocturnal and nomadic, it is normally solitary, preferring but not confined to the semi-arid savannas.

The brown hyena (*H. brunnea*), maximum length slightly more than 2½ ft., weight 125 lbs., inhabits arid lands. It wanders extensively, however, and may appear on beaches, where it feeds on marine carrion. It is seldom seen because of its secretive habits. The brown hyena erects its light mane when threatened but is less aggressive than the spotted hyena and rarely fights. Botswana and South-West Africa are its main strongholds.

AARDWOLF (FAMILY PROTELIDAE)

The aardwolf (*Proteles cristatus*), maximum length 20 in., weight 30 lbs., is closely related to hyenas and is sometimes included in the same family. In the course of evolution, the aardwolf has adapted to a diet of insects, feeding almost exclusively on termites but also eating other insects and small animals. It has weak jaws and small teeth. Shy, inoffensive and nocturnal, the aardwolf inhabits open savannas. It lives alone or in small family units.

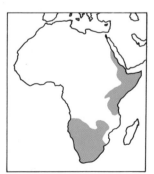

■ *Aardwolf*

Sloth bear and cubs

BEARS (FAMILY URSIDAE)

Bears are stockily built, with a large head, short but powerful limbs, broad flat feet bearing large claws, almost no tail, small ears and eyes and long, coarse fur. They have excellent hearing and sense of smell but poor sight. They range in size from the sun bear weighing up to 100 lbs. to the Kodiak bear, the heaviest of the land carnivores, which may weigh 1,600 lbs. Males are invariably larger than females.

Despite their size, bears are agile both on the ground and in climbing. They are omnivorous, eating carrion, freshly killed animals and fruits.

Bears are usually inoffensive unless provoked—when they can be formidable opponents. They are normally solitary except during the breeding season or when food is particularly abundant in a certain area. Bears of cool temperate regions feed voraciously in autumn, accumulating fat that tides them over the winter months when food is difficult to obtain. Most bears spend the winter in a den in a state of dormancy. They are not true hibernators, however. They sleep deeply, rousing and moving about a number of times during the winter.

Females give birth while in the winter den, after 6–9 months of gestation and commonly involving delayed implantation. Newborn cubs are extremely small, weighing less than a pound. They accompany their mother for at least a year before becoming independent. Mortality of cubs is high during the first year— about 50 percent. Females are sexually mature at 2 years, males at 4–6 years. Adult females breed only every second or third year. Bears may live up to 30 years in captivity, less in the wild.

The bear family is largely confined to the Northern Hemisphere and to temperate regions, but bears may be found both in the tropics and in Arctic regions.

Sun bears and cubs

SLOTH BEAR *(Melursus ursinus)*, maximum length 5½ ft., has small teeth with a gap in front (no incisors), a long snout and large claws—adaptations for its diet of insects, principally termites. The bear tears a nest open with its claws, then sucks up the termites through the gap at the front of its mouth. It may also eat honey, fruit and other vegetable matter.

Breeding occurs in June in the north and probably earlier in Ceylon. One to three cubs are born in a den after a 7-month gestation period. Cubs are said to ride on their mother's back when they leave the den 3 months later. Both parents care for the cubs, which remain with them for several years.

Nocturnal, the sloth bear is a competent climber but spends most of its time on the ground. It is inoffensive and slow-moving, except when pursued. It has become rare throughout its range.

SUN BEAR *(Helarctos malayanus)*, maximum length 4 ft., has strongly curved claws and no hair on the soles of its feet. An excellent climber, it spends most of the day sleeping in a crude nest of branches high in a tree or basking in the sun. It becomes active at night. Omnivorous, the sun bear has a special fondness for fruit and honey, using its claws to open a nest and its long tongue to reach into cavities. It also eats termites in the same manner.

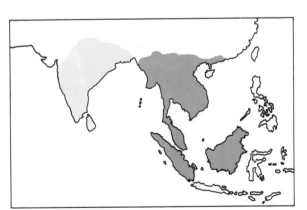

▢ *Sloth bear* ▨ *Sun bear*

Alaskan brown bear

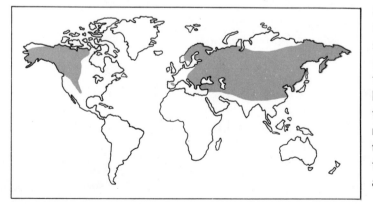
Black bear and cubs

BROWN BEAR (*Ursus arctos*) is the most widely distributed of all the bears, adapted to habitats ranging from semideserts to the Arctic tundra and from sea level to high mountain country. The many races range in size from the mountain-dwelling Syrian brown bear, weighing less than 200 lbs., to the North American grizzlies (maximum about 1,000 lbs.) and the Kodiak (maximum more than 1,600 lbs.), giants that stand as much as 9 ft. tall.

Brown bears are distinguished by the prominent hump between their shoulders and by their hollow or scooped-out facial profile. Despite their tremendous size and need for great amounts of food, brown bears do not usually tackle large prey like the grizzly. They are nocturnal; and while they are not ordinarily aggressive, they are unpredictable, their tempers flaring quickly. When attacking, they bite and use the powerful claws on their front paws. They may rise and shuffle toward their opponent on their hind legs in an awesome display. Unless cubs are present or the bear is wounded, their usual reaction when brought face to face with man is to flee. Most had been exterminated by the 11th century, and today small numbers can still be found in the mountain ranges and remote forests.

Spectacled bear and cubs

BLACK BEAR *(Euarctos americanus)*, maximum length 5 ft., is normally black but may be reddish brown, white or bluish. It usually weighs less than 200 lbs. but may weigh as much as 500 lbs. More adaptable and even-tempered than the brown bear, it is a good climber. It may live in close proximity to man, and though heavily hunted—encouraged for a time by federal bounties—the black bear remains well distributed over most of its original range.

Black bears are more diurnal than brown bears and the two species seldom meet in the wild. It is usually solitary except in June at breeding time. The male does not help rear the cubs. Black bears sleep through the winter after acquiring a thick layer of fat.

In 1902 Theodore Roosevelt took a black bear cub as a pet. It was used as the model for the first stuffed toy Teddy bear.

SPECTACLED BEAR *(Tremarctos ornatus)*, maximum length 5 ft., along with the sun bear, is the only member of the bear family in the northern part of the Southern Hemisphere. The markings vary and may be totally lacking on some individuals. Primarily a forest dweller, the spectacled bear occurs in a variety of habitats, from tropical savannas to 10,000 feet in the Andes. It is said to be more herbivorous than other bears, eating grass, fruit and roots. Reports of spectacled bears killing llamas and vicuñas are probably unfounded. Hunting and destruction of habitat have made this species rare except in undeveloped areas, particularly in Ecuador and, it is believed, Bolivia.

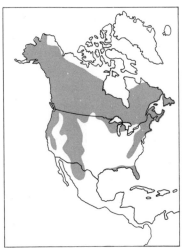

■ *Black bear*

Asiatic black bear

ASIATIC BLACK, or HIMALAYAN, BEAR *(Selenarctos thibetanus)*, maximum length 6 ft., has a black coat in winter that becomes brown in summer. It inhabits forests from the foothills to the timberline at about 12,000 feet. It is sedentary in undisturbed areas but may wander when food becomes scarce. It remains active during mild winters but hibernates in the colder climates of Russia and China. As a result of deforestation and also because of its limited predation on domestic livestock, the Asiatic black bear is now rare.

POLAR BEAR *(Thalarctos maritimus)*, males maximum height 5 ft. tall at the shoulders, weight 1,500 lbs., is exceeded in size only by the Kodiak race of the brown bear. It is distributed throughout the polar region. The polar bear's broad feet have thick, furry soles that serve for insulation and for better traction on the ice. The front paws are partially webbed, and the neck is noticeably longer than in other bears.

The polar bear spends much of its life on the pack ice and in the surrounding waters. An exceptionally good swimmer, it is at home in the sea.

Unlike other bears, the polar bear is almost totally carnivorous. Its principal prey is the ringed and bearded seal, which it stalks on the pack ice or hunts in the open water. Young walruses and fish are also eaten. Polar bears will eat carrion, however, and are attracted from long distances to the carcasses of dead whales. They may also munch on seaweeds.

When the pack ice breaks up in summer, the polar bear may move ashore. On land, food is scarce for the big bear. Thus summer, which is the season of plenty for most animals, is the lean period for the polar bear, who must turn to berries, fish or any small animals it can find; some raid rubbish dumps.

Polar bear and cub

Males do not den in winter unless the weather becomes very severe. Several females may den together on land during the winter to give birth to their cubs, which are born after a gestation period of 8 months. Newborn cubs weigh less than 2 lbs., and their eyes do not open for about a month. Females stay with them (usually twins) until they are 2–3 months old and are large enough to follow her outside the den. During this period, the female exists on reserves of fat. The cubs stay with her until the following season, so females breed once every two or three years. Males do not help rear the cubs and may even kill and eat them if given the opportunity.

The total polar-bear population is estimated at about 10,000, found mostly in the Canadian Arctic. Except for subsistence hunting by Eskimos and other native peoples, the polar bear is now given protection, varying from partial to total, over most of its range.

Hunting for pelts and for sport is now controlled. The decline in population since the turn of the century appears to be leveling off. The most recent threat is indirect but more serious: potentially lethal doses of insecticide have accumulated in their bodies and in the bodies of seals, the bear's main source of food.

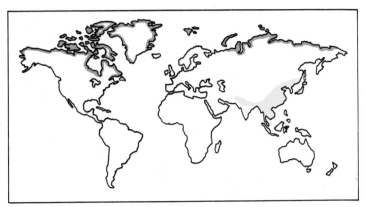

Asiatic black bear   Polar bear

Coati

RACCOONS, COATIS AND KIN (FAMILY PROCYONIDAE)

This largely New World family is sometimes included with the bears. All are predators of small size, except the giant panda, and most have a long tail, usually bushy and ringed. They walk on the soles of their feet as bears do.

Pandas (see pp. 164–165), the only Old World representatives of the group, are often placed in a separate family or subfamily.

KINKAJOUS *(Potos flavus)*, maximum body length 2 ft. with a 1½-ft. prehensile tail, live in South American tropical rain forests. The most arboreal member of the family, it rarely comes to the ground. It uses its long tongue to get at the soft flesh of fruit. It travels alone or in pairs slowly through the treetops. Females bear a single young (sometimes two), and the gestation period is 12 weeks. Kinkajous are sometimes sold as pets, but their nocturnal habits and unpredict-

able temperaments make them difficult to live with.

COATIS *(Nasua,* 3 species) have long, mobile muzzles and typically carry their ringed tails high over their backs. They usually rest and sleep in trees but hunt for food on the ground, using their long snout to poke into forest litter for earthworms, insects and other invertebrates. They are most active in early morning and evening. They travel in bands of six to several dozen animals—two features that differ from other members of the family. Coatis are territorial, and the range of two neighboring troops seldom overlap. Females bear four to six young after a gestation period of about 74 days.

■ *Coatis*

Raccoon

RACCOON *(Procyon lotor)*, maximum body length 20 in., inhabits woodlands, preferably near streams, lakes or ponds. It wades but seldom swims. It gets much of its food—mainly fish, crayfish and frogs—from the water, but it is omnivorous, eating almost any small animals in addition to fruits, nuts and green plants. Raccoons often use their forepaws to catch and eat their food. Their sense of touch is particularly well developed.

The raccoon spends most of the day resting in a tree before hunting at night. In winter it becomes semidormant. Though heavily hunted, it remains common, even in and near cities. Females give birth to three to six young; the gestation period is about 65 days. Cubs travel with their mother for the first year. Crab-eating raccoons *(P. cancrivorus)* have shorter fur.

CACOMISTLE, or RING-TAILED CAT *(Bassariscus astutus)*, maximum body length 1 ft., looks like a slim raccoon with a long (1½-ft.) tail. It is also nocturnal but is more agile and active. The cacomistle occurs in southwestern United States, Mexico and Central America. The Mexican cacomistle *(B. sumichrasti)*, rare and more arboreal, is found only in the subtropics and tropics. Cacomistles are heavily trapped for their pelts and killed because of their raids on poultry. Gold miners and settlers often had cacomistles as pets and reported that they hunted mice.

OLINGO *(Bassaricyon gabbii)* is the same size as the kinkajou, which it resembles. Its tail is hairy, ringed and not prehensile. The olingo is social and moves about in groups, sometimes mixing with kinkajous while feeding in fruit trees.

░ *Crab-eating raccoon*   ▨ *Raccoon*

Red pandas

PANDAS are Asiatic representatives of the raccoon family, the only members occurring naturally in the Old World.

RED, or LESSER, PANDA (*Ailurus fulgens*), maximum body length 2 ft., has a bushy, ringed tail and looks somewhat like a brightly colored raccoon. The face is triangular in shape and has a dark stripe covering the cheeks to the chin. It lives in the mountains at elevations between 7,000 and 12,000 feet. During the day it rests in the branches of trees, becoming active at dawn and dusk.

An agile climber, the red panda is more at home in trees than on the ground, where it moves with a rolling shoulder gait. Believed to be strictly a vegetarian, it feeds principally on the leaves, tender shoots and stalks of bamboo.

The red panda has large teeth and powerful jaws, two adaptations for chewing the fibrous bamboo. With its prehensile thumb on each front paw, it can grasp even the smallest shoots. When threatened, this normally peaceful animal will rear up, strike with both paws or bite.

The red panda normally lives in pairs or in small family units. The litter size is one or two (usually two), the births occurring in a rocky den or in the hollow of a tree. A straying cub will make a bleating sound until the mother finds it. The gestation period is 90 days, and young are born blind.

GIANT PANDA (*Ailuropoda melanoleuca*), maximum length 6 ft., weight 300 lbs., is sometimes classified with raccoons and sometimes with bears, which it also resembles superficially. Its skull is much wider than a bear's head, but like bears, at birth the young are helpless and a tiny fraction of their adult size. It has only a stump of a tail, which is another characteristic shared with the bears. The giant panda is solitary in habits, except briefly during the mating season.

Giant pandas and cubs

Like the red panda, the giant panda is a vegetarian, subsisting almost solely on bamboo in thickets at elevations of 5,000 to 13,000 feet. Immense quantities must be eaten because of the low nutritional value of the bamboo, and pandas spend 10 to 12 hours a day feeding in the dense thickets. They are also reported to eat flowers, grasses and small animals. The unusually long radial bone in the wrist has evolved into a padded, fingerlike "thumb" that helps the giant panda grasp bamboo stems. The giant panda sits on its haunches while eating.

The giant panda can climb, but because of its bulk it spends most of its time on the ground. It is active mostly during daylight hours. During periods of intense cold in winter, the giant panda may take shelter in caves or in the hollows of trees, but it does not hibernate. Like the red panda, the giant panda's fastest movements are a kind of jog-trot. Lacking speed, it is protected by its inaccessible habitat and powerful jaws.

The giant panda normally has only a single young (rarely two), born after a gestation period of about 150 days. The young is born in a nest of bamboo shoots.

Because of its restricted range and habitat, the giant panda is not common. It was discovered only in 1869. It does not appear to be endangered, however, and is stringently protected by the Chinese, who call it the beishung, the white bear.

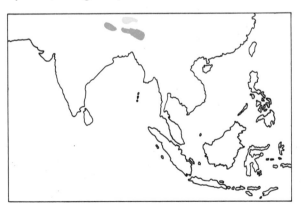

Giant panda   Red panda

Stoat, winter coat

Stoat, summer coat

WEASELS, SKUNKS, OTTERS AND THEIR KIN (FAMILY MUSTELIDAE)

Despite their small size, many members of this family are among the most aggressive and fearless of all the predators. Their success is reflected in their wide distribution; they are found on every continent except Australia and Antarctica, plus Madagascar. They are most abundant in the temperate regions of the Northern Hemisphere. In the tropics they are replaced largely by mongooses, civets and their allies.

These animals prey mainly on rodents, birds and insects. They sometimes are destructive to game birds and poultry but compensate for this by their control of rodents and insect pests. Several species are important commercially for their pelts.

Males are substantially larger than females. Most species have anal scent glands; the scent is used to mark territories and for defense.

STOAT, or SHORT-TAILED WEASEL, or ERMINE *(Mustela erminea)* is about 12 in. long including its 4-in. tail. It is called ermine in the northern part of its range, where it turns white in winter. But even in its winter pelage, the tip of its tail is black.

A solitary animal, the stoat is active mainly at dusk and at night. Mice and voles are its principal prey, but it also feeds on shrews, moles and insects or other invertebrates. Mating occurs in late spring or early summer, implantation not taking place until the following spring. The gestation period is 30 days, with six to nine young per litter.

The least weasel *(M. nivalis)*, maximum length 9 in. including the tail, is the smallest of all carnivores. Lithe, agile and swift, it attacks animals far larger than itself, following them along their runs and into their burrows. Females bear two

European polecat

American mink (see text, p. 169)

litters of four to eight every year, with a gestation period of 6 weeks. Implantation is not delayed. The range overlaps the stoat's but extends farther south. It was introduced to New Zealand and is now firmly established there.

European polecat *(M. putorius)*, about 2 ft. long including a 6-in. tail, lives in woodlands, often in close proximity to man. It is solitary and nocturnal. Remarkably lithe and speedy, the polecat can escape most pursuers. If necessary, it squirts its foul-smelling liquid at an attacker. If caught, its dense fur and loose skin make it almost impervious to bites.

The polecat itself kills with a well-placed neck bite, followed by violent shaking. Because it preys on poultry, it has been exterminated except in the most remote parts of its range.

The European polecat's relatives include the very rare blackfooted ferret *(M. nigripes)* of North America and the Asiatic polecat *(M. eversmanni)*, both in-habitants of open grasslands. The ferret is a semidomesticated Asiatic polecat. The marbled polecat *(Vormela peregusna)* lives in the arid Asiatic steppes, and the zorilla, or African polecat *(Ictonyx striatus)*, is widely distributed south of the Sahara.

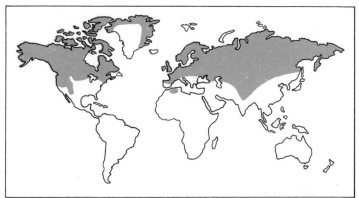

■ Stoat

Pine marten

Beech marten

MARTENS *(Martes,* 6 species) have powerful claws for climbing and a long, bushy tail for balancing. They share the short legs and elongated body characteristic of the family Mustelidae, but the head of martens is more triangular, and the round ears are large. They commonly pursue prey through the treetops and are more nimble than squirrels, which are a common prey. Mostly arboreal, they may also hunt on the ground and eat nuts and berries in season. Males patrol their territories along arboreal and terrestrial pathways marked with scent and urine.

The sable *(M. zibellina)* and the fisher *(M. pennanti)* (see illustration, p. 170) are the largest (maximum length 3 ft.) of the group and also the least arboreal. The fisher kills porcupines by turning them on their backs to get at the soft undersides. It has also been known to kill deer stranded in snow drifts.

Martens are active all winter, the gestation period varying from a year for the

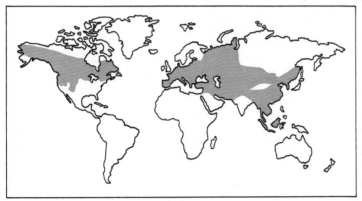

fisher to as little as 9 weeks for the beech marten *(M. foina).* Litters vary from three to six. Young are weaned at 6–7 weeks and are independent at 3 months.

Pelts of these animals, particularly those of the sable, are among the world's most valuable fur. Some were nearly trapped out of existence until given stringent protection.

Tayra

Grison

MINK *(Mustela,* 2 species) are solitary, nocturnal and equally at home in water or on land. Both the American mink (*M. vison*) (see illustration, p. 167), maximum length 28 in. including its 8-in. tail, and the slightly smaller European mink (*M. lutreola*) feed on fish, frogs, muskrats and other small animals. In the nesting season they may prey on the eggs and nestlings of waterfowl.

Mink litters in the wild average four or five; in captivity, as many as ten. The gestation period is 1½–3½ months. The young are weaned at 5 weeks and are independent at 2 months. Both sexes are capable of breeding before they are 12 months old.

Mink are widely farmed for their fur. Platinum and blue are among the several color variations that have been developed. The larger American mink was introduced to European fur farms. It escaped in some areas and is now well established in the wild in these areas, displacing the native species.

TAYRAS *(Eira barbara)* are the South American equivalents of martens. They are agile climbers. The extent of the buff coloration of the head and neck varies with the individual.

GRISON *(Galictis,* 2 species) are strikingly patterned South American mustelids related to the ferrets. They live in burrows and are active at dusk and dawn in forests and grasslands. Grison are sociable; they forage in groups, trotting along in single file.

■ *American mink* ■ *Tayra*

Fisher (see text, p. 168)

170

Wolverine

WOLVERINE, or GLUTTON *(Gulo gulo)*, maximum body length 3 ft. with tail to 1 ft., is the bulkiest and most bearlike member of the weasel family. It measures about 15 in. tall at the shoulders. Sparsely distributed within its wide range, the wolverine lives on the open tundra, or taiga, and other conifer areas year round.

The wolverine is solitary. Males occupy large territories that they share with two or three females. It is mainly terrestrial but can climb trees. Powerful and fearless, the wolverine may attack any animal except man. Wolverines are said to attack fawns and bear cubs and to drag away carcasses several times their weight. Primarily a scavenger, the wolverine robs traps to feed on the animals and wreaks havoc with camps of hunters and trappers to get their food. This has caused the wolverine to be unjustly feared and hated—and destroyed over most of its range. It is now rare except in the most remote areas.

Females breed every 2–3 years, with the gestation period 60–120 days or longer, the variation in length due to delayed implantation. Litters usually number two or three. The young are fully furred when born and are weaned at 2½ months but remain with the mother until they are 2 years old. Then they are driven from the parental territory.

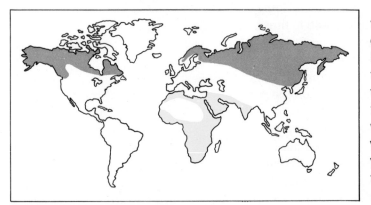

■ *Wolverine*　　■ *Ratel*

Zorilla

Ratel

RATEL, or HONEY BADGER (*Mellivora capensis*), maximum body length 2½ ft. and tail 10 in., is unusually pugnacious. It will attack animals far bigger and more powerful than itself, grabbing its victim in its powerful jaws and then hanging on like a bulldog. The ratel's coarse hair and exceptionally loose skin give it effective defense against fangs and claws. The ratel has strong claws on its front feet, and, like other members of its family, it is equipped with anal scent glands.

The ratel lives in a variety of habitats, from rain forests to open grasslands, even in deserts. In dry regions it digs holes in the sandy beds of rivers to get water, thus benefiting other animals that also need water. Ratels are normally solitary (sometimes they travel in pairs) and terrestrial. They are capable of climbing when necessary. They dig burrows or may live in burrows dug by other animals. Underground by day, they are active at dusk and at night.

A ratel will eat almost anything that comes its way—from small mammals, birds and reptiles to scorpions, termites and sometimes carrion. It also eats fruits, berries and nuts. The ratel has a special fondness for honey. Its association with the honey guide, a bird that leads it to bee nests, is well known. The ratel breaks open the nest—its thick hide impervious to the bee stings—and then both the bird and the ratel feast on the bees, honey and wax.

ZORILLA *(Ictonyx striatus)*, 22 in. long, is an African polecat that looks like a skunk. It uses its pungent anal glands to startle an attacker and then feign death.

BADGERS (8 species), best known for their speed at digging, have powerful front legs and long claws. They also have strong jaws and teeth and can fight ferociously. Unless cornered, however, they are placid and will try to escape without a fight. In general build, all badgers are somewhat bearlike, their squat

Chinese ferret badger

Hog badger

bodies almost wedge-shaped and their heads flattened. Both their eyes and ears are small, but they have a keen sense of smell.

During the day, badgers sleep in their burrows. From time to time they remove their nests and replace them with new materials. At night, badgers come out to hunt their food—insects, birds, rodents and fruit. The Eurasian badger (*Meles meles*) may also eat nuts and fruit, but the American badger (*Taxidea taxus*) is carnivorous. Both have coarse fur of limited value (generally used only for trim). Years ago, however, the coarse hairs were highly prized for making shaving brushes.

Badgers have scent glands that give off a musky odor. This happens only when the animals are disturbed or excited, and the smell is much less potent than in other mustelids.

The Eurasian badger is 3 ft. long, the tail 6 in.; it may weigh as much as 30 lbs. Its legs are so short, however, that it stands less than 1 ft. tall at the shoulders. In the colder parts of its range, the Eurasian badger sleeps during most of the winter. It prefers hilly, wooded country, though it may also live in open fields.

Its burrows contain many chambers, most commonly at three levels. Together the burrows may be as much as 300 feet long, and there are often many, sometimes several dozen, entrances. Some badger burrows have been occupied for decades, a few even for a century.

Mating occurs in late summer or early autumn, but as a result of delayed implantation, the twin or triplet cubs are not born until late winter or early spring. At birth the cubs are blind and naked. They do not venture above ground until they are about 2 months old.

Eurasian badger

American badger

The American badger, maximum length 30 in., weight 20 lbs. or less, is similar to the Eurasian badger in habits but usually lives in open country. Females bear one to five cubs in March and April. Delayed implantation prolongs the apparent gestation period, for the mating takes place in late summer or autumn. The young are weaned in about 6 weeks, and they leave the parents before the next winter. American badgers feed mainly on rodents that they dig out from their burrows. Excess food may be buried or taken underground for later use.

Other closely related species include the Japanese badger (*Meles anakuma*), with shorter, softer fur. Ferret badgers (*Melogale*, 3 species) also have fur of commercial value. The ferret badgers are partly arboreal. The hog badger (*Arctonyx collaris*) of India has a long snout. It roots piglike in the ground to get insects or their grubs and retires to burrows during the day. Stink badgers (*Mydaus*) of Borneo, Java and Sumatra are broadly striped with white. They also give off a foul odor, more potent than that of other badgers. Their scent-gland secretions are used as a perfume base, like those of civets.

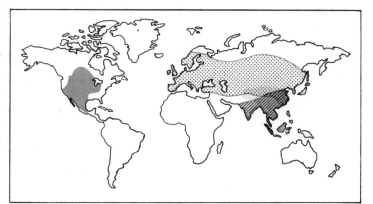

Hog badger   *Stink badger*

Eurasian badger   *Ferret badger*   *American badger*

Hog-nosed skunk

Striped skunk   Spotted skunk

SKUNKS, occurring only in the New World, can climb but are basically terrestrial, spending the day in burrows. They are usually solitary, but several females and typically only one male may share a den in winter, when they become fat, lethargic and semidormant. Skunks are mainly insectivorous but occasionally eat small birds, mammals, fruit or even carrion.

A disturbed skunk arches its tail high over its back and may also hiss, growl and paw the ground. If these warnings fail, it ejects a fine, well-directed spray of foul-smelling fluid that can cause intense irritation. Most widely distributed is the striped skunk (*Mephitis mephitis*), maximum length 40 in. including the tail. It has been heavily trapped for its fur. Females bear three to eight young (usually five); the gestation period is 60 days. They are blind and almost naked at birth, their eyes opening in about 3 weeks. They are weaned at 6 weeks, are independent at 6 months and mature in 12 months. The closely related and similar hooded skunk (*M. macroura*) has a longer tail.

The spotted skunk (*Spilogale putorius*), maximum length 22 in. including its tail, favors semi-arid brushlands.

The hog-nosed skunk (*Conepatus mesoleucus*), about 28 in. long with the tail, is one of about half a dozen species in its genus, some of which live as high as 13,000 feet in the Andes. With its hoglike snout, it roots for beetles and other insects. Females bear one to four young per litter.

■ Hog-nosed skunk   Striped skunk   ■ Spotted skunk

Sea otters

OTTERS, including river otters, are the most aquatic members of the weasel family. They have short, dense underfur, webbed feet and a slim, sinuous body. Both the ears and nostrils can be closed when the animals are underwater.
SEA OTTER (*Enhydra lutris*), maximum length 6 ft., weight 80 lbs., was hunted for its pelt until it became nearly extinct. By 1910 its total population was estimated at less than 2,000, but this has now increased to about 50,000.

In Alaska, sea otters may come ashore to sleep and bear young, but on the California coast they are exclusively marine. The front paws are mittenlike, the claws semiretractile and the fingers agile. The thickly webbed hind paws are like flippers but have a peculiarly elongated fifth digit. Sea otters, among the few mammals that use "tools," bring flat stones from the bottom and rest them on their chests, using them as anvils for breaking open shells. The stone is tucked under the arm while the otter dives for another clam or urchin. It pries clams loose with its paws. Sea otters need to eat more than 20 percent of their weight every day to provide the necessary energy to maintain their body temperature in a cold marine habitat.

Sea otters are social and live in closely knit groups. No strict hierarchy exists, and fighting is rare. They float on their backs in kelp beds when not feeding. Females bear a single young (rarely twins) after a gestation period of 9 months. Females bear young every two years.

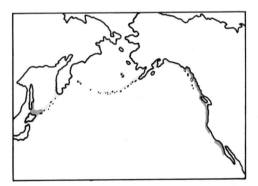

■ *Sea otter, former range*   *Sea otter, present range*

Canadian otter

Eurasian otter

RIVER OTTERS (6 genera, 12 species) live mainly along streams or lakes and only rarely appear in coastal areas. The Canadian otter (*Lutra canadensis*) measures almost 2 ft. long plus a tail almost 1½ ft. long, and the males weigh as much as 30 lbs. The females are shorter and weigh less. The Eurasian otter (*L. lutra*) is slightly smaller. Often nocturnal, and solitary except during mating, they may travel 10 miles or more in a single night on their hunts for fish, frogs and crayfish.

Female Eurasian otters bear one to five cubs (usually two or three) after a gestation period of about 60 days. These may be born at any season of the year. The female Canadian otters have the same number of young, but the gestation period is 9–12 months because of delayed implantation. The embryos lie dormant in the uterus until about 2 months before the young are born. The cubs, blind and helpless at birth, are protected fiercely by the mother. They leave the nest when they are about 2 months old, and they must be taught to swim.

Otters are victims of fur trappers, destruction of habitat and pollutants. The Eurasian otter has become rare, as has the Canadian otter, which has disappeared from much of its original range. Like other predators, otters are vulnerable to overhunting and, due to small litter size, recover slowly.

The spot-necked otter (*Hydrictis maculicollis*), an exceptionally proficient swimmer, has a very narrow head, short whiskers and thin webbing between the toes. It is known to prey largely on fish and occurs in the same areas as the African clawless otter.

The Indian smooth-coated otter (*Lutrogale perspicillata*) is heavily built and has very short, dense fur. The tail is flattened and the paws are thickly webbed. It lives in marshes and also frequents seacoasts.

Smooth-coated otter   *Short-clawed otters*

Smallest of the otters, only 2½ ft. long and weighing about 12 pounds, is the Asian short-clawed or clawless otter (*Amblonyx cinerea*). Its front paws are only partially webbed, and it has long fingers that are used like a raccoon's to search for prey under stones. It inhabits the quiet waters of ditches and rice paddies.

The African clawless otter (*Aonyx capensis*) also has webless front paws with long fingers that are used to manipulate objects with great dexterity. Even the thumb is semi-apposable. More terrestrial than other otters, it often roams far inland and gets its food on land as it travels from one body of water to another. The African clawless otter also has a wide repertoire of sounds. It feeds mainly on crayfish, birds and fish.

Rarest of the otters, listed as one of the world's endangered species, is the giant Brazilian otter (*Pteronura braziliensis*), maximum length more than 5 ft., weight as much as 50 lbs. Because of its diurnal habits and general fearlessness, it was easy prey for pelt hunters. Its tail is flattened like a beaver's and its hind feet are so thickly webbed that it travels on land with difficulty. Little is known about its habits in the wild.

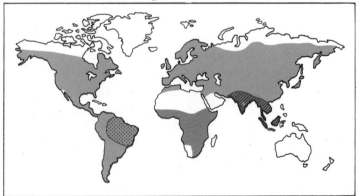

■ *Eurasian otter*
⁛ *Giant Brazilian otter*
▨ *Indian smooth-coated otter*   *Asian short-clawed otter*   ■ *African clawless otter*

Small-toothed palm civet

Masked palm civet   African palm civet

CIVETS, GENETS, MONGOOSES AND KIN (FAMILY VIVERRIDAE)

All members of this family (37 genera, 75 species) are natives of the Old World, principally subtropical and tropical Africa and Asia, where they occupy the same niche as the mustelids or weasel-like mammals of cooler regions. Most of these small and medium-sized carnivores are forest dwellers, their spots and stripes helping to camouflage them from predators. Many have well-developed anal scent glands and have been hunted for the use of this valued musk in the perfume industry. They are not valuable for their fur.

 • Most viverrids, one of the most highly varied carnivores in habits and physical features, are active hunters, preying on rodents, birds and other small animals. Others eat fruits, nuts, roots and tender shoots; still others are omnivorous. They share some features with cats, including retractile claws in some species, but they have five toes on the hind feet. Their senses of sight, hearing and smell are well developed. Typical members have a long, slim muzzle, a long tail and short legs.

Dwarf mongooses (*Helogale*) are the smallest members of this family. The shaggy binturong (*Arctitis*) is the largest. Many of the 37 genera of viverrids are little known. The African water civet (*Osbornictis*), for example, has never been seen alive.

Viverrids have well-developed anal scent glands under the tail, which secrete a strong-smelling musky fluid. This musk is obtained commercially from several species of civet in Africa and Asia and is used as a base for perfume and local medicines. Musk can be removed several times a week, each animal yielding 1/10 oz. in that time. This industry dates back to before King Solomon and probably originated in Ethiopia, where it is still practiced.

Small Indian civet

CIVETS (several genera, about 15 species) look much like weasels, are catlike in habits and have an odor that in some species ranks with that of skunks.

The African civet (*Civettictis civetta*) has a stout body 2½ ft. long plus a 1½-ft. tail ringed with black and white. The legs are short. Solitary and nocturnal, it is rarely seen even in areas where it is abundant. During the day it stays in hiding, often in the abandoned burrow of some other animal. It climbs and swims well.

The large Indian civet (*Viverra zibetha*), about the same size as the African civet, and the small Indian civet (*Viverricula indica*), only slightly smaller, are both similar in habits to the African civet.

All three species bear two or three young in an underground burrow or in dense vegetation. Little is known about their breeding habits.

Palm civets (7 species—6 in Asia, 1 in Africa) differ from true civets in being less carnivorous and in having claws more strongly developed for climbing. The best known is the Indian palm civet, or toddy cat (*Paradoxurus hermaphroditus*), maximum body length 2 ft. plus tail about the same length. It commonly lives near houses, and if disturbed, it gives off a foul odor. Omnivorous, it feeds on rats and mice, but it may also make raids on stored foods. It gets its common name from its fondness for fermented palm sap (toddy).

The African palm civet (*Nandinia binotata*) is sometimes called the two-spotted palm civet because of the pale spots on its shoulders.

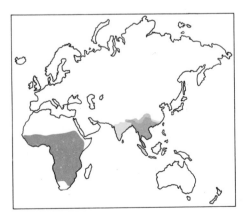

■ African civet   ■ Small Indian civet   ■ Large Indian civet

Banded linsang

Spotted linsang

GENETS (2 genera, 6 species) have white facial markings and black spots on the body. Best known is the feline, or small-spotted, genet (*Genetta genetta*), maximum body length 22 in., tail 18 in. It is slender and graceful, its movements catlike and its claws retractile. A crest of still black hairs along the middle of the back is raised when the animal is disturbed. Nocturnal and mostly solitary, it is terrestrial but a good climber. It can be seen rapidly making its way along the network of treetop branches, sometimes descending to dart across a trail, body held low. Genets feed on rodents, birds and insects, stalking their prey like a house cat and pouncing to deliver a fatal neck bite. Females bear two or three young with a gestation period of 10–11 weeks. In some areas females have two litters per year.

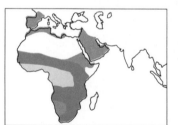

■ *Feline genet*
▧ *Large-spotted genet*

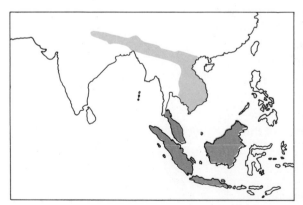

LINSANGS (*Prionodon*, 2 species) are arboreal—the most catlike of the viverrids. Similar to the genets in habits, they are about 2½ ft. long, including the tail, and their claws are retractile. Nocturnal and solitary, they prey on birds, small mammals and insects.

The banded linsang (*P. linsang*) has six broad, blackish bands across its body, while the spotted linsang (*P. pardicolor*) is marked with dark spots on its orange-brown coat.

■ *Spotted linsang*   ■ *Banded linsang*

Feline genet

Binturong

BINTURONG, or BEAR CAT *(Arctictis binturong)*, is the largest of the viverrids, its body 2–2½ ft. long. The bushy tail, almost as long as the body, is slightly prehensile. It is used as an aid in climbing but probably is not capable of supporting the adult's full weight (about 30 lbs.). The young, however, may hang by their tail. The kinkajou (see p. 162) is the only other carnivore with a prehensile tail. Both animals use their tail as a braking device when descending a tree head first.

The binturong has black ear tufts, white on its ears and face and very long whiskers. The hairs on its shaggy black coat are tipped with brown or gray, and the hairs on its tail are distinctly longer than those on the body. The fur of the binturong is used for making hats and garments.

The nocturnal binturong sleeps during the day curled in branches in treetops. Occasionally it rouses to move onto branches where it can bask in the sun. Unlike most carnivores, the binturong eats mainly fruit, tender young shoots and leaves. Sometimes it may hunt birds, rodents or other small animals. It moves awkwardly on the ground and is a slow and deliberate but skilled climber in trees. Most civets and their kin are virtually silent, but the binturong howls loudly. It is still fairly common in its mountain habitat.

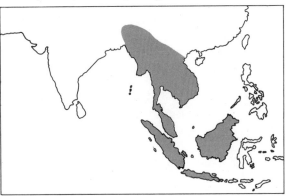

Binturongs tame easily and become affectionate pets, but if provoked they may bite with their powerful jaws.

Banded mongoose

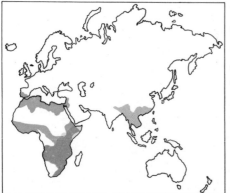

Crab-eating mongoose

MONGOOSES (several genera, about 48 species) are all similar in general appearance and habits, with short legs, slim muzzles and a tapered, bushy tail. Their small, rounded ears are almost hidden in their fur. Most have five toes on each foot, and the claws cannot be retracted. They can climb but not well, and they spend nearly all their time on the ground.

Mongooses attack with lightning speed and accuracy. Their battles with cobras are legendary. Mongooses are rarely ever bitten but are not immune to snake venom.

The Egyptian mongoose, or ichneumon (*Herpestes ichneumon*), maximum body length 2 ft. plus 1½-ft. tail, was sacred to the ancient Egyptians. They called it Pharaoh's cat.

A closely related species in Asia is the crab-eating mongoose (*H. urva*), about the same size as the Egyptian mongoose. It feeds on crabs, fish and frogs. The Indian mongoose (*H. edwardsi*) and the small Indian mongoose (*H. auropunctatus*) are both smaller, the body and tail each reaching a length of 1–1½ ft. The small Indian mongoose was introduced to Jamaica and other West Indies islands to prey on rats and snakes, which it did—in addition to exterminating native birds and mammals and making raids on poultry. Mongooses have a fondness for eggs, too, often holding one in their front paws and then throwing it backward between their hind legs to smash it against a tree or rock.

■ *African dwarf mongoose*

■ *Egyptian mongoose*   ■ *Crab-eating mongoose*

Meerkats

African dwarf mongoose

Smallest of the mongooses is the African dwarf mongoose (*Helogale parvula*), rarely exceeding 1 ft. in total length and usually smaller. It drinks by dipping its front paw into the water and then licking it. The dwarf mongoose lives in abandoned termite mounds or in the burrows of other animals.

Most mongooses are uniformly gray or gray-brown, sometimes lightly speckled. The banded, or zebra, mongoose (*Mungos mungo*) is distinctive in having dark zebralike stripes over its body.

Little is known about the breeding habits of mongooses. Most have two to four young per litter; the gestation period is about 60 days.

MEERKAT, or SURICATE (*Suricata suricatta*), body 10–14 in. plus a 7–10 in. tapered tail, is a slender, specialized mongoose that lives in colonies of two dozen or more on dry, sandy plains. With its powerful front legs, it digs burrows with numerous entrances leading to the passages. The burrows may be as much as 10 feet deep and may be shared with ground squirrels and other mongooses. The meerkat uses its keen sense of smell to find its prey—insects, rodents, birds or other small animals—which it holds in its front paws squirrel-like when eating. After its meal, the meerkat leans back with the paws on its belly to bask in the sun. Females bear two to four young. The gestation period is 75–80 days. Both parents help rear the young, which look like diminutive adults within two months. Hawks and eagles are the main predators, and meerkats rush underground whenever they see one overhead. Like other social mongooses, they have a large repertoire of sounds and constantly chitter to one another as they dig for grubs and roots.

■ Meerkat

Margay

Ocelot

CATS (FAMILY FELIDAE)

All cats have short, powerful jaws and long canine teeth for holding and puncturing. Except for the cheetah, their sharp, curved claws can be retracted into protective sheaths. Cats have excellent eyesight and hearing; their good sense of smell is used selectively. They normally stalk their prey, then make a sudden rush from close range, killing with a bite deep into the neck or back of the head.

Most cats are solitary and nocturnal. They are most abundantly represented in the tropics but occur throughout the world, except Australia, Madagascar, the West Indies and Antarctica. Wild cats are essentially terrestrial but are competent climbers. They usually take shelter in the hollows of trees, in caves or among boulders. In small species the gestation period is 9 weeks, the litters averaging two to four kittens. The kittens are weaned at about 4 months; small species are sexually mature at 12 months, larger ones at 2–3 years.

SMALL NEW WORLD CATS live mainly in the tropics and subtropics. The habits of most of these smaller species are not well known. Most are only slightly larger than domestic cats.

The ocelot (*Felis pardalis*) ranges from Texas through Central America to northern Argentina, the margay (*F. wiedi*) from Mexico to northern Uruguay and the little spotted cat (*F. tigrina*) from Central America to southern Brazil and northern Argentina. All inhabit rain forests.

The fur of these three species is valued, and they are hunted locally for their meat and pelt. Deforestation has reduced their prime habitat and, along with hunting, has now made them uncommon and even rare. If given reasonable protection from excessive hunting, they could probably adapt to the changes in their environment. These cats have been kept as pets.

Pampas cat

Jaguarundi

Geoffroy's cat (*F. geoffroyi*) ranges from the Bolivian Andes to Patagonia in southern Argentina. The Chilean mountain cat, or kodkod (*F. guigna*), is restricted to the Andes of Chile. Both are woodland species. The Andean cat (*F. jacobita*), the rarest and least known of the South American cats, inhabits the higher elevations in the Andes, as high as the snow line, from southern Peru and northeastern Chile to southwestern Bolivia and northwestern Argentina. It is larger than the others—maximum length 4 ft.

The pampas cat (*F. colocolo*) ranges from western Brazil through Peru, Bolivia, Chile and Argentina as far south as Patagonia. It is essentially an inhabitant of the Andean valleys but is sometimes found in coastal regions or high on mountain slopes. Though exceptionally handsome, its pelt has no commercial value. For this reason it remains comparatively common except in areas of intensive settlement where it is now rare. Little is known about its habits except that it is terrestrial and nocturnal.

The jaguarundi, or otter cat (*F. yagouaroundi*), occurs from southern Arizona and Texas to Paraguay and northern Argentina, inhabiting both tropical and subtropical forests. The jaguarundi is about twice the size of a house cat. It frequents dense underbrush and thickets but is also found on open grasslands and savannas. Although it is normally terrestrial, the jaguarundi is an agile climber and an excellent swimmer. It is primarily nocturnal but may hunt during the day.

The jaguarundi's predation on poultry has made it a pest in settled areas. Because its pelt is of low quality, however, it is not hunted commercially. The species appears generally to be safe at the moment.

Leopard cat

Pallas's cat

Wild cat

SMALL OLD WORLD CATS are even more diversified than those of the New World. Most of the species are about the size of the domestic cat.

The wild cat (*Felis silvestris*), one of the probable ancestors of the domestic cat, has an exceptionally wide range: the greater part of Africa and most of western Eurasia. It has adapted to habitats that range from deciduous forests to steppes and open savannas.

The leopard cat (*F. bengalensis*) lives in the forests of southern and eastern Asia, including the Philippines. In most of this region it is the most common cat.

Desert-dwelling cats include the sand cat (*F. margarita*), ranging from southern Iran through Arabia to the northern and central Sahara. It is a true desert inhabitant. The thickly furred pads on its feet aid it in traveling over loose sand.

The black-footed cat (*F. nigripes*) occurs only in the Kalahari sand plains and similar areas. During the day it rests in holes in the ground or sometimes in old termite mounds.

The Chinese desert cat (*F. bieti*) occurs from southern Mongolia to Kansu and Szechwan, along the fringes of the Sino-Tibetan steppe. Here it must tolerate seasonal and daily temperature variations ranging from intense heat to excessive cold.

Pallas's cat (*F. manul*) lives in rocky and mountainous country in Tibet and Siberia. Its long fur and very short ears help it to withstand climatic extremes in a variety of habitats ranging from open steepes to forests and from lowlands to more than 15,000 feet on the Tibetan Plateau.

The fishing cat (*F. viverrina*), found from India and Ceylon through Southeast Asia to Sumatra and Java, lives near rivers, streams and tidal creeks. Fish and mollusks form part of its diet. Though it is always close to water and has a

Serval

Golden cat

suggestion of webbing on its front paws, the fishing cat has never been seen swimming like tigers. It uses its paws to scoop up fish. Bold and ferocious, it may attack animals much larger than itself.

The flat-headed cat (*F. planiceps*) lives along rivers and other waterways in southern Thailand, Malaya, Sumatra and Borneo. This rare species is reportedly more dependent on fish than any other cat.

The jungle cat (*F. chaus*) ranges from southern China and Southeast Asia through India, Afghanistan and lower Egypt. It frequents thickets and reeds along rivers and other waterways but may sometimes be found in open country. It is a good climber, like the domestic cat.

The serval (*F. serval*) occurs in Africa south of the Sahara. One isolated race is found only in eastern Algeria. It resembles a small cheetah and is shy and nocturnal. It frequents woodland savannas and bush country but often moves into open grasslands to hunt. Though normally found at lower elevations, it has been seen at 10,000 feet in alpine meadows on Mount Kenya. When hunting, the serval moves silently on its tall legs through long grass, ready to pounce on any prey it sees. It leaps into the air to catch low-flying birds. Normally terrestrial, the serval will climb trees if pursued.

The name golden cat refers to two distinct species. One (*F. temmincki*) lives in Asia, from the Himalayas of Nepal and Assam through Tibet to western and southern China and Southeast Asia to Sumatra. The other (*F. aurata*) is in Africa, from Sierra Leone and Cameroon to western Kenya. Primarily a forest dweller, the golden cat occupies a variety of habitats, from woodland savannas and secondary forests to alpine meadows. It is probably the Old World equivalent of the puma.

Northern lynx

LYNXES (4 species) are medium-size cats with relatively short bodies, long hind legs, short tails and prominent ear tufts. The three species are mainly terrestrial, but lynxes are excellent swimmers and climbers, preying principally on small mammals and birds.

The northern lynx (*Felis lynx*), about 3½ ft. long including the tail and weighing up to 40 lbs., is the largest of the lynxes. Its long fur and furred paws are adaptations for the cold climates where it lives. The broad paws enable it to walk over the snow without sinking in. Its ear tufts and throat tassels are notably longer than those of lynxes living farther south.

The northern lynx is usually a forest dweller but may be seen in tundra. It is almost wholly nocturnal. Like other lynxes, it is solitary and usually shy and retiring, but if cornered it fights ferociously. All of the lynxes hunt by hearing and sight. Like other cats, they wait in ambush, then rush and pounce when the quarry is close enough.

Snowshoe hares are the northern lynx's principal prey in North America. The cat's population follows the cyclic abundance and decline of the hares. The lynx will also take deer, birds and any other animals that are available.

Males establish large territories that usually overlap the territories of several females. The usual litter size is two or three born after a gestation period of 7–9 weeks. Kittens are weaned in 2 months but remain with the mother until the end of the following winter.

The northern lynx has been greatly reduced in numbers wherever it has come into contact with man, who covets its fur and holds it responsible for preying occasionally on poultry. It has vanished from most of its range in Western Europe, except for relict populations in Spain and Scandinavia. It is relatively

Caracal

abundant in Eastern Europe and Asia. In North America, it lives only in remote northern regions.

The bobcat, or bay lynx (*F. rufa*), is slightly smaller than the northern lynx. It has prominent cheek ruffs but less conspicuous ear tufts. Bobcats favor brushy country with rocky outcrops but have adapted to conditions varying from swamps and deserts to high mountain country. It does not, however, live as far north as the lynx. Though mainly nocturnal, the bobcat is often seen during the day. Its main prey are jackrabbits, cottontails and small rodents.

The caracal, or desert lynx (*F. caracal*), about the same size as the northern lynx, has prominent black tufts on its long, black-edged ears and black facial markings. It is more closely related to the serval than to other lynxes. It prefers dry country, from grasslands to woodland savannas, semi-arid bush country and subdeserts. The caracal preys on birds and small mammals, including dik-diks.

This long-legged cat is a good runner and, like the cheetah, the rare caracal has been employed as a hunting animal. It was once used in pigeon-baiting contests, where it was trained to strike down as many birds as possible before they flew off.

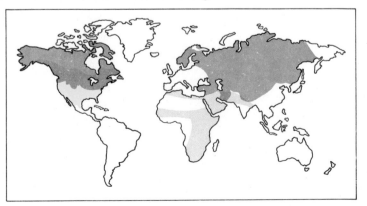

▦ *Northern lynx*

▦ *Bobcat*   ▦ *Caracal*

190

Jaguar

JAGUAR *(Panthera onca)* is the largest member of the cat family in the New World. Of all the big cats, only lions and tigers are larger. It equals the leopard in height and length but is much more heavily built. It is known to weigh as much as 350 lbs. Females are smaller than the males.

The jaguar's markings are similar to a leopard's, but in the center of each rosette, larger than those of the leopard, is a small black spot. The tail, shorter than a leopard's, is ringed with black toward the the tip. In some the yellowish background color is very light; others are almost black, the rosettes showing only faintly.

Jaguars prey on animals of all sizes. They will even tackle a river turtle, but peccaries, capybaras and deer are mainstays. They hunt at night, resting and remaining in hiding during the day. Males patrol their territory regularly, de-positing their droppings in conspicuous places and scratching trees to warn off other males. Pumas and jaguars may be found in the same areas, and they apparently co-exist peacefully.

These cats normally inhabit lowland forests but sometimes find shelter in the bushes or reeds of open grasslands. Jaguars often wander for long distances and are agile climbers. They do not hesitate to enter water and are reported to be skilled at fishing.

Adults are usually sexually mature at about 3 years. Litters normally contain two or three kittens, produced after 95–110 days of gestation. The young usually stay with the mother for about 2 years, when they leave to find mates.

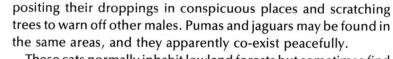

Puma

PUMA, known also as COUGAR, PANTHER, MOUNTAIN LION, CATA-MOUNT and many other names (*Felis concolor*). The largest members of the genus *Felis*, males may be 6 ft. long (excluding the tail) and weigh more than 200 lbs.; the females are smaller. As with most members of the cat family, those inhabiting the tropics are smaller than those living in cooler regions.

Once the most widely distributed carnivore in the New World, the puma now survives only in remote parts of its extensive range, its habitat varying from deserts to mountain forests. The planting of forest for pulpwood in eastern Canada favored the puma as it provided excellent habitat for two prey species, deer and the occasional grouse. Whitetail deer may make up 75 percent of the puma's diet. Pumas thus control the deer population in areas where they are numerous. Where deer have been allowed to multiply too rapidly, they have sometimes run out of food.

Pumas stalk their prey, pouncing and killing with a throat bite. Mainly nocturnal, the puma patrols its territory in search of prey, usually killing from ambush. Besides deer and elk it may also take rodents and birds. Where its natural prey has been largely eliminated by settlement of the land, the puma has turned to domestic livestock and may even attack horses. As a result, the cat has been destroyed at every opportunity and is now seldom seen.

The color of pumas varies from fawn to dark gray, depending on the race and region. The young have dark spots and tail rings.

■ *Puma, former range*   ■ *Puma, present range*

Leopard

LEOPARD *(Panthera pardus)* is powerfully built, standing almost 2½ ft. tall at the shoulders and weighing up to 180 lbs. Females are only slightly smaller than males. The black rosettes and spots stand out conspicuously against the tawny yellow background fur. Even in the black or melanistic forms—most common in Asia but rare even there—the rosettes are faintly visible. Leopards typically have green eyes, but those of melanistic forms are blue.

The leopard is the most widely distributed member of the cat family, with great variation in color and pattern among individuals and the more than a dozen races. Though primarily a forest dweller, preferring dense cover, the leopard sometimes inhabits woodland savannas or even open grasslands.

Nocturnal and solitary except during the mating season, the leopard preys on a wide variety of birds and mammals, such as impalas, gazelles and monkeys. It usually kills from ambush. The leopard, extremely agile and capable of clambering up a tree while carrying prey weighing as much as itself, commonly caches uneaten portions of its kill in the branches to keep it from scavengers. It returns later to feast on the remains. Females usually give birth to two or three cubs after a gestation period of 98–105 days.

Demand for its fur as well as killing for sport has greatly reduced the leopard population. The animal survives in numbers only in remote regions.

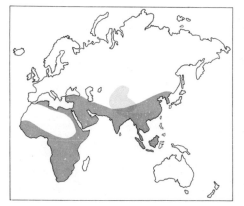

Leopard   Snow leopard   Clouded leopard

Snow leopard

SNOW LEOPARD *(Panthera uncia)*, slightly smaller than the common leopard, has a longer tail and much longer fur, especially on its underparts. The markings on the head, spine and upper part of the tail are well defined, but the rosettes, in a random pattern, are less distinct than in the common leopard. The tail is long and thickly furred, with the tip curled upward. Markings show more clearly in summer. Because of the short muzzle and long fur, the head appears disproportionately small. Unlike other large cats, the snow leopard does not roar.

Snow leopards live on the rocky slopes of central Asian mountains. They spend their summers at high altitudes (to 18,000 feet) and descend into the valleys in winter following their prey—wild goats, bharals, gorals, deer, boar, marmots and sometimes domestic dogs and livestock. They hunt by stalking and then making a sudden rush; they may also wait in ambush for victims. Snow leopards are the least aggressive of the large cats and rarely attack man.

Female snow leopards normally bear two or three cubs after a gestation period of 93–110 days. Born in spring or summer, the cubs remain with their mother through the following winter or until the next litter is born 2 years later.

Snow leopards have been heavily hunted for their pelts, the most attractive and most valuable of the wild-cat furs. As a result of this continued pressure and the scarcity of prey species, snow leopards have become very rare.

CLOUDED LEOPARD *(Neofelis nebulosa)*, smaller than the snow leopard, has short legs and broad pads on its paws. The canine teeth are exceptionally long. The blotches, spots and rings are distinctively dark-edged. It is found only in southeastern Asia.

The habits of the now rare clouded leopard, nocturnal and arboreal, have not been studied in the wild. The normal litter size in captivity is two.

African lions

LION *(Panthera leo)* is a massive carnivore. Males, larger than females, may be tall at the shoulders and weigh as much as 450 lbs. Some lions are dark brown, others tawny yellow, but all have a long tail with a black tuft that conceals a sharp, horny tail spur. Only the male has a mane, which is darker than the body color and covers the head and shoulders, sometimes extending onto the belly.

Lions are found in Africa south of the Sahara and in Asia, where they are now restricted to the Gir Forest in India. The relict population in Iran is now believed to be extinct. Lions once ranged over parts of Europe but were eliminated long ago. Because the lion comes into conflict with man wherever the land is settled, the population has been greatly reduced. They now survive mainly in national parks and reserves, which are the principal remaining large undeveloped areas.

Lions prey on grazing animals as large as buffaloes. Their principal prey in Africa are wildebeests and zebras. Lions stalk their prey, usually at night and often working in groups, or they commonly wait in ambush at waterholes. Lions rarely pursue their prey far, and one kill may last them for a week or more. Females are usually the ones to stalk and kill, but the dominant male eats first.

Despite their size and fearsome reputation, lions are generally inactive,

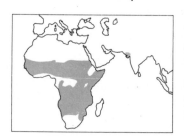

spending up to 20 hours a day resting or sleeping. They live in family groups called prides, consisting of a dominant male plus several females and their cubs and one or more young males. Two to six cubs are born with spotted coats after 3½ months' gestation. They are weaned at 3 months, then spend 9 months perfecting their hunting techniques; consequently cub mortality is very high. Adults may kill and eat cubs when food is scarce.

Cheetahs

CHEETAH *(Acinonyx jubatus)* is the most doglike of all the cats. Males stand almost 30 in. tall at the shoulders and weigh up to 130 lbs.; females are slightly smaller. The legs are exceptionally long, and there are no sheaths into which the claws can be retracted as in other cats. Cheetahs have a small head with a distinctive black stripe from the inner corner of each eye to the upper lip. The hair on the neck forms a crest or short mane. Cheetahs have a generally gentle disposition. They tame easily when young and have been used in hunting.

Cheetahs occur mostly in open savannas in Africa. They once occurred also in southwestern Asia but have been eliminated there except for several small populations in Iran. They have fared better in Africa but have become localized because of their inability to tolerate alterations in their habitat.

The cheetah's prey ranges from birds to small and medium-size antelopes, such as Thomson's gazelles, impalas and oribis. It relies on its superior speed— the cheetah is faster than any other mammal, capable of running at 60 miles per hour—to overtake and pull down its prey. But the cheetah tires quickly and can maintain this speed only for short distances. Almost wholly diurnal, it hunts alone by sight rather than scent, and never in pairs or in small groups as do lions. It may also hunt by moonlight. Unlike other big cats, cheetahs rarely return to a kill to feed after the first meal.

Females give birth to two to four cubs after a gestation period of 84–95 days. Cubs are born with a silvery mane, which disappears when they are about 2½ months old.

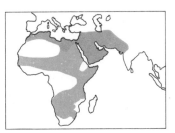

■ *Cheetah, former range*　　■ *Cheetah, present range*

TIGER *(Panthera tigris)* is the largest of living cats. Some males from the temperate regions of the northern hemisphere are more than 3 ft. tall at the shoulders and extend to a length of 13 ft., including the tail. They average 400 lbs. and may weigh 600 lbs. Females are smaller, seldom exceeding 300 lbs.

Tigers from the northern limits of the animal's range—the Siberian tigers—have longer, paler coats than do the Bengal tigers of the tropics. The black stripes on the tawny coat are like shadow marks, effective camouflage in the animal's forest habitat. Considerable variation in size and color occur among the half-dozen races. While typical tigers have yellowish eyes, aberrant white tigers have blue eyes.

Usually a forest dweller, the tiger also lives in tall grasslands but rarely comes into the open. It wanders by day in undisturbed areas but it is regarded as nocturnal. Tigers are solitary hunters that stalk their prey or lie in ambush. Tigers preys on animals of any size, from baby elephants to deer, gaur and wild pigs. If it is hungry, the tiger will even eat the smallest rodent. Portions of larger animals left after the first meal are dragged into the brush, and the tiger will return on successive days until all is consumed. Elimination of their natural prey and destruction or modification of their forest habitat are other reasons for the decline in the number of tigers.

Tigers have been heavily hunted, which in India includes the indiscriminate use of poisoned baits. The exportation of tiger skins has been prohibited by law, but this conservation measure is far from adequate protection for these magnificent beasts. With now fewer than 2,000 believed to exist in India, tigers are an endangered species. The race on Bali is believed extinct.

Indian tigers (foreground) and Barasingha deer (background)

Soviet authorities have established reserves—the Sudzukhe and Sikote Alin reserves—to protect the Siberian tigers, but despite the large size of these reserves, they are only partially effective, as tigers are nomadic and regularly range beyond the boundaries of the sanctuaries.

Tigers can climb—but not well. They are excellent swimmers, however, and regularly cross rivers, lakes or bays to explore new hunting grounds. Like most other big cats, the tiger can purr and roar. It does not roar as often as a lion, but it may roar as a threat. An uneasy tiger makes an unusual "pok" sound that can be mistaken for the Sambar deer's alarm bark. It is not known why the predator imitates the sound of its prey.

Tigers in the wild become sexually mature in 3–4 years. Females usually produce two to six cubs per litter after a gestation period of 98–110 days. The cubs are born blind and remain with their mother for 2 to 3 years, and during this time of caring for her young, she does not come into heat again. Mature females thus breed only every second or third year. Cubs learn to kill on their own at seven months. As with lions, cub mortality is very high, and only one or two cubs survive. A tigress may have 10 litters in her lifetime and leave 20 viable descendants.

Tigers have long been among the favorite animals for exhibit in zoos. Siberian and Bengal tigers do well in captivity but do not breed as prolifically in zoos as lions do. Tigers raised in captivity may live to be 20 years old. Hybrids between tigers and lions have been produced. The offspring of a male tiger and a female lion are called tiglons; those of a male lion and a female tiger are ligers.

Elephant seals (see text, p. 201)

SEALS (ORDER PINNEPEDIA)

Seals are essentially marine mammals but are not as completely aquatic as whales. They spend a substantial part of their life cycle ashore, principally for breeding. Their hind limbs are flippers, differing in size, shape and effectiveness according to the family. Those of the eared seals are the most versatile—long and capable of being turned forward for use like a pair of oars, aiding the foreflippers that are the principal source of propulsion. The hind flippers of earless seals trail helplessly on land but are the main source of power in water. The walrus can use its flippers like an eared seal.

Seals are most abundant in Arctic and Antarctic regions. The annual movements of many species are governed by the movement of pack ice, which necessitates seasonal migration toward warmer waters. They return closer to the poles to breed. Adult male fur seals arrive first at breeding grounds called rookeries and establish territories in readiness for the females, who come about a month later. Earless seals in the Antarctic have limited seasonal migrations.

Defense of his territory is such a consuming occupation that the dominant male cannot leave the rookery even to feed. In some species the female also goes without food until her offspring has been weaned. Both male and female subsist on fat accumulated during months at sea. A single young is the rule. Mating takes place soon after they arrive at the rookery. Delayed implantation postpones development of the fetus for about 4 months.

Some seals are very large. Elephant seals and walruses weigh a ton. In all species except Weddell and leopard seals, males are larger than the females.

There are three families: eared seals (Otariidae), earless or common seals (Phocidae) and the walrus (Odobenidae).

California sea lions

EARED SEALS (FAMILY OTARIIDAE)

Eared seals, which have small external ears, are divided into two groups: fur seals (8 species), with dense, soft underfur; and sea lions (5 species), with coarse hair. Both are highly gregarious, their well-developed social organization based on a harem system controlled by a dominant male. Fur seals and sea lions prey mainly on fish but also eat squid and shellfish.

NORTHERN FUR SEAL (*Callorhinus ursinus*), maximum length 7 ft., breeds on Pribilof, Commander and Robben islands in the Bering Sea. It winters along the Pacific coasts southward to California and Japan. Once almost annihilated, the Pribilof population has grown from a few dozen to a population now estimated at 1.5 million. This is an outstanding example of practical conservation.

SOUTHERN FUR SEALS, of which there are 7 species, are all of the genus *Arctocephalus*. Except for the Guadalupe Island fur seal (*A. philippii*), they are confined to the Southern Hemisphere.

All fur seals were once very abundant. An estimate of their original numbers can be made when it is known that over 30,000 pelts were harvested annually for over 300 years. This uncontrolled exploitation was stopped only when too few remained in a given area to make harvests profitable.

Two of the 5 species of sea lions inhabit the Northern Hemisphere, 3 the Southern. STELLER'S SEA LION (*Eumetopias jubatus*) ranges on both sides of the Pacific from the Aleutians to California and Japan. Bulls may be 10 ft. long and weigh 2,000 lbs., making this species the largest of the sea lions.

CALIFORNIA SEA LION (*Zalophus californianus*) lives in warmer waters off the offshore islands of California as well as on the Galápagos Islands and coastal Japan. Males measure as much as 7 ft. long.

Harbor seals and pup

Gray seals

EARLESS, OR COMMON, SEALS (FAMILY PHOCIDAE)

In addition to lacking external ears and having hind flippers virtually useless out of water, earless seals have short, coarse fur without dense underfur.

In the Southern Hemisphere, the WEDDELL SEAL (*Leptonychotes weddelli*), maximum length 9 ft., ranges nearer to the South Pole than does any other seal. It does not migrate, nor does the little-known and rare ROSS SEAL (*Ommatophoca rossi*), maximum length 9½ ft., which lives on the landward edge of the Antarctic ice. The LEOPARD SEAL (*Hydrurga leptonyx*), maximum length 13 ft., summers on the seaward edge of the pack ice, then migrates toward the north during the winter months.

The highly gregarious CRAB-EATER SEAL (*Lobodon carcinophagus*), maximum length 8½ ft., is the most abundant of the Antarctic seals, with a total population estimated at about 15 million. Despite its name, it does not eat crabs, but krill, the small shrimplike crustaceans that are the main food of blue whales. Like the whale, the crab-eater seal swims openmouthed through the krill. Its elaborately shaped molars form a sieve that screens the krill from the water.

In the Northern Hemisphere, the RINGED SEAL (*Pusa hispida*), maximum length 4½ ft., lives in the most northerly part of the Arctic, mainly coastal areas but sometimes on firm ice extending to the North Pole. The CASPIAN SEAL (*P. caspica*) and the BAIKAL SEAL (*P. sibirica*) live in fresh waters, as do subspecies of the ringed seal in Finland. The BEARDED SEAL (*Erignathus barbatus*), maximum length 8 ft., lives in Arctic waters. A bottom feeder, it eats mollusks and crustaceans and hence remains close to land. In contrast, the HOODED SEAL (*Cystophora cristata*), maximum length 10 ft., ranges far out to sea in Arctic waters. It

Harp seal and pup

is solitary in habits, congregating only during the breeding season. Mature males have a prominent nose pouch that can be inflated like a balloon. It is erect when the seal is aggressive.

The RIBBON, or BANDED, SEAL (*Histriophoca fasciata*), maximum length 5½ ft., lives in the Bering Sea and cold North Pacific. Its banded coat is distinctive among seals. Like the hooded seal, and unlike most seals, the ribbon seal tends to be solitary.

The HARP SEAL (*Pagophilus groenlandicus*), maximum length 6 ft., breeds on ice floes off Newfoundland and in the Greenland and White seas. Its total population is estimated at about 5 million, making it the most abundant seal in northern waters.

The COMMON, or HARBOR, SEAL (*Phoca vitulina*), maximum length 6 ft., lives in cool to temperate waters of the North Atlantic as far south as Nantucket and in the North Pacific as far south as Japan and California. The GRAY SEAL (*Halichoerus grypus*), maximum length 9½ ft., also lives in the North Atlantic but is easily distinguished from the common seal by its generally larger size and bigger nose.

ELEPHANT SEALS (*Mirounga*, 2 species) are the largest of the earless seals. Adult males may be 15 ft. long and weigh as much as 4 tons; females are smaller—11 ft. and 1 ton. The male's trunklike snout usually hangs limply over the mouth, but during the breeding season it is inflated into a large proboscis. The northern elephant seal (*M. angustirostris*) breeds on islands off the coast of central California. The southern elephant seal (*M. leonina*) inhabits subantarctic islands from South America to New Zealand.

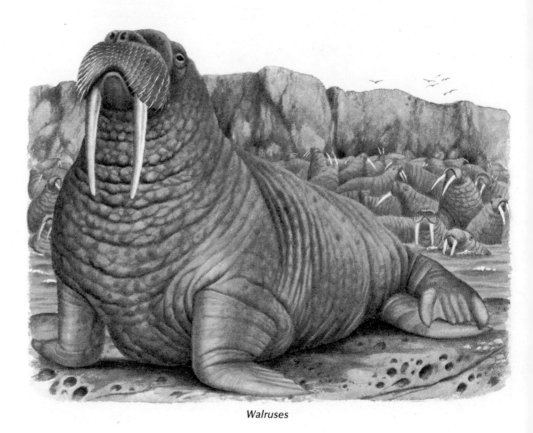

Walruses

WALRUS (FAMILY ODOBENIDAE)

The walrus (*Odobenus rosmarus*) lacks external ears but can bring its hind flippers forward. Adult males may be 13 ft. long and weigh 2 tons; females are smaller. The almost hairless skin is thick and wrinkled. The tusks, maximum length 3 ft., are not used to root in the sea bottom for clams and mussels but as a support when hauling out of the water onto the ice. They continue to grow throughout the life of the males. An adult male's tusk may weigh 10 lbs.; the female's is always lighter and more slender. The stiff bristles on the upper lip hold the molluscs in place while the soft insides are sucked out. They also help the walrus feel its way in murky waters. Because of its shellfish diet, the walrus inhabits comparatively shallow coastal waters.

Walruses live in large mixed herds on islands, sea ice and in isolated coves.

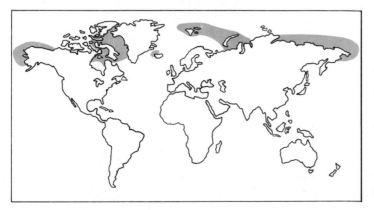

Their seasonal movements are governed by the advance and retreat of the pack ice.

Females give birth to a single young after a gestation period of 13–15 months. The calf is suckled up to 3 years, until its tusks grow and it can feed by itself.

Eskimos have hunted walrus for centuries and made use of every part of the animal.

Aardvark

AARDVARK, OR ANT BEAR (ORDER TUBULIDENTATA)

The aardvark, or ant bear (*Orycteropus afer*), is the only species in its order. The African name, based on the Dutch word, means "earth pig." Features that the aardvark shares with New World anteaters are attributable to evolutionary convergence.

The aardvark's head and body measure 3½–5 in. long, the tail 2 ft. Its primitive teeth, which occur only in the cheeks, lack enamel, and their upper surfaces are honeycombed with tubelike cavities. The teeth grow continuously, falling out and being replaced by other molars. The thick skin is sparsely covered with coarse hair. The tail, thick at the base, is naked.

The stout limbs have strong hooflike claws with which the animal can dig with incredible speed. When it is burrowing, the aardvark's large, mulelike ears are folded down. The snout is long, with a velvety muzzle. After breaking into an ant or termite mound with its claws, the aardvark inserts its long, sticky tongue into the galleries, as do New World anteaters.

Found only in Africa, south of the Sahara, the aardvark inhabits the open savannas—wherever it can find ants and termites, its almost exclusive food. It is inoffensive and solitary, except for females with their single young.

Due to their nocturnal habits and wariness, aardvarks are seldom seen. During the day they sleep in a burrow. The holes they dig are evidence of their presence but not a reliable indication of their numbers, since each aardvark digs a great many holes—some as "homes" but most when searching for food. The holes are of considerable ecological importance, however, for they are utilized by many other animals—birds and reptiles as well as mammals.

Asiatic elephants

ELEPHANTS (ORDER PROBOSCIDEA)

The two living species of elephants are the largest, most powerful land mammals. They are remnants of a once large and diverse group. In the past, elephants occurred on every continent except Australia and Antarctica.

The elephant's trunk, an extraordinarily versatile extension of the muzzle, is an organ of both touch and smell. The elephant's sense of smell and hearing are developed, but its sight is not acute. The trunk serves also as a highly flexible "arm," enabling the elephant to lift food and water to its mouth and to reach objects on the ground or high in trees. It combines strength with deftness, for it can pluck a single leaf from a tree or lift a huge log. A foraging elephant may consume 500 pounds of food in a day.

Except for its tusks, which are greatly enlarged incisors, the elephant has only four functional teeth at one time—two molars in the upper and two in the lower jaw. Each may be 12 inches wide. As a tooth wears down, it is gradually replaced by another, a total of five replacements being possible during an elephant's lifetime.

Elephants range from equatorial primary forests to semi-arid bushveld and from hot coastal plains to high mountain forests and cool, alpine meadows. They require water regularly and are rarely far from a good source.

Elephants are gregarious animals whose social organization is based on a family unit commanded by a mature female. These families frequently join to form herds of up to a hundred animals. Young bulls form separate bachelor herds; old bulls are frequently solitary. Herds may roam over great distances.

Females are generally mature at 14–15 years, males at up to 25 years. Gestation is about 22 months, and a single calf is usual. It is suckled for about 4 years,

African elephants

sometimes longer, but remains with its mother even if another calf is born, which is generally every 4 years.

Elephants have been either reduced in numbers or exterminated over much of their original range.

AFRICAN ELEPHANT *(Loxodonta africana)*, found in Africa south of the Sahara, is the larger of the two species of elephants. Males may stand 11 ft. tall at the shoulders and weigh 6 tons. The tusks, present in both males and females, may be 11 ft. long and weigh 200 lbs. A subspecies lives primarily in the forests.

Despite its great bulk, an elephant can move with surprising silence and is capable of high speed. An elephant bearing down at 25 miles per hour, with its ears extended and screaming with rage, is a formidable sight.

The African elephant has a concave back, large ears and a coarse skin. The forehead is flattened, and the trunk ends in two fingerlike projections.

ASIATIC ELEPHANT *(Elephas maximus)*, of southeastern Asia, does not exceed 10 ft. in height at the shoulders and is usually shorter. The back is convex, the forehead bulbous, with a trough between the two bulges. The trunk has only a single projection, or finger, at the tip. The tusks are smaller than those of the African elephant but may still be large—nearly 9 ft. in length and each weighing as much as 150 lbs. Females usually lack tusks, as do many of the males.

The Asiatic elephant has been used as a work animal for centuries. The African elephant does not submit as readily to training.

Adult male Asiatic elephants discharge a dark oily substance called musth from glands on the temple. Musth is discharged when the level of the male hormone (testoterone) in the blood is high. The bulls become extremely aggressive at this time.

Tree hyrax

HYRAXES, OR DASSIES (ORDER HYRACOIDEA)

Hyraxes resemble tailless marmots with protruding upper incisors. On the back is a bare gland surrounded by a fringe of long guard hairs, more prominent in some species than in others and differing in color according to the locality. When the animal is agitated, the hair around the gland becomes erect.

Hyraxes are a puzzle to anatomists: Their teeth resemble those of rhinoceroses and hippopotamuses, their stomach is like a horse's and their feet and brain are similar to those of elephants. The hyrax is in fact a living fossil—it preceded all the hoofed animals we know today.

The gestation period of hyraxes, unusually long for small animals, is 7½ months. The one to three young are well developed at birth.

Usually ignored by large carnivores, hyraxes are preyed on regularly by leopards, small predatory mammals, snakes and birds of prey. Verreaux's eagle feeds almost exclusively on hyraxes. The animals are hunted also by man, both

for meat and for pelts used in making the karosses worn by the African natives. Despite this heavy and constant predation, rock hyraxes remain common and widespread. Tree hyraxes are greatly reduced in numbers due to deforestation in parts of their range.

There are three genera: rock hyraxes *(Procavia)*, maximum length 20 in.; tree hyraxes *(Dendrohyrax)*, maximum length 18 in.; and *Heterohyrax*, with intermediate features.

One hyrax, the Syrian hyrax *(Heterohyrax syriacus)*, is mentioned in the Bible under the name cavy or guinea pig. This was a mistake in translation.

Rock hyraxes

ROCK HYRAXES *(Procavia, 3 species)* are widely found throughout Africa and extend into the Arabian Peninsula and the Middle East.

Rock hyraxes are terrestrial, only occasionally climbing trees. They may be active on moonlight nights but are diurnal, living in open, semi-arid or even desert country. They occupy rock piles or boulders at the base of rocky hills *(kopjes)* that are prominent in the otherwise flat bushveld. Their colonies may be composed of 50 or more animals.

During the heat of the day, the hyraxes rest in their burrows or bask in the sun on rocks and ledges, constantly alert and ready to dash to safety underground. They can go for long periods without drinking. Large mounds of droppings, always deposited in one place, leave white stains on rocks as telltale evidence of their presence.

TREE HYRAXES *(Dendrohyrax, 4 species)* are primarily nocturnal, solitary and more placid than rock hyraxes. They live in the hollows of large forest trees and occasionally descend to the ground. For this reason, unspoiled primary forests are essential for preservation of the animals. River and montane forests are especially favored habitats. They feed on fruits, leaves, berries and shoots.

At higher elevations—above the treeline to 15,000 feet—tree hyraxes have adapted to living among the rocks in the open country. There they are frequently mistaken for rock hyraxes.

Rock hyraxes have a wide repertoire of calls and are particularly vocal in early morning and late evening, when they are most active. The call of tree hyraxes is louder, commencing with a series of harsh croaks and culminating in a long, drawn-out, high-pitched scream.

Manatee   Dugong

MANATEES AND DUGONGS (ORDER SIRENIA)

Sirenians are wholly aquatic, like whales. They have lost their hind limbs and external ears, have small eyes protected by an oily secretion and have horizontal tail flukes, round in manatees and crescent-shaped in the dugong. Their young are born underwater. Despite these similarities to whales, the two groups are unrelated, having evolved from entirely different origins.

The DUGONG (*Dugong dugon*), 10–12 ft. long, lives in tropical waters on the fringes of the Indian and western Pacific oceans. The three species of MANATEES (*Trichechus*), measuring 7–12 ft. long, inhabit both sides of the Atlantic.

Manatees have only molars, which are replaced when worn down in the same way as an elephant's. Male dugongs have a pair of tusklike incisors measuring as much as 9 in. long. Both sexes have horny plates in their mouth, and they use the stiff bristles on the muzzle as aids during feeding.

Sirenians are mainly nocturnal. They live alone or in small groups, though dugongs sometimes assemble in large herds. They are essentially marine, but manatees may enter estuaries of large rivers.

Unlike whales, sirenians are vegetarians, feeding on plants that grow only in coastal waters. These shallow waters protect them against large marine predators, but sirenians are extremely vulnerable to human predation and to changes in water temperature; an extended cold spell can prove fatal.

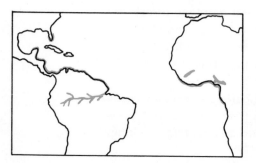

■ *Manatees*

Przewalski horses and foal

ODD-TOED HOOFED MAMMALS (ORDER PERISSODACTYLA)

All the mammals forming this group are large and have an odd number of digits on their feet. The tips of each toe are enclosed in a horny sheath or hoof.

Tapirs, the only representatives of the order in the New World, have four toes on the front feet but only three on the hind feet. Rhinoceroses have three toes on all feet. Horses and their near relatives, the asses and zebras, support their body weight on the third toe of each foot; the other toes have atrophied to rudimentary splints. This was an adaptation for swift running on the open plains.

Man took advantage of the horse's intelligence and amenability to domestication. As a result the horse, more than any other animal, helped to shape the history and progress of mankind.

HORSES, ASSES AND ZEBRAS (FAMILY EQUIDAE)

PRZEWALSKI'S HORSE (*Equus przewalskii*) is the only surviving wild horse. A stockily built animal, standing as much as 4 ft. tall at the shoulders, it has a large head and an erect mane. In the wild it lives in small herds consisting of about a half dozen mares and their young commanded by a stallion who defends his harem against rivals. Colts driven from his herd join bachelor herds until old enough to establish their own harems.

Deliberate slaughter, disease and interbreeding with domestic ponies contributed to its decline, but more important was the gradual exclusion of the horse from the limited sources of water as land areas were settled and fenced.

The few remaining wild Przewalski's horses live in a small area fringing the Gobi Desert between Mongolia and China. About 180 exist in zoos.

Mongolian wild asses

ASIATIC WILD ASSES *(Equus hemionus)* vary in color from sandy yellow to chestnut and are darker in winter. They display a dark stripe along the spine.

The five races are separated geographically: the dark-yellow onager, from Turkmenia and northern Iran; light-chestnut kiang, from the Tibetan Plateau and the Himalayan region; sandy-colored Indian wild ass, or ghor-kar, from Little Rann of Kutch in western India; rusty brown Mongolian wild ass, or kulan, from the steppes of central Mongolia; and light-fawn Syrian wild ass, believed now extinct. The severe winters of 1879 and 1891 are thought to have been responsible for the latter's demise. Although wild asses prefer high plateaus, blizzards may seriously hamper their movements and bury their food supply.

Wild asses have been used in the service of man for longer than the horse. Foals were in constant demand for stud purposes to breed draft animals or riding asses. The spread of livestock grazing brought the wild asses into increasing conflict with man. The wild ass cannot exist without drinking regularly and thus had to compete with domestic livestock for the limited supplies of water.

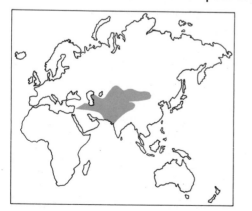

This was the crucial factor in the decline of the wild populations. The speed and stamina of wild asses made them difficult to hunt with primitive weapons, but modern firearms changed this situation, favoring the nomadic pastoralists. Wild asses are also susceptible to diseases transmitted by domestic livestock.

Wild-ass meat is highly esteemed. The hide is used for leather, and other parts of the animal are credited with medicinal properties. The combination of these factors forced the wild ass from favored parts of its range into arid areas less frequented by man.

Somali wild asses

AFRICAN WILD ASSES *(E. asinus)* are smaller and have relatively larger ears than do the Asiatic wild asses. The two surviving forms are the pale fawn Somali wild ass from northern Somalia and northern Ethiopia and the pale gray Nubian wild ass from the Red Sea Hills of the Sudan and eastern Eritrea. The Somali wild ass has only a faint spinal stripe and no stripes on the withers, but it has a series of dark bands on the lower legs. The Nubian wild ass has a withers stripe but no leg markings. Pockets of so-called wild asses scattered on the fringes of the Sahara Desert are believed to be domestic asses gone feral.

Both the African and the Asiatic wild asses are hardy animals, capable of withstanding bitter climatic extremes of their range. Their social organization is different from that of wild horses. An older female leads a herd of mares and younger males. Stallions live apart for most of the year. In autumn, family units join to form herds of a thousand or more animals that remain together all winter. Mature stallions break away in early spring and forage in small independent groups until the rutting season in late April, when they assemble their harems and fight with rival males. Their diet varies seasonally: Grass is grazed in the spring, and herbs and bushes are browsed during the summer. When the temperatures rise, wild asses feed during the cooler evening hours.

Wild asses become sexually mature in 2–3 years. Mares bear their first foal a year later, after a gestation period of 11½ months. When foaling, mares congregate in a favored area to gain protection from predators. In only a few days, however, colts run with the mares.

A mule is not a wild ass but the offspring of a male domestic ass and female donkey; a hinny is a cross between a female ass and a male donkey. Both are sterile and cannot breed. Mules have remarkable endurance and a well-known stubbornness.

Mountain zebra   *Grant's zebra*

BURCHELL'S, or PLAINS, ZEBRA *(Equus burchelli)* is the most widely distributed of the three species of zebras. In Kenya and South-West Africa, its range overlaps that of both Grevy's and the mountain zebra. Grant's zebra is one of the several varieties of Burchell's zebra.

Like wild horses, zebras are creatures of the open plains, but the three species nevertheless live in different environmental conditions. Burchell's zebra favors relatively lush grasslands; Grevy's and the mountain zebra, arid and semi-arid lands.

Zebras are grazing animals; but when fodder is scarce, they may browse. It is an unusual characteristic of zebras that they can look fat and sleek even under poor conditions. Zebras must also drink at frequent intervals and are therefore seldom far from a source of water.

Burchell's zebra remains in one area most of the year, migrating only when there are seasonal shortages of water or vegetation on which to graze. The best-known and most spectacular migrations occur on the Serengeti Plains of Tanzania when thousands of zebras and other animals trek to fresh pastures.

For safety, zebras rely on their keen eyesight and speed, but they will use their hooves and teeth for defense when necessary. They associate with wildebeest, hartebeest, tiang, oryx and other grazers on the plains, gaining protection in numbers.

Zebras are slow breeders. A single foal is born between October and March after a gestation of 11–12 months.

■ *Mountain zebra*   ■ *Burchell's zebra*   ■ *Grevy's zebra*

Grant's zebra
and hunting dogs

Grevy's zebra

GREVY'S ZEBRA *(E. grevyi)* tends to be larger than the other species. It may stand 4½ ft. tall at the shoulders, the others about 4 ft. tall. Also the black stripes on the spine extend onto the tail.

Grevy's zebra inhabits arid and semi-arid country. In the more arid parts of its range, where the few waterholes may be used by domestic livestock, it may migrate long distances to get water. Grevy's zebra is confined to northern Kenya and adjacent parts of Ethiopia and Somalia. Basically a grazer, it will browse when fodder is scarce and will also dig for roots and tubers.

Burchell's and Grevy's zebras have different social organizations. A Burchell herd consists of a dominant stallion and his closely knit family group. Grevy zebras have no permanent bonds. Stallions defend territories 1 to 4 square miles in size when mares are in estrus and flock together in grazing groups at other times.

MOUNTAIN ZEBRAS *(E. zebra)* are the smallest zebras. They are distinguished also by having a small dewlap, or fold of skin, under the throat. In addition, the stripes tend to be broader than those of other zebras. The striped pattern of zebras makes the animal less conspicuous in the open areas by breaking up the outline of their body. Mountain zebras are far less common than Burchell's zebra. The mountain zebra is restricted to the dry regions of South-West Africa and Cape Province. Often it gets water by digging with its hooves in the river beds into which seeps the water from just beneath the surface. These small waterholes benefit other kinds of wildlife that are not equipped for digging.

Although closely related to domesticated horses and wild asses, the zebra has not been domesticated. This is probably due to its lack of stamina compared to the donkey. Zebras offer the advantage of being immune to horse sickness.

Malayan tapir and calf

TAPIRS (FAMILY TAPIRIDAE)

Early explorers of the New World thought tapirs were giant pigs and classified them with the hippopotamus. They are in fact closer to horses and rhinoceroses.

Tapirs are stockily built animals with four toes on the forefeet, three on the hind. Each toe is tipped with a small hoof. The snout is extended into a short, flexible proboscis that helps pluck foliage while browsing. Tapirs have an acute sense of smell and excellent hearing but poor eyesight. Their range is remarkable for its discontinuity—one species in Asia and three in the Americas.

Tapirs are active at night, hiding in thickets or dense undergrowth during the day. Although solitary, tapirs may move in pairs through the almost impenetrable jungles along tunnel-like trails made from their regular use of these paths. Jaguars and spectacled bears are said to prey on South American tapirs; the tiger is the main predator of the Malayan species.

Tapirs are inoffensive, shy and retiring creatures. They cannot tolerate disturbances and do not adapt readily to changing environmental conditions. They are solitary, but individuals may roam over wide areas.

Tapirs grunt in piglike fashion when disturbed. In the mating season they give shrill whistles. Mating pairs remain together for several weeks, then separate. The rearing and caring for the young becomes the female's responsibility.

MALAYAN, or SADDLE-BACKED, TAPIR *(Tapir indicus)* is the largest of the four species. It may be as long as 8 ft. and weigh 500 lbs.

As with tapirs of the New World, the encroachment of civilization—the spread of agriculture and grazing, construction of roads and deforestation—has contributed to the decline of the Malayan tapir's population.

Mountain tapir

Brazilian tapir

BRAZILIAN TAPIR *(Tapirus terrestris)* is the most widely distributed of the tapirs. Most tapirs inhabit dense tropical rain forests. They are partial to swamps and spend much of their time wallowing. They are excellent swimmers and can remain submerged for long periods. If attacked, their natural inclination is to run to the nearest water and plunge in. Tapirs wear down paths through the swamps and thick undergrowth that are used by the natives as convenient hunting trails.

A single calf, rarely twins, is born at any time of year after a gestation period of 13 months. The calf remains with its mother for about a year, during which time it has horizontal stripes and spots.

MOUNTAIN TAPIR *(T. pinchaque)* lives in subtropical to temperate forests in the higher parts of the Andes—at elevations above 8,000 feet. It occupies two distinct types of habitats: the almost impenetrable montane mist forests that extend about 12,000 feet and plateau meadows up to 13,000 feet.

This is the least well known of the tapirs. It is sometimes called woolly tapir because its body is covered with curly hair.

BAIRD'S TAPIR *(T. bairdii)* also lives at high elevations—to 6,000 feet—but may move down to sea-level forests.

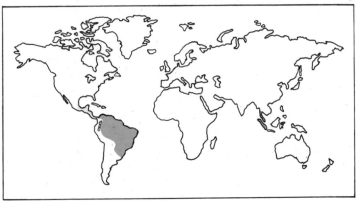

■ *Malayan tapir*   ☐ *Baird's tapir*

▨ *Mountain tapir*   ■ *Brazilian tapir*

White rhinoceros   *Top and right: Black rhinoceroses*

RHINOCEROSES (FAMILY RHINOCEROTIDAE)

In addition to their bulk and their thick, usually hairless skin, rhinos are set apart from other animals by their unique horns—located on the snout rather than on top of the head and composed of skin derivatives, like fingernails, instead of bone. The African and Sumatran rhinos have two horns; the Indian and Javan rhinos have only one.

African rhinos inhabit dry country. The white, or square-lipped, rhino is a grassland grazer; the black favors thornscrub. Asiatic rhinos live in rain forests. The Indian rhino inhabits swampy jungles at the foot of the Himalayas, feeding mainly on grass and swamp vegetation. Javan and Sumatran rhinos are browsers, living in dense forests but feeding at the fringes or in clearings.

A prime need of all rhinos is water, not only for drinking but also for their mud wallows. The wallowing helps cool them and provides protection from hordes of biting flies. In the dry season, African rhinos take dust baths.

Most rhinos are solitary except for the mother-calf relationship. The African square-lipped rhino, less pugnacious than the black rhino, may assemble in small herds. Males are generally more aggressive than females. Despite their size, rhinos are remarkably swift and agile. They have poor eyesight but a keen sense of smell. White rhino males use scent-marking with urine and dung to mark their territory; the Indian rhino does not.

Sexual maturity is reached at about 5 years of age, and mature females generally breed every 3 years. The gestation period is 15–17 months. The single calf is weaned at 2½ years and is driven away by the mother before her next calf is born. It may rejoin her later.

Sumatran rhinoceros

Indian rhinoceros

All rhinos, but particularly the Asiatic species, are endangered. The reported power of powdered rhino horns as an aphrodisiac, making them astronomically valuable, has fed their exploitation.

WHITE, or SQUARE-LIPPED, RHINOCEROS *(Ceratotherium* simum) is the largest of the rhinos, standing 6½ft. at the shoulders and weighing as much as 3½ tons. It has a broad mouth and a prominent shoulder hump. The total population is estimated to be about 2,000.

BLACK, or HOOK-LIPPED, RHINOCEROS *(Diceros bicornis)*, maximum height 5 ft., weight 1½ tons, is the more widespread and abundant of the two African species. Its total population is estimated to be about 12,000.

INDIAN RHINOCEROS *(Rhinoceros un-icornis)*, maximum height 6 ft., weight 2½ tons, has thickly folded skin covered with tubercles. The 650 existing animals live in sanctuaries in India and Nepal.

JAVAN RHINOCEROS *(R. sondaicus)*, maximum height 5½ ft., weight 1½ tons, is the most rare, with only 40 animals existing.

SUMATRAN RHINOCEROS *(Didermocerus sumatrensis)*, maximum height 4½ ft., weight ½ ton, is the only rhino with a hairy coat. Only about 150 animals remain.

White rhinoceros

Black rhinoceros

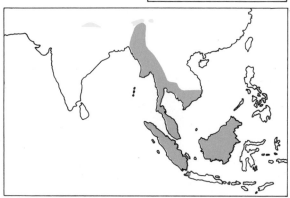

Indian rhinoceros

Javan rhinoceros   Sumatran rhinoceros

EVEN-TOED HOOFED MAMMALS
(ORDER ARTIODACTYLA)

These animals typically have two toes on each foot and each toe tip is encased in a hoof. Some have four toes, but the outer toes are high—not touching the ground and thus not aiding in support of the body except in hippopotamuses. Many have antlers or horns, and most have a complex, or four-compartmented, stomach. These animals ruminate, or "chew the cud." Exceptions are pigs and the hippo, both nonruminating.

NEW WORLD PIGS, OR PECCARIES (FAMILY TAYASSUIDAE)

Peccaries (*Tayassu*, 2 species) differ from Old World pigs in having a rudimentary tail and three toes on the hind feet (two of which are functional). The upper tusks grow downward, and there is a large musk gland on the back near the rump. The stomach is divided.

The stockily built collared peccary, or javelin (*T. tajacu*), 20 in. tall at the shoulders, ranges from deserts to rain forests, preferring dense ground cover. It travels in groups of 10 to 20. The white-lipped peccary (*T. peccari*), maximum height 24 in., lives in herds of as many as 100 and inhabits primary forests.

Peccaries run quickly when frightened; if cornered, they will crowd together and stand ground. Though able to tolerate the hunting pressure, they cannot survive the loss of habitat.

■ *Collared peccary*   *White-lipped peccary*

European wild boar and young

OLD WORLD PIGS (FAMILY SUIDAE)

Old World pigs have a flat, disklike snout used for rooting, a feature they share with New World peccaries. In Old World pigs the upper canines turn upward as tusks, and there is also a lower pair of tusks, often curved. There are four toes on each foot, only the front two functional. The stomach is two-compartmented, and the sparse hair on the thick skin is bristly. The senses of smell and hearing are well developed.

Primarily vegetarian, pigs will also eat small animals and carrion. They are land dwellers but are excellent swimmers and are fond of wallowing. They are gregarious and travel in small groups. Males are larger than females, and the young of most species are striped.

Wild pigs and feral domestic pigs often destroy crops. In many parts of the world they are hunted for sport and food.

EUROPEAN WILD BOAR *(Sus scrofa)*, ancestor of the domestic pig, stands to a maximum height of 40 in. at the shoulders and may weigh as much as 400 lbs. It has been introduced to the United States and other areas.

Wild boars become sexually mature in 18 months but may not attain full size until 5 or 6 years old. Females bear litters of five to eight piglets after a gestation period of 4 months. The wild boar's tail is straight and hangs, instead of being lifted and coiled as in domestic pigs.

■ *European wild boar*

Giant forest hog

Bush pig

ASIATIC WILD PIGS include the rare and bizarre babirusa (*Babyrousa babyrussa*), measuring 31 in. tall at the shoulder and weighing 200 lbs. The male's upper tusks (maximum length 17 in.) grow through the skin of the snout, then curve back toward the eyes. The short lower tusks do not contact the upper tusks and hence are not sharp. They are not used in rooting and are probably sexual attributes like the antlers of a stag; natives call babirusa "pig-deer." They are nocturnal and move about in small groups. When alarmed, they run quickly and are strong swimmers. Unlike most wild piglets, babirusas are not striped at birth. Hunting and deforestation have greatly reduced the babirusa population.

The pygmy hog (*Sus salvaninus*), slightly larger than a European hare, is the smallest of the pigs. Living in remote swamps, it is shy and nocturnal and was believed extinct until its rediscovery in 1972 on a tea plantation in Assam.

AFRICAN WILD PIGS include three species occupying different habitats. Their populations do not compete or come into conflict even where their ranges overlap.

The bush pig, or red river hog (*Potamochoerus porcus*), 30 in. long and 200 lbs., has a coat of bristly hair, a pronounced mane and long, pointed ears. Mainly a nocturnal animal, it lives in bushy woodlands and at forest edges where it digs for roots and tubers. It uses its snout for grubbing in the soil and its tusks for prying out the roots. In settled regions it may be a pest of crops. The bush pig, of which there are several races, produces litters of three or four young after a gestation period of 4 months.

■ *Babirusa*

Warthogs

Babirusa

The warthog (*Phacochoerus aethiopicus*), maximum length 31 in., weight 250 lbs., appears to be hairless but in fact has a narrow mane, tail tuft and bristles over much of its body. Its name comes from the two or more wartlike protuberances on its cheeks. The massive upper tusks vary from 10 in. to 2 ft. in length; the lower tusks, only about 6 in. long, are kept sharp by constant honing against the upper tusks.

When the warthog moves rapidly, its tail is held straight up. It lives in burrows dug by aardvarks or other animals. Almost invariably it backs into the hole. A diurnal animal, the warthog grazes in the savannas and specializes on cropping the shorter, more succulent grasses. To do so, it kneels on its forelegs while eating and may shuffle forward while still on its knees. Its eyes, placed high on its head, still give it protective vision. Males are usually solitary, while the females can be seen during the day rooting around, followed by their offspring. Female warthogs produce litters of two to four young after a gestation period of about 6 months. Lions prey heavily on warthogs, as do leopards and hunting dogs.

The giant forest hog (*Hylochoerus meinertzhageni*), extending to 36 in. and 500 lbs., has tusks less well developed than those of the warthog. Its litters of two to six young are produced after a gestation period of 4½ months. As its name implies, the giant forest hog lives in the forests and is active in the twilight hours of dusk and dawn, browsing on leaves, fruit and shoots as well as eating grass in the clearings. It is rarely seen in the wild.

■ Giant forest hog
■ Bush pig

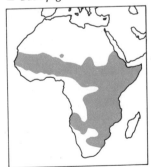

■ Warthog

Hippopotamuses

HIPPOPOTAMUSES (FAMILY HIPPOPOTAMIDAE)

Hippos are exceeded in size among the land-dwelling mammals only by elephants and rhinoceroses. Belonging to the same order as pigs, they have four toes on each foot, all aiding to support the bulky body on its short, column-shaped legs.

Common hippos are more at home in water than on land, where they move ponderously, their bellies almost scraping the ground, though they can trot at a surprising speed when necessary. They swim with ease, and in the water they often laze at the surface with only their ears and their bulbous eyes and nostrils above the surface. The nostrils are equipped with valves so that they can be closed when the animal submerges. Sometimes a hippo walks along the bottom.

The thick, smooth and almost hairless skin may account for as much as 20 percent of the animal's total weight. Its bluish gray to muddy color makes it inconspicuous in the water. Hippos are most active at night.

HIPPOPOTAMUS *(Hippopotamus amphibius),* maximum length 14 ft., 5 ft. tall at the shoulder, weight 2½ tons, has a wide range in Africa. This has been greatly contracted, however, the species now being confined mainly to the equatorial regions of eastern Africa.

The common hippo is the most amphibious of the two species. Its dung has an incidental effect of fertilizing the water and thus enriching the fishery. In the water, a hippo may remain submerged for 4 minutes or longer without having to surface to breathe. The common hippo is sociable, associating in groups of a dozen or more animals. At dusk the hippos emerge from the water to graze on land, sometimes traveling long distances and over rough terrain to reach favored grasslands.

Pygmy hippopotamus and calf

Because of intensive hunting, the declining numbers of hippos have become increasingly wary, hiding during the day in vegetation or below the surface. Unfortunately for the hippo, it is attracted to cultivated fields. A hungry hippo can devour more than 100 pounds of food daily and will destroy even more as it forages. This has not put it in good favor with man.

The common hippopotamus bears a single calf after a gestation period of 8 months. Births occur on land or in water. The calves are weaned at 12 months. Hippos become sexually mature when about 9 years old. Males establish territories that are defended from intrusion by other males, while females and their calves generally occupy a central nursery area surrounded by the males and their territories.

A yawning hippopotamus displaying its canine tusks (they may be 5 in. long in some) and its long, straight incisors is not being lethargic. Rather it is showing its weaponry. The yawn is an aggressive threat signal that may provoke a fight. Fights between males frequently result in serious wounds.

PYGMY HIPPOPOTAMUS *(Choeropsis liberiensis),* maximum height 2½ ft., weight 500 lbs., is less amphibious than the common hippo. Neither its eyes nor its nostrils is bulbous.

The pygmy hippopotamus lives in swamp forests and in the dense vegetation along rivers. Here it browses on shoots, twigs, leaves and fruit. In the forest it moves along tunnel-like trails, kept open by usage. Solitary and secretive, the pygmy hippo seeks refuge in the forest when disturbed. It is rare, and its habits are not well known.

■ *Hippopotamus*   ▨ *Pygmy hippopotamus*

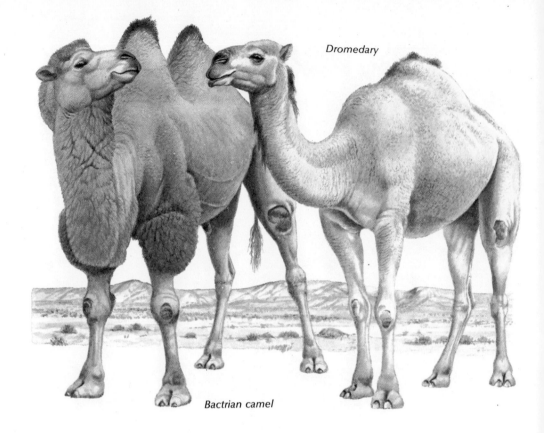

Dromedary

Bactrian camel

CAMELS, GUANACOS AND KIN (FAMILY CAMELIDAE)

Camels and their kin have two toes on each foot. Rather than hooves, they have thick, leathery pads that support the body weight, providing a nonskid surface for animals that climb and protection from the hot sand. The legs are slim, the neck long and the upper lip deeply cleft. The stomach consists of three chambers. Camels have humps; guanacos and their relatives do not.

CAMELS are natives of the Old World. There are two species—the one-humped Arabian camel, or dromedary (*Camelus dromedarius*), and the more heavily built, two-humped bactrian (*C. bactrianus*). About 500 wild bactrians live in the Gobi Desert. Hybrids (called tulus) occur in some areas, and camels introduced to Australia are now feral. Wild camel populations suffered from excessive hunting, but their exclusion from sparse pastures and limited water supplies were responsible for their decline.

Among the characteristics that made camels valuable as domestic animals in the desert include their ability to tolerate extremes of heat and cold. Their efficient utilization of water enables the animals to go for long periods without having to drink. They avoid excessive loss of water by regulating their body temperature. When food is plentiful, the fat is stored in the hump.

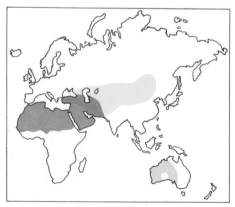

Bactrian camel

Dromedary camel, natural range

Dromedary camel, introduced range

Llama   Vicuña

GUANACOS *(Lama guanaco)*, maximum length 43 in., weight 200 lbs., and VICUÑAS *(Vicugna vicugna)*, 33 in., weight 100 lbs., are the only free-living members of the camel family in the New World. Two other members of the family, their exact ancestry not clear, are domesticated: the llama *(L. glama)*, maximum length 46 in., weight 250 lbs., used primarily as a beast of burden; and the alpaca *(L. pacos)*, maximum 36 in., weight 150 lbs., which produces top-quality wool.

Both the guanaco and the vicuña live in arid parts of the Andes. The guanaco ranges from the deserts and pampas to the alpine meadows. The vicuña inhabits a more restricted range and lives higher in the mountains—in the altiplano zone, from 13,000 to 18,000 feet at the upper limits of the treeline. The vicuña's red fleece blends remarkably well with the rocky, red earth terrain.

Both species live in small harem units consisting of 5–15 females and their young, which are under the control of a dominant male. Younger males are expelled from the herd after a year, when they reach sexual maturity, and live in bachelor herds. During the spring rut, males engage in fierce battles, kicking and biting each other. A single foal is born 10 months later. At the end of the breeding season, family units join to form large flocks that in the past contained a thousand or more individuals.

Heavy exploitation for their superior wool has reduced the vicuñas from an estimated population of 400,000 to 18,000. Also, their fragile habitat has been overstocked with domestic animals. The Incas considered the vicuña sacred, and it was strictly protected then as it is, once again, today.

■ Vicuña   ■ Guanaco

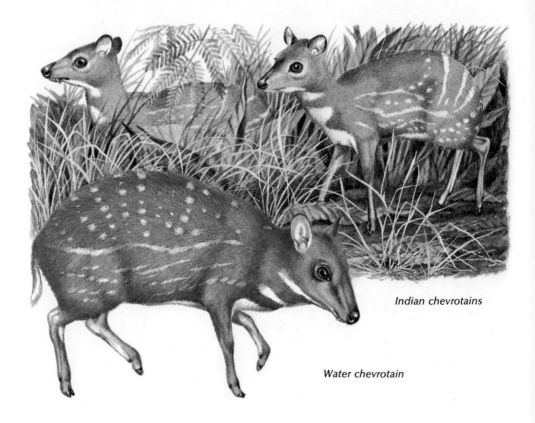

Indian chevrotains

Water chevrotain

CHEVROTAINS, OR MOUSE DEER (FAMILY TRAGULIDAE)

Chevrotains are the smallest hoofed mammals. Surviving remnants of a group of primitive ruminants, these hare-size animals are not true deer. They are probably more closely related to camels. They do not have horns or antlers; they have four well-developed toes on each foot, exceptionally slender legs, a pointed nuzzle and upper canines elongated into curved tusks that protrude below the lips in males. The stomach has only three divisions.

Water chevrotain, or mouse deer (*Hyemoschus aquaticus*), 14 in. tall at the shoulder, inhabit equatorial rain forests in Africa. Three Asian species—Indian chevrotain (*Tragulus meminna*), maximum height 12 in.; larger Malay chevrotain (*T. napu*), maximum 13 in.; and lesser Malay chevrotain (*T. javanicus*), maximum 11 in.—also live in equatorial rain forests. All live close to water and are good swimmers. Elusive, solitary and nocturnal, they mainly eat plants. Females give birth to a single young.

They were once described as "tiptoeing deer" because of their dainty gait. Chevrotains are so shy that they are rarely seen. African chevrotains readily take to water if pursued; the Asian species disappear into the undergrowth. The mouse deer is often mentioned in Southeast Asian folklore.

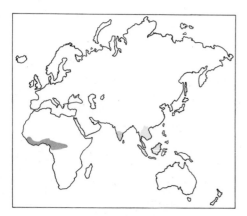

Indian chevrotain

Water chevrotain   Malay chevrotains

Musk deer

TRUE DEER (FAMILY CERVIDAE)

Males of most true deer have antlers. Female caribou are also horned. Bony outgrowths of the skull, antlers are at first tender and covered with a thin layer of skin (called velvet). This dies and is rubbed off when the antlers, used for defense and to defend territories, are fully grown. Antlers of mature males may be large and much branched; yearlings have unbranched "spikes." Antlers are shed after the breeding season.

True deer and all the following families of even-toed hoofed mammals are ruminants—that is, their stomach has four compartments, and they chew a cud.

MUSK DEER *(Moschus moschiferous)*, maximum height 20 in., is found in central and northeastern Asia. Males lack antlers; instead, the upper canines are strongly developed, forming tusks up to 3 in. long that protrude below the jaw. Mature males have an abdominal musk gland that excretes a waxy substance used in perfumes and medicines. To get this substance, musk deer have been hunted relentlessly, and in China they are farmed. Females and young do not yield musk. Musk deer are solitary and are active mainly at dusk and dawn. They prefer high mountain forests and brush land.

CHINESE WATER DEER *(Hydropotes inermis)*, maximum height 21 in., lack antlers, and the males have tusks like the musk deer. They inhabit swamps and the lowlands along lakes and rivers. Solitary and diurnal, they rely on concealment for safety.

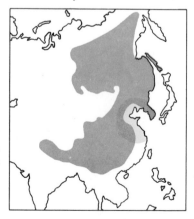

■ *Musk deer* ■ *Chinese water deer*

Indian muntjac family group

MUNTJACS, or RIB-FACED DEER, or BARKING DEER *(Muntiacus,* 4 species and a number of races), are small deer. They have tusks like the musk deer, but the males also have single-tined antlers that grow on pedicels almost as long as the antlers. The frontal bone forming the pedicels appears on the forehead as a pair of corrugated outgrowths that have given these deer the name rib-faced deer. They are also called barking deer because their sharp ''barking'' noises constitute their alarm cry.

Muntjacs are nocturnal and solitary forest dwellers, predominantly browsers but sometimes grazers feeding at the forest edges or invading field crops. They are hunted throughout their range, both for meat and for hides. In some areas they are considered pests because of their habit of chewing the bark on trees.

Females typically give birth to a single young (occasionally twins) after a gestation period of 6 months.

The four species in the genus *Muntiacus* are: the Indian muntjac (*M. muntjak*), maximum height 22 in. at the the shoulder; Reeve's muntjac (*M. crinifrons*), maximum 24 in.; and Fea's, or Tenasserim, muntjac (*M. feae*), maximum 20 in. Even when common, these shy deer are seldom seen.

TIBETAN, or TUFTED, DEER (*Elaphodus cephalophus*), maximum height 24 in., is closely related but has unbranched antlers so small they are almost not visible, and they lack pedicels and the forehead ridges. The coat is bristly, and the forehead is crowned with a tuft of hair.

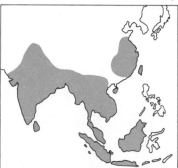

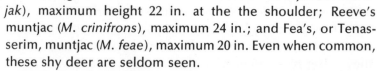 Muntjac

Fallow deer   *Axis deer*

FALLOW DEER *(Dama dama)*, maximum height 37 in., have antlers with flattened tips in males. Both sexes have a dewlap, but it is more pronounced in males. Color variations are greater than in any other deer—a result of semidomestication and breeding. Originally there were probably only three colors: black, white and the normal fawn.

The fallow deer inhabits open woodlands where it both grazes and browses. It is gregarious, assembling a large herd of females and young males. Older males remain separate except during the autumn rut, the mating period. Females bear a single fawn after a gestation period of 8 months.

AXIS DEER, or CHITAL *(Axis axis)*, maximum height 37 in., inhabits open grasslands but may also browse in woodlands. Herds of a hundred or more are common. Chital are tolerant of other ungulates and can be seen feeding with blackbuck, nilgai and swamp deer. Females produce a single fawn, rarely twins; the gestation period is 7½ months. The mother stays close to her fawn, usually hiding in dense cover until it is strong enough to follow her back to the herd. Stags may shed their antlers at any time of the year, then leave the herd to form all-male herds until new antlers have grown. The alarm call is a short high-pitched bark. Axis deer will readily take to water and are reported to be strong swimmers.

The hog deer *(A. porcinus)*, maximum height 29 in. is stockier, short legged and more solitary.

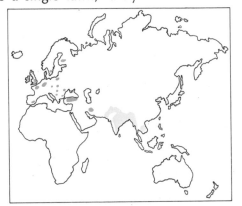

▨ *Axis deer*   ▪ *Fallow deer*

Roe deer, summer coat

Red deer

RED DEER, or EUROPEAN STAG *(Cervus elaphus)*, 54 in. high at the shoulder, varies in size and color over its wide range. It occurs in a number of races. It has been introduced to Australia, New Zealand and South America.

Basically a woodland species (deciduous and coniferous), it has adapted to many habitats and both browses and grazes. A gregarious animal, its herds contain only a few dozen individuals in woodlands but up to a hundred or more in the open country. Mature stags live in bachelor herds or separately, establishing harems during the rutting season. Shifts in stag dominance may occur after battles during the rut. The stag will roar to signal other males to challenge him or keep away from his harem. While the ruling stag may be ousted during the course of the rut, the herd movements are controlled year round by an older female.

Females are mature at 3 years of age, males at 4. Normally a single fawn is produced after a gestation period of 8 months.

SAMBAR *(C. unicolor)*, a widely ranging species in southern Asia, is divided into 16 races ranging from 25–55 in. in shoulder height. The Sika deer *(C. nippon)* is more northern, its races varying from 25–43 in. It shows a white rump patch when alarmed. Spotted like the fallow deer, the sika has a white tail instead of a black one. During the September rut the stags can be heard calling. This modulated whistle ends in a grunt that they repeat several times.

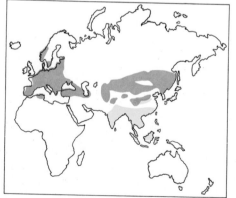

▓ *Sambar*　　▓ *Red deer*

Top: Swamp deer   Sambar stag

ROE DEER *(Capreolus capreolus)*, maximum height 30 in., prefers deciduous woodlands but lives wherever cover is adequate. It has no visible tail. It feeds mainly at night, both browsing and grazing, and is solitary except during the breeding season, when the bucks mark their territories with urine and scent from special glands and defend them from rivals. The bucks vigorously defend their territory. Instead of locking antlers, the two rivals face each other and scrape their antlers against the nearest tree.

Roe deer are foxy red in summer and in winter have a thick gray coat with a prominent white rump patch. They mate in summer, but implantation does not occur until 3–4 months later. The period of gestation is 5 months; twins are fairly common and triplets have been observed. The fawns mature in about 16 months, usually staying with their mother through the first year. They do not get antlers until their second year. The roe deer's alarm call is a bark.

SWAMP DEER, or BARASINGHA *(C. duvauceli)*, maximum height 55 in. at the shoulder, has handsome antlers that may be more than 40 in. long. This rare deer is found in forests, plains and swamps in northern and central India. Like the red deer, the stag collects a harem during the December breeding season, which he defends from other males. The stag's roar is said to resemble the braying of a donkey. At other times of the year, the barasingha travels in groups of the same sex and age.

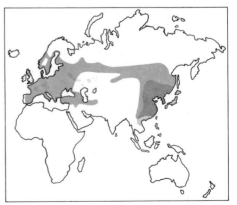

Sika deer, original range

Roe deer   Sika deer, introduced range

Moose   Whitetailed deer

WHITETAILED DEER *(Odocoileus virginianus)* is distinguished by its "flag"—the white underside of its tail that flashes clearly when the deer lifts its tail and runs. The different races measure from 25 to 42 in. at the shoulder. The whitetailed deer inhabits woodlands, favoring brushy areas that provide food for browsing. It has adapted to a wide variety of habitats over its extensive range.

Whitetailed deer associate in small groups of about a half dozen animals, the males and females generally separate. Females produce one or two fawns following a gestation period of 7 months. For the first few weeks, the spotted fawns stay in dense cover, and the does return to suckle them. They are weaned at 1½ months but remain with the mother for 1–2 years.

Excessive hunting greatly reduced the population of whitetailed deer. Now, after careful management and game laws and also the increase of browse, whitetails are again abundant in many areas—despite heavy hunting.

MULE DEER *(O. hemionus)*, 36 to 42 in., have large mulelike ears. A grasslands animal, it grazes during the wet season but turns to browsing during the dry months. In social organization, it is different from the whitetailed deer. It tends to associate more in herds and also migrates seasonally to feeding grounds.

The blacktailed deer *(O. hemionus columbianus)* is a slightly smaller subspecies. The underside of tail is black rather than only tipped with black, as in the mule deer.

■ *Whitetailed deer*

■ *Mule and blacktailed deer*

Wapiti   Mule deer pair

MOOSE, or ELK *(Alces alces)*, maximum height 92 in. at the shoulders, weight 1,800 lbs., is the largest of the living deer. In Europe it is called the elk. Its huge palmated antlers, shed annually, may span 70 in. across. The "bell," or dewlap, beneath the throat is present in both sexes but is longer in males.

The moose lives and browses in marshy forests of willow, aspen, birch and mountain ash. By standing on its hind legs it can reach up to 12 feet for leaves. During the winter and spring, aspen bark may be eaten. It also feeds on aquatic plants, kneeling to get those that grow close to the water or wading to get floating plants while at the same time escaping biting insects. The availability of food is the factor most limiting its abundance.

Moose can swim long distances and are often seen crossing lakes. Where wolves still exist, they are the main predators of moose. Bears and coyotes may occasionally kill a moose calf.

During the mating season, both bulls and cows bellow. In mid-September the males begin to follow females, emitting a low grunt as they travel through the forest. Bulls do not form harems but will fight with other bulls. Each seeks a female in heat and will fight other bulls for her. Females bear one to three calves (usually two) following a gestation period of 8 months. Calves remain with their mother for 2 years. Females are sexually mature in 2 years, males in 3.

WAPITI, or AMERICAN ELK *(Cervus canadensis)*, maximum height 60 in. at the shoulders, resembles red deer in behavior and habits.

▇ *Moose*   ▇ *Wapiti*

Reindeer and Laplanders

CARIBOU *(Rangifer tarandus)* and the domesticated reindeer of Eurasia are the same species, which includes half a dozen races. Those living in the wild in the tundra lands may stand 50 in. tall at the shoulders, with females smaller than males, and weigh up to 600 lbs. Domesticated reindeer are usually smaller—about 45 in. maximum height. Otherwise the two are not distinguishable.

Domesticated reindeer serve as draft animals and also as a source of meat, milk, skin and various artifacts for the Lapps and other peoples of the Arctic, whose cultures are founded on reindeer pastoralism. Reindeer are extremely economical, as they require no stables and can find their own forage, even in winter. Laplanders have herds sometimes numbering thousands of animals, which they control with only a few dogs. Reindeer may leave the herd and become feral and shy. Each animal has a small notch on its ear so that the owner can recognize it. The number of domesticated reindeer exceeds the number of animals in the wild. Eskimos have not attempted to domesticate the wild caribou but use it for food and clothing. At the end of the 19th century reindeer were introduced to Canada and have displaced resident caribou in some areas.

Caribou are the only deer in which both sexes have antlers. The female's are usually smaller, sometimes no more than spikes. Their broad, flat hooves are an adaptation for walking in wetlands and in snow, for they live farther north than any other deer. Their coats are thick, and even their muzzles are hairy rather than naked, as in the whitetailed deer. The ears are small and well furred.

The barren northern grounds where caribou live force them to make seasonal migrations up to 600 miles. They tend to summer at higher elevations to avoid the mosquitos found on the tundra.

Caribou

In summer their herds may consist of several dozen cows and their calves. Bulls tend to live apart, associating with the cows only when rutting in the fall. At this time, a bull moves in to dominate a harem, often with 30 or more cows, and will defend it against rivals. After mating, the bulls go back to their independent life. The small herds join to form larger groups—sometimes to several thousand—as they prepare for their southward migration to wooded areas for the winter. Bulls join in this spring trek and usually travel behind the cows. Whole herds may cross lakes and estuaries.

In winter the caribou feed primarily on reindeer moss, a lichen, which is often buried under the snow that must be scraped away by pawing with the hooves. Reindeer moss may be a limiting factor in the abundance of caribou. In spring the herds move back to their grazing grounds.

Man's excessive burning of the winter ranges, overgrazing with introduced domesticated reindeer and the increased hunting efficiency of the Eskimos since they acquired sophisticated modern weapons are factors that have contributed to the reduction of caribou populations. In some areas the wild animals have been eliminated purposely in favor of the domesticated. More recently, the caribou have become victims of radioactive fallout. The reindeer moss accumulates radioactive substances that are passed on to animals and become concentrated in their bodies.

Female caribou produce a single calf after a gestation period of 8 months. Most of the calves are born in early June within a two-week period. Calves are able to walk well enough to follow their mother within only a few hours after birth. They are weaned in 2 months and become sexually mature in 16 months. Calves join the herd for the fall migration.

Marsh deer

Pampas deer

MARSH DEER *(Blastocerus dichotomus)*, maximum height 46 in. at the shoulders, is the largest South American deer. It is a wetland species, inhabiting marshes and lowlands along rivers, favoring particularly the papyrus belt, or *pantanal*. During the dry season, the populations concentrate in the remaining suitable wetlands; in the rainy season, they disperse.

Marsh deer are nocturnal, feeding on grass and aquatic vegetation. Females bear a single young after a gestation period of 9 months.

GUEMALS, or ANDEAN DEER *(Hippocamelus,* 2 species), are upland animals, summering on alpine pastures close to the treeline (13,000 to 14,000 feet), descending to lower elevations in winter. Guemals stand 34–39 in. tall at the shoulders and have two-pronged antlers and long coats. Mainly nocturnal, they normally associate in groups of about a half dozen.

PAMPAS DEER *(Ozotoceros bezoarcticus)*, maximum height 27 in. at the shoulders, is now confined mainly to central and southern Brazil because of eradication of the tall pampas grass over much of its original range. In Argentina it was the most abundant deer a century ago but is now rare. As with other South American deer, a further ecological disruption has been the introduction of the red and axis deer. Losses have occurred also due to anthrax and to foot-and-mouth diseases transmitted by domestic livestock. Pampas deer have a long breeding season extending over six months of the year. The female remains with her fawn, mostly in the long pampas grass.

Pampas deer

Marsh deer   *Guemals*

Red brocket

Pudu

PUDU *(Pudu,* 2 species) are forest dwellers like brockets. The Chilean pudu *(P. pudu),* the smallest of living deer, stands only 14 in. tall at the shoulders. Nocturnal and mostly solitary, pudus stay in hiding in dense forests (elevation to 12,000 feet) during the day. Pudus have survived intensive hunting partly because they do not break cover when they are pursued by dogs, but they can do so only as long as suitable habitat remains.

BROCKETS *(Mazama,* 4 species) are small deer, varying in height from 19 to 27 in. and living from sea level to 15,000 feet. Their antlers are small, unbranched spikes, rarely more than a few inches long. The fawns are spotted and white, like those of the whitetailed deer. One species *(M. americana)* has a reddish coat; the others are brownish.

Brockets frequent almost impenetrable thickets of subtropical and tropical forests. They are shy, staying in cover by day but moving afield at night to browse on leaves and twigs. When alarmed, they crash headlong through the undergrowth, showing the white underside of their tail. Fawns tame easily and can often be seen in Indian villages, where they are kept as pets.

In the Amazon Basin, brockets are particularly vulnerable to hunting during the annual flooding that maroons them on small islands of high land. Despite intensive hunting throughout their range for these solitary, elusive animals, brockets are not endangered. But they may not able to survive the destruction of their habitat, their greatest current threat.

■ *Pudu*   ■ *Brockets*

Giraffes

GIRAFFE AND OKAPI (FAMILY GIRAFFIDAE)

Two species comprise this family, distinguished by short, unbranched horns that are bony knobs covered with skin. Often there is also a median horn, and some giraffes have a second pair behind the first. Both have long necks consisting of seven vertebrae, the normal number of all mammals. The tongue is long and prehensile. Giraffes typically run by moving both legs on each side in unison.

GIRAFFES *(Giraffa camelopardalis)*, the tallest animals, have excited man's curiosity since antiquity. Bulls may stand 17–18 ft. tall, the females about 2 ft. shorter. Their long legs carry them at speeds up to 20 miles per hour and their height gives them a commanding view of the open savannas where they live.

Giraffes are browsers, feeding on leaves that are out of the reach of most other animals. With their thick, leatherly lips and prehensile tongue extending to 1½ ft. in length, they can pluck acacia leaves, their main food, from the thorny branches. Giraffes can go for long periods without water but will drink regularly when water is available. To bend down, they must spread their legs wide; in this position, they are most vulnerable to attackers.

A giraffe's first defense is running, but if forced to do so, it will fight, giving devastating blows with its front legs. When sparring or fighting among themselves, they swing their long necks and heads against one another.

Giraffes, whose sounds are limited to grunts or whistlelike cries, normally live in small units of cows, their dependent calves and sometimes a mature bull. Occasionally they assemble in herds of up to 70, although 12 to 15 is the norm.

Giraffes do not compete with domestic livestock (though they do damage

Okapis

wire fences), but this has not spared them from being heavily hunted. Tribes-
men use the thick hide for making tough leather and the tail tuft for fletching
arrows. Giraffes are themselves vulnerable to rinderpest, a periodically
epidemic disease transmitted by cattle. The more than half a dozen races of
giraffes have varied color patterns. The most common are the reticulated,
baringo, Nubian and Masai. Females give birth to a single calf after a gestation
period of 14–15 months. The calf is weaned in 6 months but accompanies its
mother for about a year. It becomes sexually mature at 3–4 years.

OKAPIS *(Okapia johnstoni)* were not known to science until 1901, although
the African pygmy tribes have hunted them for centuries. Only the males have
horns, and the animals are much shorter than giraffes, standing only about 5 ft.
tall at the shoulders. The okapi bears a strong resemblance to the extinct
short-necked giraffe that lived 10 million years ago in Europe and Asia.

Okapis live in the dense equatorial forests of Zaire. They are nocturnal and
solitary, spending the day in the seclusion of thick cover and browsing on leaves
and fruit at night. Little is known about the behavior of these animals as it is
extremely difficult to observe them in the wild. They can hear hunters approach-
ing and quietly disappear into the forest. The okapi's camouflage pattern blends
so perfectly with its background that it becomes virtually invisible when standing still. They feed on young shoots and leaves, using their tongue to pluck them
from the trees like giraffes. Okapis have been kept and bred in zoos but are
prone to parasitic infections. The single young is born after 15 months gestation
and looks like an adult in miniature.

Pronghorns

PRONGHORN (FAMILY ANTILOCAPRIDAE)

The only living representative of this exclusively North American family is the pronghorn (*Antilocapra americana*). Its antlers consist of bony core encased in a horny sheath that is shed every year.

The pronghorn is the fastest North American mammal. It has been clocked at 60 miles per hour. Its original population, estimated at 30–40 million, was exceeded only by the bison. Bison are grazers, pronghorns browsers. The two did not compete for food, and as both species are nomadic throughout the summer, pastures were not overgrazed.

Settlement and development of the Great Plains, including the erection of fences which the pronghorn was not able to jump, combined with excessive hunting, reduced the pronghorn population drastically—to 30,000 by the 1920s. The remnant population, driven into the less suitable sagebrush country, has since built up again to about 400,000. The greatest threat now is large-scale eradication of sagebrush through the use of herbicidal sprays.

Pronghorns live in unsegregated herds during most of the year. Bucks fight for and assemble harems of 5–15 females during the 2- to 3-week mating season. Afterward, the horns are shed, and the harems amalgamate into herds of hundreds of animals. Females typically give birth to twins, the gestation period lasting 8 months. As soon as they are strong enough, the fawns join their mothers. A four-day-old fawn can outrun a man. Does mature in 16 months, bucks at 24 months.

Sitatunga

Nyala

ANTELOPES, WILD CATTLE, SHEEP AND GOATS (FAMILY BOVIDAE)

All the males in this diverse family have horns, as do the females of some species and also some domestic breeds. Hollow, unbranched and never shed, the horns are added to every year. They are attached to the skull on bony bases. Members of the family lack upper incisor and canine teeth.

NYALA *(Tragelaphus angasi)*, as much as 42 in. tall at the shoulders, is a browsing antelope almost always found near water. The male's horns may measure 2½ ft. long on the curve. The smaller, hornless female is rufous with white stripes and lacks the shaggy fringe of hair that distinguishes the blue-black male. A single young is born after a gestation period of 7½–8 months. Basically diurnal, nyalas become nocturnal if disturbed. Nyalas are considered to be among the most attractive of the antelopes.

SITATUNGA *(T. spekei)*, 36–40 in. tall, also goes by the name of marsh buck because its exclusive habitat is marshes and swamps. It is said to elude pursuers by submerging and leaving only its nostrils still above the surface. The males are dark brown or grayish; the females, which lack horns, are reddish. Both may have white stripes on the body, or they may be lacking. In both the hooves are greatly lengthened, giving the animals more support in the soft ground.

MOUNTAIN NYALA *(T. buxtoni)*, maximum height 50 in., lives at elevations of 9,000 feet or higher. It is more closely related to kudus than to sitatungas and is the rarest of the three species.

■ *Sitatunga*　　■ *Mountain nyala*　　■ *Nyala*

242

Lesser kudu pair

Greater kudu

KUDUS are handsome antelopes, the greater kudu (*Tragelaphus strepsiceros*) standing 53 in. tall at the shoulders and the lesser kudu (*T. imberbis*) reaching 40 in. tall. Males have spiraled horns; the females are hornless. The greater kudu's horns may be 5 ft. long, the lesser kudu's about 3 ft.

The greater kudu inhabits bush country and open woodlands. It appears able to get by on water from succulent plants, but where possible it stays close to a good source of water. The lesser kudu inhabits the *nyika*—the dry thornbush country of eastern Africa.

Both species typically stay in dense cover during the day, feeding mainly in twilight hours. They are basically browers but sometimes graze. Most of the year their social organization consists of several cows and their calves, usually about half a dozen animals. Bulls live alone or in small bachelor herds. During the mating season, males join females in herds of 20–30 animals but leave when the calves are born. Cows bear a single calf following a gestation period of 7 months.

Both species are highly susceptible to rinderpest disease, and during outbreaks their populations are greatly reduced.

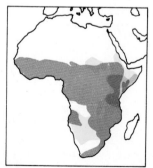

BUSHBUCK *(T. scriptus)*, maximum height to 33 in., varies in color with locality and with the age of the animals. Probably the most widely distributed of the spiral-horned antelopes, it occurs wherever there are forests for protective cover—from lowlands to 10,000 feet. Secretive, solitary and essentially nocturnal, it spends the day in dense undergrowth. The alarm call is a hoarse bark.

■ Bushbuck

□ Greater kudu   ▨ Lesser kudu

Bongo

Bushbuck

BONGO *(Boocercus eurycerus)* is one of the least known of the large African antelopes. Standing up to 50 in. tall, the bongo inhabits the equatorial rain forest, where it browses on foliage and shoots. Both sexes have large spiral horns that can be used to dig up tubers or probe deep in the mineral-rich soils of natural salt licks. In East Africa the bongo is found in several isolated mountain areas, living principally in bamboo forests near the treeline. Sometimes it descends to lower elevations, or it may move onto alpine meadows above 10,000 feet. It rarely leaves the forest. It has a remarkable ability to fade swiftly out of sight in the forest at the first hint of danger. It browses mainly at dawn and dusk, resting and ruminating during the hottest hours of the day.

From what is known about the bongo's social organization, it appears that the cows and their dependent young live together. A single calf is born in December after 9½ months' gestation and is also striped like the adult but with a lighter buff coat. They sometimes assemble in small herds of several dozen animals. Mature bulls are solitary except during the mating season. Bongos enjoy wallowing in the mud and then rubbing their flanks and horns against tree trunks.

In the Mau Forest the population of bongos is controlled naturally by setyot *(Mimulopsis solmsii)*, a forest vine that flowers only once every seven years. The vine is a favorite food of the bongo, but two-year-old vines are highly toxic, killing large numbers of bongos (also giant forest hogs). This governs the rhythmic rise and crash of bongo populations.

Bongos are seldom seen in zoos. Their shy, retiring nature makes them difficult to keep, although several zoos have recently managed to maintain and breed them successfully.

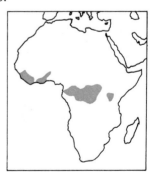

Nilgai female (left) and male

NILGAI *(Boselaphus tragocamelus)* is the largest Asiatic antelope, the males reaching a height of 56 in. at the shoulders. It lives in woodlands and open savannas, where it is mainly a browser but may also graze. During the hottest part of the day, it rests in the shade, feeding in the cooler hours of morning, evening and night. It can subsist for rather long periods without water.

Cows and calves form herds of a dozen or so animals, the bulls living alone or in small bachelor herds. The mating season starts in March so that the young are born after the rainy season in December. Only the bulls have horns, which are small. This has spared the nilgai from being sought as a sporting trophy. Also, the Hindus give it protection for religious reasons because of its resemblance to the sacred cow. These tolerances are changing, however. In one area, a bounty is now offered to reduce the number of nilgai where they are competing with domestic livestock and are also destroying crops.

FOUR-HORNED ANTELOPE, or CHOUSINGHA *(Tetracerus quadricornis)*, maximum height 25 in. at the shoulders, is distinguished by the male's two pairs of horns (the front pair is small). The female is hornless. The four-horned antelope's range is similar to the nilgai's, and it also inhabits woodlands and savannas. The usual twin set of horns have made the chousingha a coveted hunter's trophy.

It is solitary and shy, dashing into the undergrowth when alarmed. It drinks regularly, hence is seldom far from water. Mating occurs during the monsoon; up to three young are born 6 months later. In Asia, it occupies much the same niche as the duikers do in Africa.

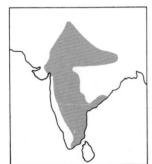

■ *Nilgai*

Cape elands

ELANDS *(Taurotragus,* 2 species) are the largest and most cowlike of the antelopes. Both the Derby or giant eland *(T. derbianus)* and the Cape or common eland *(T. oryx)* stand about 70 in. tall at the shoulders. The giant eland is so named because of its longer, heavier horns, present in both sexes. Both species live in open savannas and bush country and from near-desert lands to alpine meadows. They are basically browsers.

Eland herds are composed of about two dozen females and their calves plus one or two bulls. Other bulls live apart except at the mating season. The herds are constantly on the move, sometimes amalgamating in large numbers for migration to more favorable feeding grounds. Despite their large size, elands have great stamina and can maintain a steady trot for long distances. From a standing start, they can clear 6-foot fences.

Elands are more susceptible to rinderpest than are any other antelopes. Heavy losses from this disease as well as from excessive hunting have greatly depleted their numbers. The giant eland is now scarce throughout its range, and the common eland has largely disappeared from southern Africa except where it is protected in parks and reserves.

Elands are valued locally for their meat, milk and hides. Amenable to semidomestication, they can thrive on marginal pastures and are less dependent on water than are cattle.

Females produce a single calf after a 9-month gestation period. Females become sexually mature in 2 years, males in 3 years.

■ *Cape eland*
□ *Giant eland*

American bison

AMERICAN BISON *(Bison bison)*, the largest land mammal in America, is distinguished by its prominent hump and forequarters, accentuated by the thick, almost black hair covering the head, chin, neck and chest. Bulls stand 5 ft. tall at the shoulder and may weigh 2,000 lbs.; females are smaller. Both sexes are horned.

Bison, or buffaloes, were once the most abundant large mammal in North America. The total population, numbering about 50 million, was concentrated in the Great Plains, though bison ranged over most of the area east of the Rockies. By the 1880s, the great herds had been destroyed by market hunters. Only about

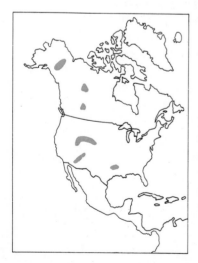

550 animals remained. Under protection, the population has built up to about 25,000. Bison are grazing animals, adapted to life on the open prairie. Originally they were nomadic, moving south in winter and north in spring.

The herds are now decentralized to avoid epidemics and to keep breeding populations in well-separated locations.

Females breed when about 3 years old, males at age 5. During the breeding season, from July to September, the bulls leave their all-male herds and join the cows. Calves are born in May and June, after a gestation period of 9–9½ months. Typically only a single calf is born, and it remains with its mother until it is sexually mature. The hump is already visible two months after birth, and the reddish coat begins to darken to a deep brown. Bison may live up to 20 years in captivity.

European bison bull and calf

WISENT, or EUROPEAN BISON *(Bison bonasus)* is taller (maximum height 6 ft. at the shoulder and longer-legged than the American bison. The hump and forequarters are less massive, the hindquarters comparatively better developed. The smaller head is carried higher; the mane is lighter, the horns shorter, less curved and more slender. The wisent is more wary than the American bison.

The wisent's original range coincided with the deciduous forests of Europe, and it declined in numbers as the forests were cut. By 1900, free-living herds were found only in the Caucasus and in the Bialowieza Forest in Poland.

Both herds were destroyed during World War I. Only the few animals in European zoos and on private preserves survived. From these, two males and three females were selected to reestablish the Bialowieza herd. Only 46 of these animals survived World War II, after which five breeding centers were established. Since 1952, wisent from these centers have been released to free-ranging conditions in Bialowieza Forest and have also been reintroduced to the Caucasus, where they are protected in several national parks.

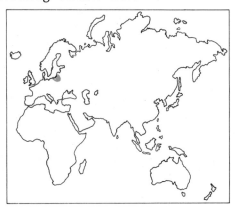

The wisent is a browser rather than a grazer. It eats the leaves, shoots and bark of some trees and shrubs, but when they are available, it feeds only on acorns. Less gregarious than the American bison, wisent herds rarely contain more than 20 or 30 animals.

African buffalo   *Red buffalo*

AFRICAN, or CAPE, BUFFALO *(Syncerus caffer)* are large wild cattle, the only members of the family living in Africa. The bulls may reach a height of 60 in. at the shoulders and weigh more than 1,800 lbs. Their horns span 5 ft. and form a thick boss over the forehead.

The African buffalo occurs in a number of races, usually inhabiting grasslands and open savannas but sometimes ranging onto coastal plains or high in the mountains. It avoids arid country, always living near a source of water used both for drinking and for wallowing (to escape the hordes of insects). One race, the red, or forest, buffalo (*S. caffer nanus*), occurs only in equatorial rain forests. It is small—standing no more than 3½ ft. tall at the shoulders and rarely weighing more than 600 lbs.

African buffalo are principally grazers but may sometimes browse. They feed at night and early morning, staying in dense cover chewing their cuds during the day. They can live in herds of several hundred to a thousand or more animals. During the dry season they stay near rivers or other permanent sources of water.

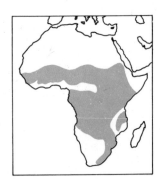

When the rains come and water is plentiful in temporary pools and streams, the herds become nomadic as the animals go in search of fresh pastures.

Though they are bold and courageous—African buffaloes are the most dangerous animals when injured or provoked to anger—they are not normally aggressive. In the mating season the bulls assemble small harems, driving the younger bulls away. Mating occurs in January, the cow bearing a single calf after a gestation period of 11 months. The average life span is 17–20 years.

■ *African buffalo*

Asiatic buffalo

African buffalo are highly susceptible to rinderpest disease transmitted to them by domestic cattle. During the epidemic outbreak in the 1890s, they were nearly annihilated. Because they are not compatible with intensive farming, large numbers have also been killed wherever the land has been settled for agricultural use.

ASIATIC BUFFALO, or WATER BUFFALO, or ARNA *(Bubalus bubalis),* reaches a height of 64 in. at the shoulders, and the bull's broad backswept horns may measure as much as 77 in. along the curve. It inhabits seasonally flooded grasslands and floodplains but is now rare in the wild. The total population is estimated at about 2,000, occurring mostly in the Brahmaputra Valley (Assam) but a few in the lower reaches of the Gadvari River (India) and the Saptkosi River (Nepal). It has been widely domesticated and used principally as a draft animal. The domesticated Asiatic buffalo may have pink, gray, black or white coloration, with white spots on the throat, limbs and chin; in the wild they are black.

Like the African buffalo, it is gregarious. In the wild it may breed throughout the year, but a breeding peak occurs at different times, depending on the area. In Asia most young are born in the fall after a gestation period of 310 days.

The rare TAMARAU *(Bubalus mindorensis)*, 39 in. tall at the shoulders, lives only in the swamps of the mountainous Mindoro island in the Philippines.

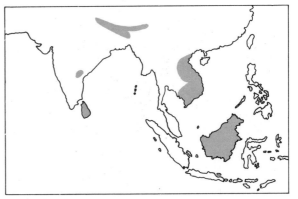

■ *Asiatic buffalo*

Gaur

Lowland anoa

GAUR *(Bos gaurus)*, maximum height 76 in. at the shoulders, has a distinctive hump. It lives in small herds of cows, calves and one or two bulls. Other bulls live alone or in bachelor herds. A forest dweller, both grazing and browsing, the gaur lives in the foothills of the Himalayas, peninsular India across to Malaysia. Gaur survive today in scattered remnant populations due to loss of habitat, hunting and diseases contracted from domestic cattle. Females bear a single calf; the gestation period is 9 months. The smaller gayal *(B. frontalis)* is believed to be a domestic version of the gaur.

The very rare BANTENG *(B. banteng)*, maximum height 69 in., has a white rump patch. It is now found only in the plains and lowlands of Thailand and Burma, migrating to higher land during the monsoons. The kouprey *(B. sauveli)*, maximum height 75 in., is also endangered. Fewer than 70 koupreys are believed to exist now—in eastern Cambodia and western Vietnam.

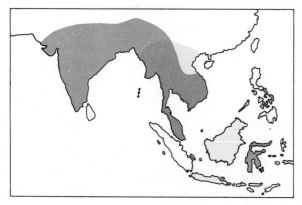

Asiatic dwarf cattle are more solitary than the larger species, and all three species are rare, due to deforestation, the draining of lowlands and uncontrolled hunting.

The LOWLAND ANOA *(Bubalus depressicornis)*, maximum shoulder height 34 in., and the mountain anoa *(B. quarlesi)*, maximum 28 in., are found only in the Celebes. The mountain anoa inhabits wetland forests.

■ *Gaur*

■ *Anoa* ■ *Banteng*

Yak.

Banteng

YAK *(Bos grunniens)*, largest of the wild cattle, occurs also as a domesticated animal in a smaller and sometimes hornless form that is widely used as a beast of burden in Tibet and neighboring regions.

The stockily built males stand more than 6 ft. tall at the shoulder and may weigh 2,000 lbs. A male's massive horns, each measuring more than 3 ft. on the outer curve, continue to turn more inward as the animal matures. Females are smaller.

Wild yaks live traditionally at 15,000 to 20,000 feet on the Tibetan plateau, their shaggy coats and thick underfur enabling them to endure the subzero weather. These immensely powerful animals are twice as large as domestic cattle. They avoid contact with man and remain in inaccessible passes and valleys.

Mature bulls live alone or in groups of 3–5, while younger bulls reside in bachelor herds of 10–12. Females and calves may form herds of 1,000 or more as they concentrate at feeding areas. If danger threatens, they form a phalanx with the calves in the center.

Wild yaks feed in the morning and evening, resting and chewing their cuds during the day. In summer, herds are nomadic as they search for young grass. Their abundant dung on their permanent wintering grounds is used by the Tibetans as fuel in this treeless land.

Yaks mate in September. Females bear a single calf after a gestation period of 9 months. Uncontrolled hunting has reduced the wild yak to virtual extinction. No wild yaks have been reported recently, but small populations may exist in the area shown at right.

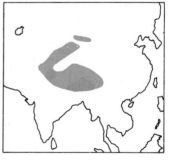

■ *Domestic yak*   ■ *Wild yak*

Gray duiker   *Yellow-backed duiker*

DUIKERS are small, mainly forest-dwelling antelopes confined to Central and South Africa. They live singly or in pairs, less commonly in larger groups. Most species are nocturnal. They are principally browsers but may occasionally graze. Their diet includes a high proportion of fruit and seeds, sometimes supplemented with insects or other small animals.

Duikers are timid, furtive animals whose small size enables them to move through the undergrowth without being seen. For protection they may hide in addition to fleeing as do other antelopes. Their name in Dutch means "diver," referring to the speed with which they crash through underbrush. Their secretiveness also explains why so little is known about their habits. They establish definite territories, however, and travel along the same trails, where they are rather easily snared. It is surprising that, despite constant persecution, some species persist in large numbers even in intensively developed areas.

Females usually give birth to a single young after a gestation period of 4 months. Duikers reach maturity in three years.

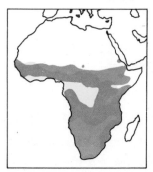

The gray duiker (*Sylvicapra grimmia*), maximum length 25 in., is the only duiker that lives in open savannas—from lowland subdeserts to the snow line in alpine meadows. It lives at higher elevations than any other hoofed mammal in Africa. Long-legged compared to other duikers, it runs on an erratic course from bush to bush when flushed. Both sexes have spikelike horns up to 6 in. long, and both have a tuft of hair on the forehead.

■ *Bush duikers* (Sylvicapra)

Forest duikers (Cephalophus)

Bay duiker   *Blue duiker*

The red duiker (*Cephalophus natalensis*), maximum length 20 in., inhabits rain forests, bush country and forest strips flanking rivers. It is the most widespread of the species.

The blue duiker (*C. monticola*), maximum length 13 in., is the smallest of the duikers. It ranges from arid to humid zones, from lowlands to highlands and from forest interiors to their fringes. Maxwell's duiker (*C. maxwelli*) is slightly larger. When alarmed, it stands still and gives a shrill whistle before dashing off through the forest.

The yellow-backed duiker (*C. silvicultor*), maximum length 31 in., is the largest duiker. It lives in the most dense parts of the equatorial rain forests of West Africa, mainly at low and medium elevations. In Kenya, it ranges into the bamboo forests at high elevations.

The black duiker (*C. niger*), maximum length 20 in., and the smaller red-flanked duiker (*C. rufilatus*), maximum 14 in., live at the forest edge and in bushy thickets from Senegal to Uganda.

Jentink's duiker (*C. jentinki*), maximum length 30. in., favors marshes and lowlands, as does also the banded duiker (*C. zebra*), maximum 18 in., of the same region. Both are limited to the Ivory Coast, Sierra Leone and Liberia and are rare, not only as a result of excessive hunting but also because of the destruction of their forest habitat. They are seldom seen in captivity.

The black-fronted duiker (*C. nigrifrons*) shows a preference for marshy country but may be found in thick mountain forests. Its broad hooves are particularly suited for walking on soft ground.

Abbott's duiker *(C. spadix).*, maximum length 26 in., has a red crest and lives up to 12,000 feet in dense mountain forests such as that on Mount Kilimanjaro.

254

Red lechwe

Waterbuck

RED LECHWE *(Kobus leche)*, maximum length 40 in., and a subspecies, the black lechwe (*K. leche smithemani*), found only around Lake Bangweulu in Zambia, are greatly reduced in numbers due mainly to hunting—both the large-scale drives (chilas) of canoe-borne native spearmen and the commercialized hunts that supplied meat to copper miners. Literally hundreds of thousands of black lechwes have been reduced to about 15,000. There are even fewer red lechwes—probably no more than 1,500, surviving principally in national parks.

Lechwes live in swamps and on the flood plains, spending much of their day in the shallow water. They are strong swimmers and commonly take refuge in the water if they are hard-pressed. With their long and narrow hooves, a special adaptation to their marshland habitat, they can bound through the swamps with amazing speed. When the seasonal floods come, the lechwes move to the peripheral grasslands but return to the richer lowlands as soon as the waters recede.

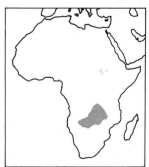

Highly gregarious, the lechwes live in large herds of both sexes during the breeding season. They separate at other times of the year. At 7 years of age, males establish year-round territories that they maintain for at least 2 years until younger males drive them out.

The Nile lechwe (*K. megaceros*), maximum length 40 in., is distinguished by its white shoulder patch. It lives in the wetlands along the Upper Nile. At present, its population is not as endangered as are those of central Africa.

■ *Lechwes*　□ *Nile lechwe*

Kobs displaying

WATERBUCK *(K. ellipsiprymnus)*, maximum length 48 in., from the eastern coasts, and the defassa waterbuck, or sing-sing *(K. defassa)*, maximum 53 in., live in the savannas, usually near water, in which they take refuge. The two species interbreed where their ranges overlap and show intermediate variations in color patterns. They are diurnal, foraging in grasslands during the day and sleeping in nearby thickets at night. Males have crescent-shaped horns with the sharp curve of kob horns.

Males establish well-defined territories and defend them vigorously. Females and their young form herds of about two dozen that are loosely associated with specific male's territory.

KOB *(K. kob)*, maximum height 36 in., and the closely related puku *(K. vardoni)*, maximum 35 in., live in open grasslands adjacent to swamps and rivers. They may enter the water during the heat of the day, but when alarmed they seek dry cover.

Kob males establish small territories within a special breeding ground. Females in heat wander from one territory to another. Each male displays and mates with the females as they pass through his territory. The strongest males have territories in the middle, while the younger males remain on the periphery. If the male leaves his ground to drink, another may usurp his area, but usually they merely display to one another along the boundary. Pukus have larger territories than kobs and do not defend them as rigidly.

 Kobs   Puku

Waterbuck   Defassa waterbuck

Bohor reedbuck   Common reedbuck

REEDBUCKS are medium-sized antelopes that are related to waterbucks. Males have curved horns, the tips faced forward; females are hornless. All reedbucks have a prominent bare glandular patch below each ear.

The common reedbuck (*Redunca arundinum*), maximum length 36 in., inhabits grasslands and savannas, never far from water. It is usually found singly or in pairs, occasionally in larger groups. When alarmed, it gives a short whistle and then runs, always staying with its group. This species is less wary than other reedbucks. Rather than run far, it pauses to look back at the source of alarm. Reedbucks may wade in the shallows to destroy their scent before usually seeking cover in the brush. Females normally give birth to a single young after a gestation period of 7½ months.

The bohor reedbuck (*R. redunca*), maximum length 31 in., inhabits wetlands. It lives in small harem groups consisting of a male and three or four females. Young males form bachelor herds. When alarmed, the group "freezes" in the grass, scattering in different directions if discovered.

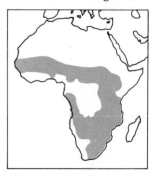

The mountain reedbuck (*R. fulvorufula*), maximum length 31 in., lives in grasslands and bush country in mountains. Herds of a dozen or more are common. Like the bohor, it will "freeze" as a defense when approached.

The Vaal rhebok (*Pelea capreolus*), maximum length 32 in., has a more woolly coat, almost straight horns and no naked glandular patch as in the reedbuck. It is also more wary. It lives in upland rocky outcroppings (*kopjes*) and meadows. During the mating season, males are particularly intolerant and pugnacious and are quick to attack intruders.

Sable antelope   Roan antelope

ROAN ANTELOPE *(Hippotragus equinus)*, maximum shoulder height 60 in., favors bush country and is usually found either alone or in pairs, sometimes in herds of a dozen or more. It is closely related but larger than the oryx. Females bear a single calf after a gestation period of 9 months. Older males may join herds of wildebeests, zebras or other grazers; young males generally form bachelor herds. Roans are courageous and will attack when pressed. Disease (principally rinderpest), excessive hunting and agricultural development have depleted their numbers. Roans have a higher mane and a longer neck fringe than sable antelope; their ears are usually tufted at the tips. Roan and sable antelope differ in behavior: When alarmed, a roan herd will run single file, whereas sable gallop off as a group.

■ Roan antelope

SABLE ANTELOPE *(H. niger)*, maximum shoulder height 56 in., has larger horns—as long as 64 in. in a subspecies that inhabits Angola (the roan's horns rarely exceed 38 in.). The sable antelope prefers woodland savannas, with thickets for resting and hiding and grasslands for grazing. It generally lives in groups of 8–40 males, their young and a dominant bull; but some herds are larger. Bulls fight fiercely to protect their harem during the rutting season. Calves are born from May to July. Old bulls become solitary after they are ousted by rivals.

Sable and roan antelopes may inhabit the same area, but they do not intermingle except at the waterholes. Sables are now very rare. One species, the blue-buck *(H. leucophaeus)* of South Africa, was exterminated in 1799, 33 years after its discovery.

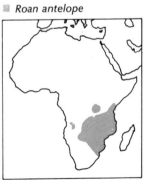

■ Sable antelope

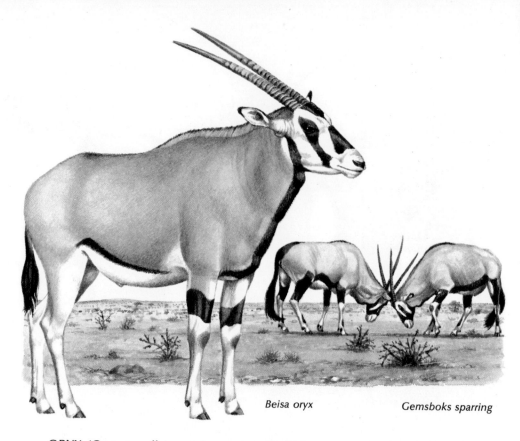

Beisa oryx   *Gemsboks sparring*

ORYX *(Oryx gazella)*, maximum length 48 in., occurs in three distinct sub-species: beisa *(O.g. beisa)*, to the north of the Tana River in Kenya; the fringe-eared *(O.g. callotis)*, to the south; and the gemsbok *(O.g. gazella)*, in South-West Africa. The Arabian oryx *(O. leucoryx)*, maximum length 40 in., has been reduced to a small population found in southern Arabian deserts, and the scimitar-horned or white oryx *(O. tao)*, maximum length 47 in., is found only in the southern Sahara. Its horns are curved rather than shaped like rapiers.

Oryxes normally live in small herds of 6–20 consisting of females, young and a dominant male. They sometimes form larger groups. Herds of a thousand or more scimitar-horned oryx were once reported but probably no longer exist. Oryxes are grazers but may browse when no grass is available. Keen-sighted and intensely wary, they live on dry, open, shrub-covered plains or sometimes in thornbush country. In drier regions they are often nomadic, traveling long distances to find pasturage. They drink water when available but can go for long periods without it, satisfying their water needs from succulent plants, roots and tubers. They feed mainly in the cooler morning and early evening hours and sometimes at night. During the heat of the day, they rest in the shade. Sometimes they dig shallow depressions in the sand to cool off.

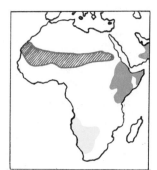

Oryx bulls fight during the rutting season, carefully placing their long sharp horns and thrusting with their forehead. A bull may also spar with a female in mock courtship battles. The female runs away, pursued by the male, stops and repeatedly locks horns with him until she is ready to mate.

Females normally give birth to a single young, but twins are not uncommon. The gestation period is 9–10 months.

Beisa oryx
Gemsbok
Arabian oryx   /// Scimitar-horned oryx

Scimitar-horned oryx

Addax

ADDAX *(Addax nasomaculatus)*, maximum length 42 in., is distinguished by its prominent black forehead tuft and by its broad, flat hooves that are special adaptations for travel in sand. The ringed, spiraled horns of the addax may measure more than 40 in. long on the curve. Both sexes are horned. Like the oryxes, they will charge if provoked, using their horns as formidable weapons.

The range of the addax overlaps that of the scimitar-horned oryx; but whereas the scimitar-horned oryx lives along desert margins, the addax is a true desert dweller, inhabiting the most arid parts of the Sahara. It is the antelope that has best adapted to desert conditions, even more so than the Arabian oryx. Like the oryx, it normally lives in small herds of a dozen or more females and juveniles with a dominant male. Addax are said to be constantly on the move in their search for grazing areas. Like the oryx, the addax does not need to drink at regular intervals. It derives moisture from succulent plants and tubers.

Both the addax and the scimitar-horned oryx have long been hunted by the desert nomads. Primitive weapons limited the number that could be killed, but modern firearms have increased the lethal capacity beyond a level the species can sustain. More heavily built than other oryx, the addax cannot run as fast or as long and is more easily overtaken by hunters on camels or in cars. When exhausted, the addax will turn and lunge with lowered horns.

The addax was once found over most of the Sahara but is now restricted to the southern parts—northern Chad, Niger and the Mauritania–Mali frontier. The remoteness and inaccessibility of their habitat that were protections in the past have been eliminated, principally as a result of oil prospecting that has opened up large areas of the desert to settlement and to motorized travel. Less than 3,000 addax remain in the wild.

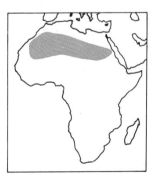

Blesbok   *Bubal*

HARTEBEESTS *(Alcelaphus)* and TOPIS *(Damaliscus)* have a conspicuously sloping back, accentuated by the narrow face and lyre-shaped horns (present in both sexes). They are among the most abundant and widespread African antelopes, inhabiting grasslands and bush country, sometimes savanna woodlands. They are normally sedentary but may form nomadic herds in the dry season, commonly associating with zebras, wildebeests and others.

There are two species: bubal or common hartebeest (*A. buselaphus*), maximum length 46 in., and Lichtenstein's hartebeest (*A. lichtensteini*), maximum 49 in. All live in small herds of about a dozen females, juveniles and a single male. Old bulls are usually solitary; young bulls form bachelor herds. Males establish and guard territories during the breeding season, often sparring but seldom doing serious battle. Females give birth to a single calf after a gestation period of 8–9 months.

Closely related is the swift topi, or sassaby (*Damaliscus lunatus*), maximum length 48 in., which is said to be the fastest antelope. Two relatives are the

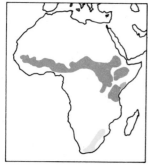

Hunter's antelope (*D. hunteri*), maximum length 40 in., and the rarer bontebok (*D. dorcas*), maximum 40 in., of which the blesbok (*D. dorcas albifrons*) is an upland race.

Hartebeests were a prime source of meat for the early African settlers. In some areas where they are protected their numbers have increased—the bontebok, for example, from 17 in 1931 to 900 in 1970. The blesbok has been so successfully managed in South Africa that domestication programs are under way.

■ *Bubal*
■ *Lichtenstein's hartebeest*   ■ *Hunter's antelope*

Topis

Brindled gnu

WILDEBEESTS, or GNUS *(Connochaetes)*, resemble hartebeests in having heavy forequarters. Sickle-shaped horns are present in both sexes.

The blue wildebeest, or brindled gnu (*C. taurinus*), maximum length 56 in., lives in the grasslands and is one of the most common animals of the plains. It generally associates with other plains animals, particularly zebras. Strictly a grazer, it favors succulent grasses; and because it needs to drink regularly, it is seldom far from water. In the rainy season the herds disperse over the plains. In the dry season herds come together, up to 500,000 animals on the Serengeti Plains, and move almost constantly in search of pastures. The sound of their mooing, a monotonous sound, is one of the most familar of the Serengeti Plains.

Males establish temporary territories during the mating season and assemble harems consisting of a few to as many as a hundred females. When they spar, they may drop to their knees like hartebeests. Violence is not excessive. After a few days, harems are reabsorbed by the larger herd.

A single calf is normal, born after 8–9 months' gestation. The calf is able to follow the mother within a few minutes after birth and stays with her until another calf is born. Heavily preyed upon by lions, hyenas and hunting dogs, only about 20 percent of the calves live to maturity.

The black wildebeest, or white-tailed gnu (*C. gnou*), maximum height 48 in. at the shoulder, occurs only in South Africa, where it was almost exterminated about a century ago as a result of excessive hunting for its meat and hides. Small herds were protected by land-owners, and the population has now risen to about 3,000.

■ *Brindled gnu*
  White-tailed gnu

Klipspringer   *Oribi*

SMALLER ANTELOPES of several species occur south of the Sahara.

KLIPSPRINGER (*Oreotragus oreotragus*), maximum length 20 in., lives among the rocky outcroppings *(kopjes)* scattered over the savannas. It feeds near their bases, rests near their summits. Leaves and grass are its principal food. If no bush is available, it will eat rock plants, succulents above all. Special hoof pads

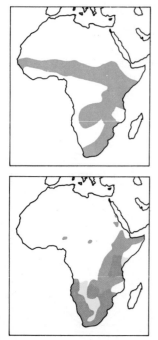

aid it in climbing the smooth rocks with the nimbleness of a mountain goat. It is said to stand nearly always on a tip of rock with all four feet close together in a delicate balance. Largely independent of water, the klipspringer travels in pairs of small groups.

BEIRA (*Dorcatragus megalotis*), maximum length 29 in., is often mistaken for the klipspringer but occupies even drier country in Somalia and adjacent parts of Ethiopia. It can apparently subsist without regular access to water. It associates in groups of about half a dozen, each group establishing a territory on a particular hill.

ORIBI (*Ourebia ourebi*), maximum length 27 in., is a grasslands species found from the lowlands to 9,000 feet. The male has short, pointed horns, but both sexes have dark glandular patches below the ear. The oribi rests in tall grass. When running, it may leap into the air to soar over the grass. It is known also for "stotting"—leaping with its legs stiff, a trait it shares with deer and other small antelopes.

Top map: ■ *Oribi*

Bottom map: ■ *Steinbok* ■ *Klipspringer*

Phillips' dik-dik

Kirk's dik-dik

Suni

Royal antelope

STEINBOK *(Raphicerus campestris)*, maximum length 20 in., and the closely related grysbok *(R. melanotis)* and Sharpe's grysbok *(R. sharpei)* are grazers. They are the same size as klipspringers. Steinboks lie flat on the ground until danger has passed and do not break cover until the last moment. They persist in developed areas despite heavy hunting.

SUNI *(Neotragus moschatus)*, maximum length 14 in., gives off a strong musky odor from facial glands. Primarily a browser, it lives in dry bush country or in thickets along rivers. Sunis have smaller horns than steinbok.

The royal antelope *(N. pygmaeus)*, maximum length 11 in., is the smallest antelope. Bates's dwarf antelope *(N. batesi)* stands only 12 in. tall. Both are nocturnal and live in lowland primary forests.

DIK-DIKS *(Madoqua,* 7 species), maximum length 12 in., live in arid bush country, frequenting the scattered thickets. Primarily browsers, they exist largely without water and are usually seen alone or in pairs. Pairs maintain territories and use well-defined paths like duikers. They have elongated and mobile snouts. When alarmed, dik-diks erect the tuft on their forehead and dash off in a zigzag pattern, giving a loud chirping call.

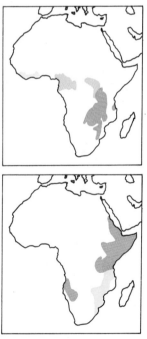

Top map: ■ *Sharpe's grysbok* ■ *Royal antelope* ■ *Bates's dwarf antelope*
Bottom map: ■ *Dik-diks* ■ *Suni*

Blackbuck: buck (left) and does

BLACKBUCK *(Antilope cervicapra)*, maximum length 33 in., is noted for the male's slender, spiraled horns that may be more than 27 in. long. Inhabiting both grasslands and open woodlands, the blackbuck is very alert and fast. It is active during the day, and for most of the year it lives in small herds of about two dozen. Males assemble temporary harems in the mating season and chase other bucks away. Young bucks and does have a brown pelage, while adult males are glossy black.

During the dry season, herds of 10,000 or more used to assemble, but the blackbuck, once the most abundant antelope in India and Pakistan, has now become rare. Oddly, it is now more abundant in Texas and in Argentina, where it has been introduced. Females give birth to one or two young after 6 months' gestation. Fawns remain concealed in grass until they join the herd.

IMPALA *(Aepyceros melampus)*, maximum length 38 in., is one of the most graceful antelopes in form and movement. When alarmed, it makes spectacular leaps—sometimes more than 30 feet horizontally or 9 feet vertically. The male's lyrate horns may be 2½ ft. long.

The impala is mainly a browser and lives in savanna and open woodlands. Its local distribution is governed largely by the availability of water.

Impala are gregarious. During the rut males have a harem, usually 15–20, sometimes 100 females, and will fight fiercely with other males. Females produce a single fawn after 6½–7 months' gestation.

Impala are often accompanied by troops of baboons, both benefiting from the mutual protection. Impala are not endangered except for the Angolan black-faced impala *(A. m. petersi)*, smaller subspecies found only near the Kunene River in South-West Africa.

Impala

Gerenuks

GERENUK *(Litocranius walleri)*, maximum length 40 in., inhabits arid thornbush country and can go for long periods without drinking. Males have semilyrate horns. A browser, it uses its long tongue and mobile lips to pluck leaves, much as giraffes do. Like the dibatag, the gerenuk often stands on its hind legs and reaches up with its front legs to pull branches within reach. When standing, it can form a straight vertical line with its hind legs, back and neck.

The gerenuk is diurnal and usually is seen alone, in family units of two or three or less commonly in harems of half a dozen animals and a single male. The very shy gerenuk will move away from a disturbance, running with its head low in a crouched position. This helps it pass under the low branches of the thornbush. Though not described by scientists until the late 1800s, it was pictured in Egyptian paintings in 5600 B.C. Natives refuse to eat gerenuks because they believe this would bring bad luck to their camels.

DIBATAG *(Ammodorcas clarkei)*, maximum length 35 in., resembles the gerenuk, but its horns curve forward like a reedbuck's. It lives in pairs or small groups in fairly dry country in East Africa, feeding on the grass of the plains and especially favoring the flower and leaves of acacia and the leaves of the *Commiphora* shrub. It holds its head and tail high when running in contrast to the gerenuk, which stretches its head and neck forward. The dibatag's ears are round, the gerenuk's are pointed. Its coloration blends in so well with the background that a motionless dibatag is virtually invisible. The dibatag is like the gerenuk in habits but has not fared as well because its restricted range (northern Somalia and Ethiopia) is an area of political unrest.

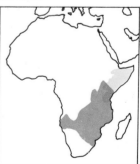

■ *Impala*   ■ *Gerenuk*

Dama gazelle

Left and background: Thomson's gazelles

GAZELLES *(Gazella,* 10 species in Africa; and *Procapra,* 3 species in Asia) are medium-size, delicately built and graceful antelopes with long legs and short tails. Their conspicuously ringed horns are slightly lyre-shaped, with pronounced variation in shape among the various species.

Gazelles range from northern and eastern Africa and the Arabian peninsula to central Asia from Turkey to Mongolia and the plains of India.

As a group, they occupy the arid-lands niche, ranging from sea level to high plateaus. Some are true desert species, living in arid conditions that few other mammals can tolerate. They drink water when it is available, but most satisfy their thirst from the plants they eat. Gazelles are highly gregarious. Some species migrate to find better pastures during the dry season.

Three basic patterns of social behavior have been observed in gazelles studied in the wild: territorial males, all-male herds and female herds. In the first case, males establish territories that they defend from rivals. They mate with females from female herds that wander through their territories. All-male herds circulate around the periphery of a male's territorial area. Occasionally a single male from the herd will challenge a territorial male, evict him and take over the territory.

A single young (twins in some species) is born after 6–6½ months' gestation. It is hidden in vegetation at first, the mother returning to suckle it until it is large enough to join the herd. Gazelles sexually mature in 1½–2 years.

While some species, such as Grant's gazelle *(G. granti),* maximum length 33 in., are still very numerous, others, such as the Dama gazelle *(G. dama),* maximum 37 in., are becoming increasingly rare. Common species include dorcas *(G. dorcas),* maximum length 20 in., and Thomson's *(G. cuvieri thomsoni),* maximum 27 in.

Springbok

Right and background: Grant's gazelles

SPRINGBOK *(Antidorcas marsupialis)*, maximum length 32 in., has lyre-shaped horns and a large glandular pouch or fold in the middle of the lower back. This contains long white hair that can be erected to form a conspicuous white fan when the animal is excited. The white patch is visible for long distances in the open country.

The name springbok refers to the animal's habit of "stotting," or "pronking"—a succession of high, vertical leaps (to 10 feet) with all four legs held stiffly, hooves close together, back curved, head down and fan extended. At rest, the fold of skin is visible as a narrow line on the back and rump.

The springbok lives in the dry grasslands of South-West Africa, extending into South Africa and Botswana. It grazes, browses and sometimes digs roots and tubers. Like all gazelles, it can go for long periods without water.

Springboks frequently associate with gemsboks, zebras, hartebeests and other species of the plains. During the dry season, it commonly assembles in large herds to search for better pastures. In the past these herds sometimes contained hundreds of thousands of animals. The last of these massive migrations was in 1896, the year of the great rinderpest epidemic. Excessive hunting, overgrazing by domestic livestock and the burning of natural ranges as land is settled have all taken their toll. The springbok, the national symbol of South Africa, is now confined mainly to national parks and private preserves. The largest of these is centered at Etosha Pan, in the Kalahari Desert.

Along with other gazelles, springboks display distinctive behavior during courtship. The male positions his extended foreleg between the female's hind legs and strokes them. This stimulates the female to mate. Females bear a single young after a gestation period of 6 months.

Male saiga

Female saiga

Gray goral

SAIGA ANTELOPE *(Saiga tatarica)*, maximum length 31 in., the Mongolian saiga *(S. mongolica)*, maximum 27 in., and the TIBETAN ANTELOPE, or CHIRU *(Pantholops hodgsoni)*, maximum 31 in., appear to be links between sheep and antelopes. The rare Tibetan antelope shares the cold deserts with the wild yak at 10,000 to 17,000 feet. All have thick woolly coats and enlarged snouts. Females are hornless. They are primarily grazers.

Excessive hunting, unusually heavy wolf predation and a series of severe winters reduced the saiga close to extermination about 50 years ago. Only a few hundred animals remained. With stringent protective measures they recovered and now number about 2 million today.

Saigas give birth to one to three (usually two) young after a gestation of 5 months. Females are mature in 8 months, males in 12 months. Male chirus dig a shallow depression that protects them from the wind and cold.

CHAMOIS *(Rupicapra rupicapra)*, maximum length 32 in., is a link between antelopes and wild goats. Both sexes are horned.

Special hoof pads make the chamois surefooted and agile for travel over the steep rock faces. In summer, it lives in alpine meadows above the tree line; in winter, it moves into the warmer forests below.

Up to 30 females and their offspring form groups; each has a sentinel, which gives a warning whistle and stamps when alarmed. Males are solitary during most of the year, joining the females in autumn for the rutting season. After the end of the rut, at the end of winter, the enlarged herds break up into their summer, females-only groups. After a gestation period of 5–7 months, females give birth to a single kid (sometimes twins), which is able to follow its mother almost immediately. Females mature in 2 years, males in 3–4 years.

Mountain goat

Chamois

MOUNTAIN GOAT *(Oreamnus americanus)*, maximum length 40 in., is the North American counterpart of the chamois, living among rocks and snow on steep mountain cliffs above the timberline from Alaska to Oregon. Males live apart and wander widely except during the mating season.

Females bear single or twin kids after a gestation period of 6 months. Bears, wolves and pumas are their main predators.

GRAY GORAL *(Nemorhaedus goral)*, maximum length 28 in., and red goral *(N. cranbrooki)*, maximum 26 in., are horned in both sexes, as are the closely related serows. Gorals live in rugged country where there is sparse cover and little grazing, traveling in family groups of about half a dozen. Males stay apart except during the mating season. Gorals feed early and late in the day. During the day, they lie on rocky ledges. They remain motionless when alarmed, breaking cover at the last minute.

The two species of serows—maned *(N. sumatraensis)*, maximum length 42 in., Japanese and Formosan *(N. crispus)*, maximum 30 in.—have facial glands, which are greatly reduced in the gorals. They are usually solitary, preferring high rainfall areas on forested or bushy slopes. Serows are hunted by the Chinese for medicinal purposes. Females give birth to one or two kids after a gestation period of 7–8 months.

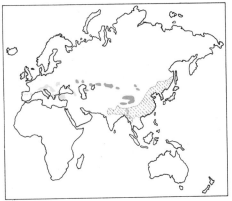

≣ Red goral   Gray goral

 Chamois   Saiga antelope

269

Mishmi takin

TAKIN *(Budorcas taxicolor)*, maximum height 42 in. at the shoulders, has sturdy horns that grow outward before bending backward and upward, measuring up to 2 ft. long on the curve. Both sexes are horned. The common and most widespread Mishmi takin (*B. taxicolor taxicolor*) has a dark coat, but the Szechuan takin (*B. t. tibetana*) that lives in southwestern China has a yellowish coat with dark markings. The third race, the golden takin (*B. t. bedfordi*), found only in Shensi Province in western China, is totally yellowish or cream-colored, with no dark coloration.

Takins (and the musk-ox) have features intermediate between wild cattle and wild sheep and are sometimes grouped with the so-called goat-antelopes. They are powerfully built animals, with short legs, heavy bodies and shaggy coats.

Takins live in rugged country at elevations of 8,000–14,000 feet—at the upper limits of tree growth where there are thickets of dwarf bamboo and rhododendrons. Gregarious animals, their summer herds are said to be large,

sometimes numbering several hundred animals. In autumn and winter, the herds fragment when the animals are obliged to move to lower elevations to find suitable forage. During the cold winter months, takins are principally browsers. In summer they graze on the grassy alpine pastures while they are free of snow. They spend most of the day in dense cover, moving out to feed in early morning and evening.

No scientific studies have been made of takins in the wild, largely because of their inaccessibility. They are said to mate during the summer, with the kid born the following spring.

Musk-ox

MUSK-OX *(Ovibos moschatus)* is a close relative of the Asiatic takin. The bulls stand up to 57 in. tall at the shoulders and may weigh more than 800 lbs. Their massive horns, measuring more than 2 ft. along the curve, form a broad, solid boss where they meet across the forehead. Females, which are smaller, also have horns.

Musk-ox live in the Arctic tundra. Their adaptations to cold include a thick, shaggy coat that hangs down the legs almost to the hooves and a dense, soft waterproof undercoat. The short tail is hidden in the heavy coat. The broad hooves enable the musk-ox to move over snow and ice with ease. They move with great speed and agility when pressed.

Musk-ox are gregarious, the winter herds consisting of up to a hundred or more animals. In summer these break up into herds of as few as a dozen. Some bulls live apart except during the mating season. As a defense against wolves, the adults form a protective phalanx around their calves, standing shoulder to shoulder. This habit led to their easy exploitation by man. Explorers and fur traders killed hundreds of musk-ox for sport and food. With strictly enforced protective laws, musk-ox numbers appear to be increasing slowly.

Musk-ox eat grasses, sedges and other plants and browse on willows, lichens, mosses and bark. Females give birth to a single calf every other year. The calf joins the herd immediately but is not weaned for 9 months. Calf mortality is high, hence the natural increase in the population is slow.

Himalayan tahr

Markhor

TAHRS *(Hemitragus,* 3 species) are close relatives of goats but have short horns and lack beards. All have a goatlike odor and are similar to goats in behavior. They are mountain dwellers.

Tahrs prefer wooded slopes where they can browse and graze. They feed in early morning and evening. The remainder of the day they rest in a sheltered place. Females live in small groups, sometimes joined by males. Males are much more nervous and secretive than females.

The Himalayan tahr (*H. jemlahicus*), maximum length 40 in., is the only tahr with a shaggy mane and long fur. The Arabian tahr (*H. jayakari*) and Nilgiri tahr (*H. hylocrius*) are now rare.

MARKHOR *(Capra falconeri)* is the largest of the wild goats, males standing up to 41 in. tall at the shoulder. Females are considerably smaller. The horns may measure as much as 5 ft. along the curve. They are tightly spiraled or corkscrewed. Males have a shaggy beard from chin to chest, the females a simple beard.

Markhors can climb and jump with great agility. Lacking heavy underfur, they cannot tolerate extreme cold; hence they winter at low elevations. In summer they are mainly grazers; in winter, they browse.

Small summer groups of four or five females and their young amalgamate to form large herds in winter. Adult males live apart except during the mating season. Females give birth to one or two young after a gestation period of 5½ months. The young become sexually mature in 3 years.

Markhors have been hunted excessively for their superb horns and meat and have also been victims of diseases of domestic livestock. The species survives precariously in remote parts of its range.

Nubian ibexes

IBEXES *(Capra,* 7 species) are wild goats characterized by beards and heavy, gnarled, curved horns in both sexes. They are different from the true wild goat in their flattened forehead, broad-fronted horns (except the Spanish ibex) and in the smaller amount of black in their coat. Males have a strong odor.

Ibexes are primarily browsers (sheep are mainly grazers). All are surefooted and agile mountain dwellers. They stay in the alpine pastures during the day but may move down into the valleys to feed at night. During the mating season in the fall, males establish herds of about a dozen females and a few older males. The remainder of the year the sexes are segregated. Males will fight to win harems, rearing on their hind legs and butting each other with their horns. Five- or six-year-old males usually win these contests; younger males do not yet have completely developed horns. The rut continues for about one week. Females give birth to one or two kids after 6 months of gestation. The mother protects her young vigorously.

Seven species are recognized: the Alpine ibex *(C. ibex)*, maximumm shoulder height 34 in.; the larger Siberian ibex *(C. sibirica)*, maximum 40 in.; two species of the Caucasian ibex, the Caucasian tur *(C. caucasica)* and the Daghestan tur *(C. cylindricornis)*, maximum 40 in. but more heavily built; the Nubian ibex *(C. nubiana)*, maximum 33 in.; the rare Walia, or Abyssinian, ibex *(C. walie)*, maximum 38 in.; and the extremely rare Spanish ibex *(C. pyrenaica)*, maximum 30 in.

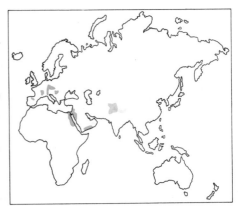

▢ *Tahrs*

▪ *Ibexes*　　▪ *Markhor*

274

Mouflons   *Barbary sheep*

MOUFLON *(Ovis musimon)*, maximum length 27 in., is a wild sheep whose numbers are greatly reduced. Eurasian wild sheep are lightly built and have longer legs than the heavier, more goatlike American sheep. The males of all wild sheep have heavy, curving horns.

Other Eurasian species are the urial or red sheep *(O. orientalis)*, maximum length 36 in., and the argali *(O. ammon)*, maximum 48 in., which includes the Marco Polo sheep with horns more than 6 ft. long. Eurasian sheep may bear twins. The gestation period is 5 months.

BARBARY SHEEP, or AOUDAD *(Ammotragus lervia)*, maximum height 44 in. at the shoulders, and the BHARAL, or BLUE SHEEP *(Pseudois nayour)*, maximum 36 in., are intermediate types between sheep and goats. The Barbary sheep's gland beneath the tail gives it the typical goat odor. It also has goatlike horns, a long beard and a mane. The bharal more closely resembles sheep, with goatlike horns curving back and inward.

The bharal is mainly a Tibetan species living at high elevations—16,000 feet or more in summer and rarely lower than 10,000 feet in winter. The several races of the African Barbary sheep are found from sea level to high desert, plateau habitats.

In social behavior, both species resemble sheep. Most old rams live a solitary life except during the mating season. Young rams form bachelor herds or may also be solitary. Herds of ewes, including young, may number from a dozen to a hundred.

■ *Mouflon, original range*   ■ *Barbary sheep*

Bighorn sheep   Dall sheep

Barbary sheep both graze and browse. Bharals are mostly grazers, feeding on grass, ferns and lichens, browsing only occasionally on juniper and other shrubs. Both are wary and can climb as nimbly as goats.

It has been reported that a sentry alerts the group in case of danger, but this is not true. An adult female usually leads the group's retreat.

Barbary sheep bear one to three lambs after a gestation period of about 5½ months. Bharals usually have a single young, the gestation period also 5½ months. The snow leopard is the main predator of the bharal.

BIGHORN SHEEP *(Ovis canadensis)*, maximum height 42 in. at the shoulder, are primarily grazers. The Rocky Mountain and California races are adapted to snow conditions; others are desert dwellers. White, or Dall, sheep *(O. dalli)*, maximum height 40 in., live only in northern Canada and Alaska. Bighorns live on the craggy slopes, sometimes above the timber line, often in precipitous terrain. In the spring, the sheep descend to feed on spruce and aspen buds and other young shoots. During the colder months they feed on berries, lichens and bark, using their hooves to dig in the snow.

Males and females live in separate flocks. The rams establish dominance by constant head-to-head butting when they are able to breed at age 4. In November and December the younger males join the females to escape the older, intolerant rams. The ram does not use its horns in serious fights, kicking with their hooves instead. The bighorn population is now less than 20,000, reduced from 2 million a century ago.

◼ Bighorn sheep

275

INDEX

279